The horse

THROUGH FIFTY CENTURIES OF
CIVILIZATION

The horse

THROUGH FIFTY CENTURIES OF CIVILIZATION

Presented by ANTHONY DENT

Holt, Rinehart and Winston
NEW YORK   CHICAGO   SAN FRANCISCO

Library of Congress Cataloging in Publication Data
DENT, ANTHONY AUSTEN.
    The horse, through fifty centuries of civilization.
1. Horses—History.   I. Title.
SF283.D43   636.1'009   73-22562
ISBN: 0-03-012781-5

*Filmset in Great Britain by BAS Printers Limited, Wallop, Hampshire
Printed in Italy by Amilcare Pizzi Spa, Milan*

Contents

1. The age of the horse

THE HUNTERS AND THE HUNTED

It is not the purpose of this book to deal with the mammal whose descendants were to become horses, either from the point when it branched off from the main stem of grass-eating animals or from the later point at which the creature first took shape whose descendants were to become zebras, asses and horses and nothing else. The successive stages of its evolution have been very fully dealt with at all levels, from the popular to the academic. Indeed it is true to say that no species except the human has had so much research lavished on its evolution as has the horse on its metamorphosis from a dog-sized many-toed forest creature to the hollow-hoofed brush-maned migrant of the steppe and the prairie.

Let us be content to believe, as Darwin and every prehistorian and zoologist since has told us, that this process took many millions of years. The most significant fact is that all the transformations of outward shape and inward construction, all the vicissitudes of size and adaptation to varying climates that befell the race between the days of the little Pliohippus, many-toed but unmistakably horselike, and the moment when the undoubted single-hoofed *Equus caballus* emerged, took place in America. Over a long period lasting from the Tertiary era of the geologists to what men of science call 'recent', wave after wave of equines crossed over the land-bridge between the north coast of Alaska and that of Siberia. Why their descendants who were left behind died out we do not know. Climatic change is unlikely as a reason. Another reason put forward is epidemic diseases. But are *continent-wide* epidemics likely?

What seems most certain is that the westward intercontinental flow of horses over the roof of the world had come to an end, and there were no more horses left in America, before the eastward migration of man out of Asia began, some time in the Old Stone Age; the first Americans came into a land where there were no horses.

What did this mean to these ancestors of the Eskimo and the Red Indians? Why, simply that there was one less kind of edible, huntable animal—a deficiency adequately compensated for by the presence of many meaty species not encountered on the other side of the Bering Strait. Even the last of these immigrants were at that stage of culture where they had no domestic animals but the dog, but most of them crossed over so late that they already had bows—a characteristic invention of the Middle Stone Age—and some of the last comers possessed that deadly East Asian invention the laminated bow, with its composite layers of horn and wood giving enormous penetrating power. The association of this type of bow with the horse was to have the most far-reaching effects on the fate of mankind in Eurasia in very early times: but that combination hardly came into play in America at all—or at least not until very late, some time in the eighteenth century AD.

Our theme is the Age of the Horse, meaning thereby the long procession of years during which it has been of prime significance to the human race, and of course vice versa. But before we broach this, it is worth setting the scene at least to the extent of defining what sort of horse this early animal was.

There has, over the last thirty years or so, been a shifting of scientific ground on this point. The monophyletic school, taking their stand on the principles of Father Darwin, swore by the beard of their prophet that the first true horses were all of one stamp, resembling as near as may be those last true wild horses of Asia: Przewalskii's Horses, or, as the simple herdsmen of Mongolia, who have lived on uneasy terms with them all these thousands of years, prefer to call them, Takis. The reasons for this were twofold. Firstly the most accessible, and the most striking, cave paintings of Upper Palaeolithic Europe, almost exclusively in France and Spain, showed a predominance of horses of Taki type. Secondly, just as there was in Europe a reindeer age, which means not the keeping of herds of tame reindeer but a hunting economy based almost entirely on the produce of the slain reindeer, so there was in some parts of Europe a horse age, in which a horse closely resembling the Taki was the chief, though never the only, prey of the hunter. The monophyletic thunder is a little damped in our day, but it has not ceased to growl away. Louder and clearer is the voice of the polyphyletes who maintain that *Equus caballus* is the descendant of at least four wild ancestors, all indubitably horses, which differed at least as much as Shetland ponies do from show hackneys, but none of

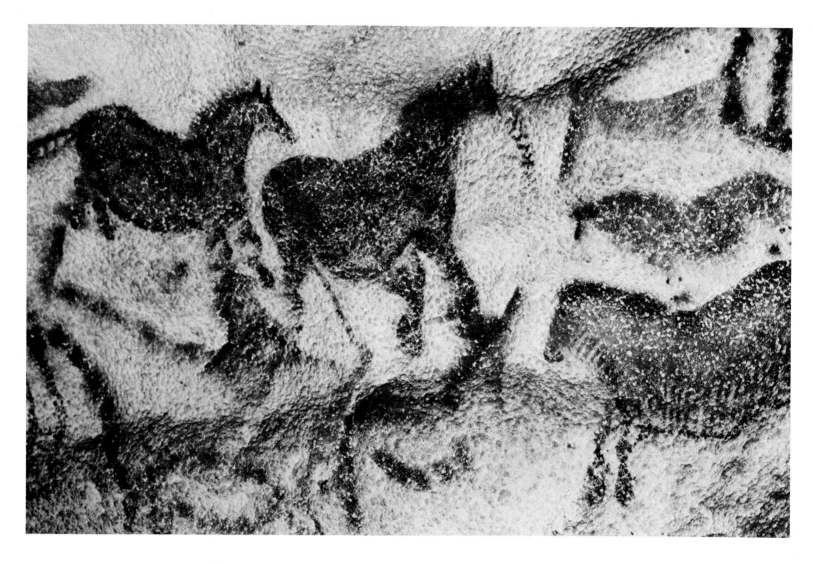

which corresponds, feature for feature, to any living breed of horse, and further that this differentiation had taken place before the great wandering from America to Eurasia began. There were two main waves. The first crossed over in a cold climatic era, having developed in North America a physique calculated to resist cold; it consisted of Pony Type I, in the latest terminology, which was able above all to resist damp cold, but was not very well adapted to life in swampy ground. It was the ancestor of all European ponies, none of which resembles it to a hair because their blood has long since been mingled with that of other equine races; it never stood more than 13 hands (1.3 metres) high at the most, more often between that and twelve; it was similar to a rather coarse Exmoor pony, and probably like it was of a brown colour with black mane and tail—horseman's brown, that is, what the Germans call *torfbraun* or *wildfarbe*; the colour of red deer in winter (French *brun foncé*). Its legs were black, there were 'mealy' patches round mouth and eyes; the belly was pale dun. Its tail at the root had longer and coarser hairs, forming a 'brush' which kept

water out of the vulnerable cleft between the buttocks. Pony Type II was likewise adapted to cold, but to dry cold. We may call it the Tundra Pony. It had a similar arrangement of tail hairs, but this was a protection against driven snow rather than rain. It was taller—say $13\frac{1}{2}$ hands (1.35 metres) at most—and heavier than Pony I. Its feet were proportionately larger and shallower. It could live in swamp because the surface of the tundra melted in summer, but it was not really proof against atmospheric damp. It was pale, sometimes rather sandy dun, with mane, tail, and legs below the knees all black; its face was darker than its body, sometimes almost black; its mane was stiff and in good health erect, with hardly any forelock. It probably turned white in winter. From its first bridgehead in Siberia it populated all Asia north of the Himalayas and all Europe north of the Alps, perhaps also the Iberian peninsula. Many regions had large populations of both races, so that wild hybrids in every degree of admixture existed.

The habitat of this first wave only overlapped at a few points with that of the second, in Eurasia. Wave two

1. Horses from the famous cave gallery (now closed) at Lascaux, in conjunction with the much-disputed structures, possibly huts but possibly corrals for capturing horses alive.

consisted of the tallest wild horses, Type III, the 'plains horse', about 15 hands high (1.5 metres) or more, with a large head, long neck, long back (having overall more vertebrae), long skull with narrow forehead, sloping croup, thin lank mane and tail, flat ('slab') sides, thin coat, poorly adapted against damp. This one and Type IV 'grew up' in America, and left there, during a warm climatic phase. Horse IV was the smallest of the wild races, only 12 hands (1.2 metres) in height (the size of a Welsh mountain pony), but in a favourable environment it could grow larger, whereas for instance Pony Type I under similar happy circumstances would only grow fatter. It had a high wither, slender legs, a straight or even concave facial profile, a high carriage of the tail, broad forehead, tapering skull with swelling muzzle, and a level croup. We may call it the primeval Arab. As to the tendency to increase or decrease in size, we may put it this way, speaking of a series of generations as if they were the history of a single horse: an Exmoor taken off the heather into lush pastures is still an Exmoor, but a gross one; an Arab taken off the desert and acclimatized to County Meath grassland becomes more and more like an Anglo-Arab in stature and conformation. Dwarf forms arise, at least in the form of shortened legs, in any breed which becomes acclimatized to life in high mountains or very cold environment, while horses of all races after long domicile on the plains develop longer legs in temperate climates. All hybrids between these four types were especially capable of increased size in favourable circumstances. Type II already in prehistoric times gave rise to a giant sub-race 18 hands high (1.8 metres, the size of a Shire horse) while living wild in certain marshy districts. The hybrid most subject to 'inflation' of this

kind was that between II and III, but as stated above, these primary types only came in contact, wild, in very few areas. The very small, thick-set pony of Shetland type existed in the wild state, or so we must believe on the evidence of Old Stone Age artists, and was simply a 'sport', arising perhaps originally on high mountains with poor grazing, of Pony Type I. It may well have been confined to such ground along the Atlantic seaboard.

We can be less positive about the colours of these latter two wild races, but they seem to have varied more than did the northern ponies. Type III seems to have varied all the way between golden dun and black, and Type IV to have been grey, bay or chestnut. Neither of these had an 'eel' (dorsal) stripe, donkey-fashion, as Type II invariably had.

This then was the equine raw material with which man, in the first instance as a hunter, was presented; in Europe primarily with Types I and II, in Asia and in North Africa (though for this the evidence is sparse and confusing) with Types III and IV.

Hunters of the Old Stone Age have left some striking memorials to their activities in the form of drawings and paintings on the walls of caves, but the finest of these are confined to a comparatively small area of western Europe and to parts of Africa where there were no horses until modern times. It is in the cave art of France and Spain that the primeval Taki—Pony Type II—so strikingly predominates in number among horses portrayed; but one fact should be borne in mind. It is an accepted fact among tradesmen of *la boucherie chevaline* that the most lucrative horse carcases are those of the modern representatives of Pony Type II—whether ponies still like the Dales and the Fjord breeds or giant varieties like the

2. Early types of wild pony and horse: Pony Type I; Pony Type II; Horse Type III; Horse Type IV.

Boulonnais and the Belgian Draft. Now anthropologists have various theories about the social—perhaps religious—purposes of Upper Palaeolithic art; but all are agreed that it is overwhelmingly concerned with the portrayal of food animals. Therefore the maestro of mural frescoes at, say, Les Combarelles, may well have taken most often as his subject Type II, not because they were the most numerous around him but because they were the meatiest. It was essentially what agricultural show catalogues call a butcher's beast; and so for that matter is its modern wild descendant, the Taki; all the pastoral tribes who hunted it in Central Asia when it was numerous enough to be worth hunting maintained that of all game it paid best in terms of dressed carcase weight: they lament its passing for reasons other than those of the zoologist.

It may be, also, that Pony Type II was the only stamp of wild horse, out of the several that were to be found in the Cantabrian region, that migrated annually at a certain season, like the reindeer. Such regular migrants are particularly vulnerable to the hunter, especially if the latter have no missile weapon but a throwing spear (note again the best of cave art is from a period before the invention of the bow). This fact cannot have been taken into account by those who maintain that the *animalier* of the caves painted all his pictures from the dead subject as he had no opportunity for close study of the living: on the contrary, the absence of the bow from

his armoury meant that he had to spend long hours in the close proximity of game, unobserved by his quarry, awaiting his opportunity to attack with short-range weapons, and meanwhile minutely observing behaviour, which would tell him when the animal became aware of his presence. Under such circumstances the lineaments of the prey were indelibly engraved upon the brain of the hunters, of whom perhaps only one of the group was able to reproduce them in carved ivory or painted limestone. This was the case when the herds were not migrating; but it is apparent from present-day observation of, say, the reindeer and the caribou, that the migrant animal is psychologically more vulnerable to the hunter, and tactically more at risk. In the first place, its mind is preoccupied with the goal of its urgent pilgrimage, and besides the herd instinct of 'safety in numbers' gives it a false sense of security. In the second place most migration routes pass through defiles of one kind or another; or they involve crossing water obstacles. The horse, like the reindeer, is a strong swimmer but utterly defenceless in the water; and a narrow pass in the mountains, or a causeway of more or less solid ground leading over a bog, provide ideal venues for an ambush, especially if the ambuscaders know that such paths have been traversed annually by the herds time out of mind.

It is most likely in the course of migration, and most certainly at the passage of some swamp or river or snow-field, that the catching alive which is the necessary preliminary to domestication must have taken place. This was a threshold of life-style most difficult to cross. The young of certain grass-eating animals are easy for the hunter to pick up—indeed he often does so by accident. The red deer hind and the roe-doe leave their fawns lying in a thicket while they go out to graze, and the instinct of these animals when very young is to cower when discovered, not to run away. It was so with the wild cow and her calf in Neolithic Eurasia. But the wild mare is different, for her foal follows her from the hour of its birth, walking where she walks, trotting where she trots, galloping where she gallops, sucking while she grazes. To run down a day-old foal is beyond the power of even the best man on his feet; and to raise a day-old foal is impossible for people not already possessing milch cows or goats or ewes. This is only one reason why prehistorians assume that the first horse-keepers must have been people who already kept some herbivorous livestock. Nevertheless there exists a tenable theory of a pastoral life-style beginning somewhere in northern Eurasia, with the horse and the horse alone—or, better, with the pregnant mare.

4. The capture of wild asses, prehistoric rock painting from the Eastern Desert of Egypt. In this way, probably, wild horses were first caught for domestication.

I say this because, supposing that the hunters do manage, at the passage of some natural obstacle, to capture a suckling mare, it does not follow that they will also secure her foal. Closely though the foal follows its dam, if she falters or fails while the herd is in flight, the king stallion will intervene. This has been seen in this century in Mongolia, during the drives organized for the benefit of Przewalskii and other fauna-collectors of the beginning of this century and the end of the last. If a foal lags behind for any reason whatsoever then the leading stallion takes its dock—the root of its tail—between his teeth and frog-marches it along without himself breaking step.

The nucleus of all tame herds, then, must have consisted of mares in foal rather than mares with foals at foot—for the reason, too, that the heavier they were in foal the slower they would be in flight. Even so, it would be rare to capture an undamaged mare. Even if they had been snared or caught in the primitive 'treadle-trap' used for catching deer by the foot, the frantic efforts to tear loose could not but result in lameness, most likely permanent, in at least one limb. So that the foundation

stock of the first herds would be all female, mostly pregnant, none of them sound. And what could man do with such stock? He could milk the mares while they lactated and in the late autumn when they dried off eat the foals which would then be at their fattest. This cycle of initial domestication seems to have been general in the case of all large herbivores, including the reindeer and the ox. Any males captured would in any case have been killed out of hand, as totally intractable.

This brought a problem in its train which matured in the spring after the capture of the first mares, and was repeated for countless years during the phase of 'meat-and-milk' husbandry as it is called: how to get the mares in foal again. Legends of many horse-raising lands from Persia to Ireland tell how it was done: by tethering the now tame mare, when she came on heat, near the grazing territory of the wild herds, so that a wild stallion would come out of the steppe to cover her. Probably the herdsmen who were still also hunters would lie in wait, to shoot him for meat after he had served the mare. We have no picture of this happening in ancient Europe. But such scenes were carved on the rocks in the Nubian desert where the African Wild Ass was first tamed under comparable circumstances (Plate 4).

This keeping of mares for milk and foals for food is a far cry from the keeping of horses for work. The lameness of the mares was an advantage to the extent that the herding of sound mares on foot was an almost impossible business in the absence of fences. But it meant that the next step—from the milking of the mare to the riding of her—was long delayed, since riding a lame mare would be no faster than walking; nor would such a ride be a comfortable one. The gap was spanned by a period of pack carriage—the most primitive form of horse transport. Imagine a man and his family and his little band of limping mares migrating over the steppe from one waterhole to the next. The day is hot and the going soft from the spring rains. Even the most primitive people acquire luggage—bedding, weapons, tools, tomorrow's food at the least. Plodding along laden beside the mare,

5. A slide-car in Ulster early in the twentieth century, used for transporting turf. The slide-car or travois was the earliest form of animal-drawn vehicle.

it occurs to someone that she is carrying nothing. So, at least drape that heavy hide sleeping-bag across her back, and there you have it: the working horse.

Among the essential baggage of all foot-nomads are their offspring who cannot walk as fast or as far as adults. Sooner or later someone will put a footsore toddler up on the mare along with the cooking-pots. Now the child is riding, probably not enjoying the experience. Nevertheless another idea is born, and grown men will also aspire to ride—on a sound horse, not a lame milch animal, and to that end some of this year's crop of filly foals will be spared the cooking-pot this autumn, and in due course will grow up to carry a living human load. Slowly over the centuries horsemanship comes to birth.

So, for that matter, does coachmanship. Far back in the Middle Stone Age, when the only domestic animal was the dog, a sketchy arrangement of rods, like a letter A, was used in summer time, one A for one dog, to take in small packets the load that in winter was carried on a sledge behind a dog team. In North America it is called a travois, in County Antrim a slide-car, in Devon two centuries ago a truckamuck. This travois was adapted, in northern Eurasia, for traction by reindeer, and probably by imitation of reindeer-herders for traction by horses at that latitude where the realms of the reindeer-herders and the horse-herders overlapped.

This primitive vehicle's history and that of its progeny is enshrined in the Russian language; *Drozhky*, which nowadays means a four-wheeled cab like the Victorian 'growler', means literally 'that which is dragged' and originally signified such a travois; nearer to us, linguistically, is the Icelandic word *drøgur* for the same thing. But it was across the grasslands of what is now Asiatic Russia that the southward progress of the travois led to the fruitful union of the horse and the wheel.

The wheel was invented, so far as we know, in Mesopotamia, and it spread simultaneously eastwards through Iran to India and northwards to the Caucasus, being used in both countries only for traction by oxen which, before its invention, had already been yoked in pairs to the plough. Somewhere to the north of the Caucasus, in the Caspian region, the outermost fringe of ox-cart men met the outliers of the Central Asian horsemen riding horses, and their wives leading mares which drew

6. A clay model of an ox-cart with solid wheels from Mesopotamia, *c.* 2000 BC.

wheelless slide-cars. The ox-men gaped. What kind of a hairy-necked hornless ox was this, so tractable it could be handled by women? Nothing like it existed in their country, nor beyond it in the Land of Twin Rivers. Some magic beast, no doubt. If one could but learn the spells that made its magic work, the—what did they call it themselves?—Horseman's Word, then the cart would move faster and further in a day, because this new animal, unlike the ox, did not need two pauses in the day's work, one to eat its bait and one to ruminate in a lying position; the new animal, it seemed, did not chew the cud.

THE AGE OF THE CHARIOTS

Only a few weeks before I took it in hand to write this essay I was privileged to see, beautifully exposed on the original site, the greatest archaeological discovery to be made in England this century. In the country of the Parisii which we now call the East Riding of Yorkshire, the road from Driffield to York crosses the line of a derelict railway track, grass-grown save where it has been made into an accommodation road, between Garton and Wetwang. A few hundred yards along this track brought us to a raw and level shelf where limestone was being quarried. Here under a transparent weather-proof shelter was the open grave of a charioteer, dead since the second century before Christ. His skull was distorted like a squashed melon with the weight of the barrow that once had been heaped over it. He lay with legs bent on the floor of his car, having been dressed for the grave in his finest clothes and jewellery, weapons to hand and food for the journey to Tir nan Og disposed within reach. The harness for his team had been draped over him.

Every shred of woodwork in that skilfully made car had disintegrated, but its 'shadow' in the shape of discoloured earth was plain to see, the long draught-pole having been chopped in two and its forward end laid crossways behind the chariot. But the metal was more enduring, the iron tyres forged in one piece and shrunk on the wheel while hot, the iron hubs and the bronze terret-rings through which the reins had passed.

The family of this Yorkshire Parisian cannot have emigrated from the Seine Valley many generations before this man was born, and quite likely on the day of his death other Gauls at the southern limit of their territory would be driving their chariots into a losing battle with the Romans whose disciplined foot, marching in step and hurling deadly volleys at the word of command, combined with their archers and slingers, and their squadrons of light horsemen on the wings of the legions, to make a fighting machine that by stages was bringing to an end the Age of the Chariots. Soon the legions would be marching up the Rhône Valley, but now they were still fighting in Cisalpine Gaul, between the Po and the Alps. In a hundred years they would have vanquished the Gauls of the north, and their reconnaissance in strength would have forced the beaches of Kent in the teeth of opposition from British chariots. But the Britons never learned to read the writing on the wall, all the way up the island. At the end of the first century of our era the Caledonian chief Galgacus was still confronting the legions of Agricola, beyond the Grampian Mountains, with a battle array of chariots: and still losing the fight. When a piece of equipment achieved such prestige as did the chariot in its day, it is hard for the military mind to abandon it and the way of life which it imposes, on the grounds of mere utility.

This charioteer of Garton, then, would bequeath to his heirs a weapon that would soon become as obsolete as the railway branch beside the barrow in Garton Slack is now.

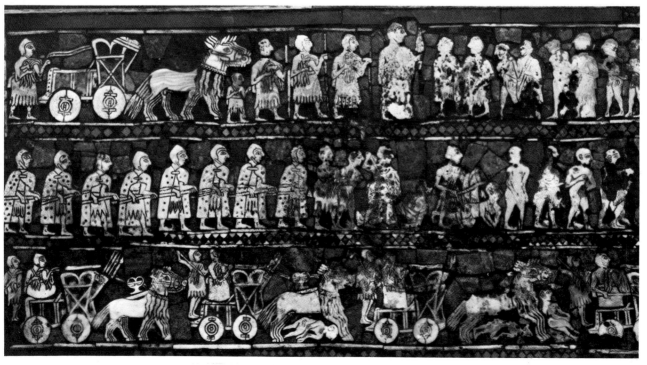

7. The birth of the war chariot—the Mesopotamian ox-cart with its solid wheels drawn by onagers, which ceased to be domesticated at all after Alexander the Great's time. Inherent difficulties of temperament and conformation made this animal unsuitable for the purpose and it was superseded by the horse as soon as its users, notably the Hittites, were able to acquire the latter from riding and horse-breeding nomads to the north of the mountains. From the Standard of Ur, Sumerian, 2500 BC.

But its history stretched back as far as the siege of Troy and beyond, to the days of the first military empires of the Near East. The first battle-cars of which we have documentary evidence belonged to the Kingdom of Ur in Mesopotamia. But these Sumerian chariots were not drawn by horses; their teams were made up of onagers— Asiatic wild asses—at the time when we first have records of them in the third millennium BC. These somewhat intractable draught animals were replaced by horses which came south over the mountains from the Iranian plateau. But what we do not yet know, and may never know, is whether they were already broken to harness and driven by Iranian charioteers, ancestors of the biblical Elamites and Midianites, or whether the drivers of the Land of Two Rivers, confronted with these mountaineers who rode a strange animal, declined to copy them so far as riding (which they probably considered indecent) was concerned, but to acquire and use these new beasts for a purpose by now long established in the low country.

This matter of altitude, and even more of evenness of terrain, is important in the history of the chariot. Its spectacular performance over the right sort of ground often led to its adoption by peoples whose home lands allowed only limited scope to the charioteer, so that the keeping of a car was often more a question of prestige than practical advantage. Indeed, this is evident in the case of our Parisian from Garton-on-the-Wolds. Next perhaps to Salisbury Plain and the Sussex Downs, the Wolds of York and Lincoln presented, in Iron Age Britain, one of the few regions where the chariot could go anywhere or do anything. Only a little way north, across the Vale of Pickering, the steep slopes and frequent bogs of the Cleveland Moors would confine the chariot to certain limited routes along the ridges, even these not passable at all seasons of the year. In the intervening vale, swamps made all wheeled movement impossible, and where the valleys had dry bottoms, thick forest would likewise confine the driver to avenues that could only be cut and maintained clear of brushwood by the orders of a very powerful chief.

Let us return to the encounter of the Caucasian carters with the horsemen from the north. The learning of the Horseman's Word proved to be a difficult and protracted exercise. As part of the deal by which the first horses changed hands to come down, eventually, into Mesopotamia, the vendors who may or may not have been also the breeders would only part with a limited amount of information. They did explain all about the use and construction of the bridle and bit: objects utterly foreign to the carters, since neither of these was used on the draught-ox. But about the management of the slide-car, in which the carters were chiefly interested, they had nothing to impart. Indeed they seemed to have no interest at all in this device, the use of which, like grinding corn and such chores, was a matter for women and slaves. It was of course impossible for an ox-person to converse directly with a mare-woman; even had there been a common language, no horseman would have tolerated such an unsuitable dialogue.

Under the new system, the slide-car was discarded altogether and ox harness was modified to fit on the horse; or rather, not ox harness but a special variant of it which had been developed in Sumeria for use on the onager, the history of whose domestication both began and ended, for practical purposes, in the third millennium before Christ. The neck carriage, almost as horizontal as that of the ox, and the shape of the withers in all asses and mules, is sufficiently like that of the ox to make the fitting of the double ox yoke possible and practical. This is not so with the equine anatomy. There had to be two individual small yokes, like inverted Vs, for the two horses, their apexes fitting into the transverse beam of the yoke proper, while their points were secured both to a girth which passed under the chest immediately behind the elbow and to a neck-strap on each horse. The idea of using one horse for one vehicle, as in the slide-car, was discarded as impracticable and was not resumed for many centuries; in any case it was utterly foreign to the thinking of people brought up in the pair-ox tradition of ploughing, sled-work and carting.

The inherent disadvantages of the yoke-and-neck-strap principle remained a limiting factor in the civilizations of the Near East and the derivative cultures in the Mediterranean until the early centuries of the Christian era. Nor were they solved by Europeans north of the Alps, such as the Celts. There was no means of stopping the yoke slipping backwards down the steep slope of the

9. Group of Tang porcelain figures about half life-size: the horseman of the steppes as seen by Chinese neighbours, and the 'heavenly horse' of Chinese tradition which carried the leaders of the Hunnish Mongol and Tartar hordes against the frontiers of all the empires bordering on the steppe from Rome to Cathay.

equine withers except by use of a neck-strap, which was flexible, and at speed pressed on both the windpipe and the jugular vessels. This meant two things. Only entire stallions, with their more massively developed neck muscles, could be used at all in this gear. And even in the stallion, pressure on the front of the neck above the breast caused the animal to throw up its head, bringing the neck erect, a posture seen in all classical representations of the chariot in motion (Plate 8). It produced in time a conformation of the neck nowadays called 'deer neck' and deplored as such: it is a goitre-like protrusion of the lower front surface of the neck. But since the horse cannot gallop unless the neck is both stretched out and lowered towards the horizontal, it meant that for the chariot to travel at speed the team must 'change up' from the walk to some gait which does not demand this neck-carriage—either a racing trot or a fast lateral pace (both legs on the same side moving together) or a 'rack' in which all the legs are moved independently one after the other like an accelerated walk: one, two, three, four. Ancient pictures—and they are many, from the rock carvings of Sweden to those of the Sahara—which show the chariot team at a 'flying gallop' with both fore legs

and both hind legs extended are not, and were not meant to be, literal and realistic. They are merely an artistic convention, a shorthand meaning 'horses at speed'.

As for bridles and bits, the prototype had been acquired from the riding, breeding, non-driving herdsmen of the steppes, and for many centuries no attempt was made to depart from their patterns, save perhaps in the use of materials. Hard metals as opposed to copper and silver were scarce on the steppe, and the cheekpieces of bits were made of bone or horn, as were the mouthpieces when they were not made of rawhide, twisted into a thin rope. So great was the respect for steppe-designed bits that long after metal ones had come into use the original material was faithfully copied in cast metal, the cheekpieces moulded to look like pieces of antler, and the mouthpieces cast in a barley-sugar spiral simulating the original rawhide rope.

One of the salient differences between ancient and modern accoutrements of the horse is that whereas in modern times there is a clear distinction between two families of bridles—driving bridles which are of stiff and comparatively rigid leather, attached to bits with solid mouthpieces and more or less elongated metal cheek-

que eulet fcauoir
que pluseure ba
rone cheualliere

pieces; and riding bridles which are flexible, holding in place bits which may be single or double, but which more often than not are of the jointed snaffle type—this distinction did not exist in antiquity. All patterns of bridle were used indifferently for riding and for driving, and all bits were of the pattern that would nowadays be comprehended under the term snaffle. The original steppe design was H-shaped, the vertical strokes being represented by the horn cheekpieces, and the horizontal by the mouthpiece of whatever material. The substitution of rings for the cheekpieces brought the design closer to the modern snaffle, and was an easy matter for people who had a bigger supply of bronze than that available on the steppes. It meant that the necessity for the side members (cheekpieces) of the bridle to end in a Y fork no longer existed. With the introduction of metal mouthpieces the innovation of the jointed mouthpiece begins at once, and besides two-piece mouthpieces of modern-looking design there are also three-piece mouthpieces both in bronze and in iron. There were also mouthpieces with so many joints that they were in practice a length of chain, and so similar to short lengths of chain used for other purposes that many of them have probably not been recognized for what they are. By the time that the La Tène phase of the Iron Age began (say 450 BC) the single-jointed snaffles then in use were virtually indistinguishable from those of today.

The evolution of the chariot itself, of which all the important stages appear to have taken place in Mesopotamia, presents baffling problems. It was vital that the whole assembly should be as light as possible, since owing to the design of the yoke and pole and the fact that what body there was had its centre of gravity in front of the single axle, the chariot was as much 'carried' as drawn by horses. The Mesopotamian ox-cart, and also the battle-waggons drawn by onagers, are shown in pictures and in three-dimensional clay models as having disc wheels built up out of three slabs of timber, immovably fixed to each end of the axle, which turned with the wheels in two staples or between four pins protruding from the floor-members of the body. Lightness with this form of construction was impossible, and it is presumed that this is the earliest and most 'primitive' type of wheel. Yet its construction demands the use of a

fairly sophisticated kit of tools, at least as much so as the earliest type of spoked wheels of which actual remains, as opposed to pictures, have been found. Most of these early spoked wheels are made of poplar (a wood so despised nowadays that it is hardly used for anything except match-sticks) and the felloe or circumference of the circle is in one piece, steamed and bent round after boring or cutting out the holes to take the outer ends of the spokes which in early examples are only four or six in number. The type of wheel-construction almost universal in the latter days of carriage building, in which the felloe was a composite of three or four arcs, joined together by the one-piece iron tyre, did of course depend on the availability of metal strips of very substantial length—at least 6 feet 6 inches or, say, twice the length of a sword. The fact that a man who had the tools to make a solid disc wheel would also be adequately equipped to make a spoked wheel may account for the fact that each new archaeological discovery tends to push the invention of the latter further and further back in time, but throws no light on the question of which came first. The conclusion is becoming inescapable that (a) these two types of wheel are entirely different inventions/conceptions, and (b) the spoked wheel may not in the first place have been designed as part of a cart—it may for instance have been a spinning wheel, a toy, a prayer wheel such as Buddhists use in the Himalayas today, or a religious symbol typifying the sun and used ritually as a working model to demonstrate the priests' idea of how the solar system worked.

The only certain fact seems to be that the disc wheel was never adapted to turn freely at either end of a fixed axle, and conversely the spoked wheel was always used to turn so on axle trees which from an early date are either metal rods fixed in the ends of the axle, and tapered, or else the ends of the axle itself tapered off and encased in metal. Independently turning wheels, which in practice were also spoked wheels, alone made turning at all but the slowest speed possible, as they afforded a differential. Once the problems of evolution from a cart operating at the walking pace of an ox to a chariot that horses could draw at a racing trot had been overcome, the way was now clear for a secondary phase of the migration of the horse as a domestic animal to begin.

10. Medieval manuscript illumination: King Richard II sets out on an expedition to Ireland.

11. Grave of the Chinese Shan Dynasty (1766–1123 BC), the very early period of Chinese history in which the chariot played a dominant part. The technique of burial and the accoutrements, together with the ceremonial arrangement of equine and human bodies in the graves, are barely distinguishable from those in the Mycenaean tomb illustrated in Plate 88.

Starting about 2000 BC from a centre midway between the Caspian, the Black Sea, the Mediterranean and the Persian Gulf, the chariot-culture radiated to all the points of the compass, but first of all eastwards through Persia to India. Then it moved southwards through Syria to Egypt, then westwards through Anatolia to Greece and the rest of Mediterranean Europe, and at the same time north-west round the Black Sea into Eastern Europe. Thus it saturated Europe north of the Alps with a chariot culture different in many physical details from that of the 'antique' Mediterranean world but ideologically identical with it in postulating a 'heroic' social class whose natural function it is to drive the chariot and steer the long-ship —and own, but not necessarily operate, the means of production.

What we know least about, and yet would provide the most fascinating story, is the means by which the chariot and all that went with it, both physically and ideologically, reached North China at a very early date. Graves

of the Shan dynasty about 1500 BC (Plate 11) contained chariots with spoke-wheels, complete sets of harness, weapons and the bones of both charioteer and team, in which the technique of both the cartwright and the 'undertaker' seem identical with those used in Mycenaean Greece (Plate 88). At the time when these interments were taking place the famous treatise on the training and keeping of chariot horses in the Hittite city of Boghazköi was being written by Kikkulis the Mittannian for the benefit of the chariot corps (see Chapter 2).

The best-preserved examples of chariots which we have are those dismantled and stacked in the antechamber of Tutankhamun's mausoleum (Plate 12). They are very light and delicately made, more like the sulkies of the modern trotting track than anything else. How far Egyptian design and standards of workmanship excelled those of other countries in Europe and Asia we cannot be certain in the absence of comparable examples in an equally good state of preservation. However, we can recognize two distinct models of 'western' chariot:

one in vogue from end to end of the Mediterranean, open at the back, in which the driver had a dashboard in front of him; the other, with semi-circular wickerwork sides, open both back and front, in which the driver sat on the right side of the floor, his right shoulder braced against the wicker side and his feet braced against the central draught-pole. This latter was the 'Celtic' model, in use everywhere north of the Alps, and probably, for some time, between the Alps and the Po also.

By far the greater number of chariot crews consisted of two men only, the driver and the 'champion' who in western Asia might be an archer but in Europe was a spearman. Again, in the Mediterranean world the driver was inferior in rank to his passenger, but in the 'Celtic' world beyond the Alps it was the prince who drove, and

the subject, who might be his brother or some close relative, who acted as 'champion'. In both styles, the champion held a shield on his left side, and in the Celtic world this was the only protection, except sometimes for helmets, that the chariot crews had, for they fought not only without armour but naked. But in 'classical' lands charioteers wore armour. There was a tradition in some countries of the Near East of three-man chariot crews, for instance among the Hittites and the Assyrians. This required a larger vehicle, and the chariots seen on Assyrian monuments, with great wheels nearly five feet in diameter, are intended for these augmented crews.

Chariots were only used in masses, whole squadrons at a time, by Assyria, Egypt, and a few more of the military powers of western Asia, because only in flat

12. Dismantled chariots found in the tomb of Tutankhamun.

terrain could they be really effective. A very modest obstacle such as a ditch or embankment would stop them. Their performance uphill was in general unimpressive because the choking effect of the neckstrap was exaggerated on such gradients. Downhill the effect was even worse, in another way. There was no breeching to the harness, nothing to prevent the chariot overrunning the team. Were it not for the girth behind the shoulder it would have the effect of pushing the yoke over their ears. And some chariot teams did not even have a girth. The growth of hilltop forts in Iron-Age Europe, culminating about the time of the Roman invasions of Britain, shows that the military engineering of even the most barbarous nations was quite capable of producing a chariot-proof stronghold.

These inherent limitations made the chariot obsolete as a war-weapon, first in western Asia, then in Mediterranean Europe, then north of the Alps. In Spain it seems always to have had a precarious footing, probably introduced by the Celtiberians across the Pyrenees, and confined to the Galician-Asturian region. Everywhere it was replaced by mounted cavalry, last of all in Ireland. But chariot-racing as a sport, originally in funeral games such as are described in the Homeric poems, lasted, for instance at Byzantium, down to the tenth century AD. Long after the Romans had ceased to use the chariot for war, successful generals drove in chariots on their official triumphs. And Roman officials throughout the Empire made use of a government network, in regular stages, of relay teams of horses drawing what were essentially chariots.

THE AGE OF THE HORSEMAN

During the four centuries and more of its existence the Roman imperial army changed from an essentially infantry formation (the Legion, of which in early times there had been only one) to a predominantly cavalry force in which infantry were only retained for special functions such as siege operations. The change was brought about by the nature of the enemy whom it faced on the frontiers. Those oriental rivals such as the Parthians and Persians who inflicted really crushing defeats on the Romans in the field, even capturing an emperor, were all cavalry armies, mostly mounted archers. The only effective counter to such opposition was more, and if possible better, cavalry. Even in the West, as time went on, the enemy tended to be mounted, along the Danube and Rhine frontier. In the continually changing kaleidoscope of Germanic tribes between the Teutoburg Forest and the Vistula, there seemed over the generations to be only one constant factor. Those tribes who had faced the Romans along the *limes*, such as the Batavians, Cherusci, Alemanni, Marcomanni, Semnones, Sugambri, Ubii, Chatti, in the days of Tacitus tended to be replaced in the front line by others coming up from the east, such as the Vandals, Goths, Lombards and Burgundians. These had long had as their neighbours the wandering horsemen of the steppe, and from them they had learned much in matters of horsemanship, both as regards riding and the building, driving and management of waggons with cross-country powers undreamed of by the Roman ox-carter with his clumsy, inflexible, fixed-hub *plaustra*. The only thing these horse-Germans did not learn was the secret of bowmanship from the saddle; if they wished to employ this weapon in conjunction with their own squadrons of mounted swordsmen they had either to ally themselves to such nations as the Sarmatians, the Alans or the Huns, or to employ some of them as mercenaries, in the same way as the Romans did.

The change of life-style could be symbolized in terms of costume: the last consuls of the Republic and the first emperors wore a toga in civil life, and on active service a laminated kilt of leather and brass, with hobnailed sandals, an infantry uniform, whereas the last emperors, whether they were effective rulers or the puppets of German generals, wore boots and breeches all the time. They had to, to stay alive.

This is not primarily a military-historical essay, but the story of horses and horsemanship is conditioned at certain points by military factors, and this is the most significant of them. The style of fighting on horseback which became peculiar to western Europe under the name of chivalry, the equipment used and the stamp of horse it demanded, were all originally evolved as a

13. Part of the Bayeux Tapestry, depicting the Norman victory at the Battle of Hastings in 1066. After 200 years the descendants of some Vikings have become gallicized Norman knights, French-speaking and militantly Christian. The descendants of others have become the ruling class of the Anglo-Danish monarchy of England, preferring in their insular way to fight on foot and conservatively wielding a Viking-style two-handed axe. Because the horse has ceased to have religious implications for the artist he draws it on a more realistic scale compared with the human figure. Note that the spears are still held overhand.

response to the challenge of the steppe-ranging mounted bowmen. The concept of an armoured horseman was not essential to encounters between 'classical' Western armies of antiquity. But the Western horseman, Roman or post-Roman, virtually without missile weapons, could not hope to close with the oriental enemy unless he wore, at least, an arrow-proof mail shirt and carried a shield more substantial than the rather flimsy leather targe which most 'Roman' (in practice mainly Spanish) auxiliary troopers had originally borne. The evolution of the Roman mailed trooper (cataphract) into the medieval knight was a very gradual process, consisting in essentials of the adoption of one 'barbarian' practice after another, but the shield was vital long before the conflict came to consist of the shock of opposing lancers. Whereas in the days of the chariot there had been a two-man team consisting of driver and fighter, there were now two-man teams comprising the weapon-wielder (*armiger* = knight) and the shield-bearer (*scutifer* = esquire).

A depressing feature of the Dark Ages is the ease with which armies continued to march and countermarch across Europe long after the ruinous state of roads and bridges had deprived them and the civilians alike of any wheeled conveyance. On a provincial scale we see this in fifth-century Britain, the Pict-ravaged outpost of the Roman Diocese of Gaul, in which south of the half-demolished frontier wall the squadrons of half-legendary Romano-British cavalry leaders like Ambrosius Aurelianus, Maxen Wledig, Uther Pendragon, Arthur of Britain, rode out against the Saxons on the right hand and the Irish on the left, between the burnt-out cities of Albion, now connected by crumbling pot-holed tracks that had once been first-class highways suitable for the fast post-chaises of the imperial messenger service. To the medieval mind these champions become, without any stretch of the imagination, 'knights'. To us they resemble more the successors to the commanding officers of such units as Ala Prima Flavia Augusta Britannica. They were, in a sense, both; the one merges imperceptibly into the other.

It was not until after the time of Charlemagne, when the Asiatic invention of the stirrup had at last been adopted on a wide scale from the Avars—yet another wave of horse-archers coming from the same steppes which in their time had vomited forth the Scythians and the Huns—that the knight took his final form as an armoured lancer; that is, a horseman not only carrying a spear (that was no novelty) but using it 'couched' under his armpit with the full momentum of the horse behind it. This demands both stirrups and a saddle of a particular 'armchair' design from which it was equally difficult to be dislodged and to disengage oneself if the horse fell. This development was not complete, in Normandy, one of the classic lands of chivalry in its practical connotation, until after the Battle of Hastings: for in the Bayeux Tapestry (Plate 13) we see the Normans using what seems to be a very light spear, overhand, on saddles that have not yet developed the pelvis-embracing cantle of twelfth-century pictures.

But the specialized warhorse is already there, and it is not just a conveyance, a 'taxi to the battlefield' as it was to the Anglo-Saxon house-carl. It is shod in front with protruding studlike nails, and the tactical ideal is to 'bear down the enemy'; quite apart from sword-cut and spear-thrust, the aim is to trample on the opposing infantry, and the heavier the horse is, the more effective the trampling will be. *The horse is now a weapon*. This is the real reason for the massiveness of the destrier or knight's first-line charger; that and the fact that the greater the weight behind the lance-point the harder it will hit. The horse-breeders of Edward I's day, say, did not breed their horses of such mass merely in order to carry the weight of armour (which has been much exaggerated by modern writers). One thing they knew as well as we do was that in order to carry weight a horse does not need to be a mountain of meat itself; for this, a short back, hard bone and sound tendons will suffice (the all-time record for weight-carrying is in fact held by a thoroughbred). Western society is henceforth endowed, and for long handicapped, with a special type of horse for which there is no alternative employment, civil or military, to carrying armour. It demands almost from the outset a host of ancillary horses, from the sumpter which carries the baggage and the palfrey which the knight rides when not in action to the rouncy which the squire rides all the time, and the courser which is for messengers and sometimes for heralds only.

Now all these types, defined by function, had their successors over a long period. The sumpter or capul gradually changed over from carrying pack-saddles to pulling carts, but this change was not complete (in northern England for instance) until the end of the eighteenth century. The courser gradually became a race-horse. The rouncy was a cob, the most generally useful of all these types. Its uses, even in feudal times, were as manifold in peace as in war. In the nineteenth century it became specialized as a harness horse and in the twentieth reverted again to work under the saddle. Like the rouncy, the medieval hackney was originally a trotting horse, but not substantial enough for military use, that is, not capable of carrying a 'half-armed' man under campaign conditions. But it might be fast. The hackney as a general-utility trotting horse was ridden, not driven, from medieval times until such light vehicles as gigs came into general use in the Macadam era. It

14. The palfrey as seen by Rembrandt in the 1630s. The travelling horse of the more affluent classes, its easy paces made it an ideal conveyance for a sick or wounded passenger. (*The Good Samaritan*, 1633)

then underwent such a specialization as a harness horse, and had such anatomical characteristics bred into it, that re-conversion to a saddle type has become, by now, almost impossible. But it is the palfrey of feudal times which had the longest history behind it, and has had the most curious destiny, since it ceased to be a member of the knightly string. It is essentially a 'western' horse and its gait and the manner of riding it were a legacy of the chariot age. The chariot team, because of the limitations imposed by antique harness with its yoke and neckstrap, did not gallop with extended neck but paced, in the manner of the modern sulky-racer, with a high neck carriage and that posture of the head known as 'stargazing'. In antiquity there was no distinction between riding and driving types of horse, and west Europeans sat far back on the horse with the legs inclined sharply forward and without stirrups, the whole technique including the use of the hands being reminiscent of the chariot-driver, to whom they looked back, rather than of, say, the Parthian mounted archer. The palfrey proceeded at either a pace, in which both legs on each side came forward together, or a rack, best described by the American expression 'running walk', in which all legs move independently in succession. A horse travelled at either of these gaits at speeds ranging from that of a walk (called 'amble' in the case of the pacer) to one equal to a gallop, accelerating from say three miles to twenty miles an hour without breaking step or 'changing up'.

Throughout western Europe all those who could afford such horses used them for all peaceful purposes such as travelling, hunting, and hawking, until the end of the seventeenth century. The breaking of these 'easy-going' horses as they were called is now a lost art in Europe, but it could not be done simply or quickly. By contrast the riding of such horses was easily learnt, and it was never the subject of formal instruction by riding-masters. The eclipse of the palfrey in the West is connected with the decline of falconry, the invention of the coach and the improvement of the side-saddle to the point where this could be used on a trotting horse without indignity or discomfort to the lady concerned. The average horseman or horsewoman at the present day in England or France or Germany or Italy has no conception of what the palfrey was like, any more than they have in Ireland or most of Spain, where for centuries the very best palfreys were bred. They survive, under various names, in a wide arc of overseas countries settled by Europeans before the ambling/racking tradition died; from Iceland with its *tjaldari* through the Tennessee walking horses and American saddle horses of the Southern States to the Paso Fino of the Caribbean,

the Caballo de Paso of Peru and the Boereperd of South Africa.[1]

In parts of northern Spain, too, and adjacent Portuguese districts, these 'easy-going' ponies are still bred and broken, neither to trot nor to gallop. This is in sharp contrast to southern Spain, the home of the Andalusian horse which works at a trot and a gallop. The Andalusian of medieval times was by definition a destrier or knight's charger, and inside the Iberian peninsula all knights bestrode an Andalusian or a part-bred approximation thereto. Outside the Hispanic region, to the far end of the Mediterranean, the Andalusian was the destrier *de luxe*, commanding top prices from Normandy to Cyprus. William the Conqueror rode one at Hastings: nobody else in his army could afford one, or if they could, cared to expose it to the hazards of a Channel crossing and the broad axes of the house-carls. Because conditions of warfare in the days and the land of the *Cid Campeador* differed greatly from those obtaining on the marches of the Frankish empire to the East, not least because the 'foul paynim' in the shape of the Moor was a light horseman but not primarily an archer, the Spanish hidalgo was less heavily armoured than his French or Bavarian counterpart and found it essential to preserve mobility faced with an enemy who put practically no infantry into the field and must be outridden if he were to be beaten at all. Not but what the noble Andalusian was quite capable of carrying all the armour that was later piled on to it.

One other Mediterranean breed commanded almost the same respect and almost the same inflated prices as the Andalusian; this was the Lombard horse of the Po valley. Today it has vanished utterly. It resembled the Spanish horse very little. As portrayed by the best equestrian artists of the fourteenth century for instance (and we simply do not know how much they idealized) it appears to have had a 'blood-like' top-line, full of quality, but otherwise to have had the same coarse and

[1] The horsemanship not only of Latin America but also of the Western United States is almost wholly of Iberian origin, but it is a mixture of the two traditions of north and south – if you like, Galician and Andalusian. The Western movie is realistic enough in this respect to show us every now and then a cow-pony ambling in the medieval manner.

15. The Stone of Hornhausen, East Germany. The mount of the seventh-century Saxon lord in this carving is a good four hands higher than what he could hope to ride in real life.

massive build as the general run of destriers throughout western Christendom north of the Pyrenees. These consisted largely of the 'poor knight's Andalusian': the all-black Frisian with an imposing front—'presence' as they say—which made it appear taller than it really was, great docility and handiness, and no turn of speed at all, even by the modest standards of the day. For the rest, all were drawn from the native stock of the North Sea–Channel area, stretching from Jutland to Brittany, or else from the Rhineland and the Danube valley: these were ancestors of the modern Noriker, Pinzgauer, Holsteiner, Ardennais, Boulonnais, and Percheron. In terms of the primeval wild strains they were all descended in varying proportions from the types Pony II and Horse III described above (page 8).

Not only was the Great Horse a weapon. In its other aspect of the High Horse it was a command post or mobile throne, and this was the capacity in which it lasted longest by far and figured earliest in the aspirations of rulers. Many pictures of Dark Age European origin show kings and princes in Germany and Scandinavia mounted on horses which in conformation are recognizable and credible granted the artistic conven-

tions of the day (Migration or Early Viking period); but in stature are sheer fantasy. They bear no relation to the horse bones recovered from the tombs of the same period in the same region, nor, unless the riders were dwarfs, to any modern breed of horse. They are wish-pictures of what every Germanic ruler hoped to breed, buy, borrow or steal, and they are a good four hands higher than what he actually got in real life.

The king as warleader on the High Horse could see all around the battlefield over the heads of friend and foe. The king in his capacity as semi-magical ruler could also be seen, if mounted on the High Horse, by even the least of his subjects in the back row of the crowd. The processional function of the horse whether in a secular or a religious context had always been of moment in its own right. The first horse known to have been kept in Egypt, about 1750 BC, before the Hyksos came, was neither ridden nor driven, but simply led in procession wearing elaborately trapped non-functional 'harness'. In certain cults the image of the god was paraded on a horse, in others the priests who impersonated the god rode the sacred horses. Thus the place of the king was on horseback if only by reason of the sacerdotal origins of his office. And what the monarch does, the aristocracy must do also, on a scale suitable to its rank. So comes into being the courser of state, with the sole function of emphasizing majesty. What this courser must have is above all presence; height, and the proper head-carriage, are of the first importance; speed is not a factor; the horse must be what the sixteenth century called 'governable' at the slightest touch, but it must also be capable of putting on a show of high spirits. Such 'great gambading horses' might be hard to find; the search however was made easier by the fact that they need not be sound in the wind, and many conditions which would soon have manifested themselves as lameness during a normal job of work would not come to the surface during the brief period when the State Horse was performing. For example, some of the more affluent warlords of the Marlborough/Eugène/Turenne

period kept a charger which they did not ride either on the battlefield or on the march but simply on those occasions when they had to make an impressive entry into some town which had fallen to them.

One little-considered effect of the Reformation in England and countries of about the same latitude was its disastrous effect on the mule. Increasingly since Carolingian times it had become the mount of ecclesiastics of high rank, both monastic and secular, so that for instance the Monk of the fifteenth-century Lydgate's continuation of the *Canterbury Tales* is shown by the illuminator riding on a mule as a matter of course, whereas Chaucer had given him a palfrey. Mules of high quality were bred for this purpose. Cardinal Wolsey had a pair of superb ones. But in Protestant countries the new senior clergy abandoned the practice, and no secular persons of similar rank took up mule

16. Reconstruction of the tapestry in the cabin of the Viking ship grave at Oseberg, Norway, done in the first half of the ninth century. Late in the history of Norse paganism horses are shown as part of a religious procession ridden and driven by priests, much greater than life-size presumably because they are sacred horses. This is in contrast to the realism with which the saddlery and the harness are shown.

riding, so that no more were bred. They lingered on, as individuals, for a few decades, for the mule is a long-lived equine. But by the end of the sixteenth century the 'mule of state' was gone from Europe outside the Mediterranean. It is not clear why the fashion for mule-riding was so widespread among Catholic clergy (not among the Russian Orthodox) at any period. It was only a fashion, being nowhere enjoined by canonical law, and must be put down to biblical influence. Perhaps it was felt that the mount ridden by anointed kings of Israel and Judah down to the times of Solomon and later was suitable for the spiritual if not the temporal leaders of Christian communities.

The history of the mule belongs more properly to that of the ass than of the horse. It suffices to say here that it impinges on our theme because where mules were available in southern Europe and the Near East certain classes of horse whose work could be done equally well or better by mules were either very scarce or absent altogether; these categories range from ploughing and very heavy draught work to elegant town hacks to carry, for instance, side-saddles at a 'soft pace'.

It is with this function of the horse—what Skelton called 'Magnificence'—that the Renaissance theorists of equitation and practical instructors are solely concerned, down at least to the time of the Duke of Newcastle. Only gradually does their avowed purpose, during the eighteenth century, condescend to more practical ends, and right to the end some element of the original purpose, namely a suitable setting for the *bella figura*, is among the unstated aims set before the graduate of the classic academies of equitation.

A more agile, more strenuous form of display riding is sparsely evident from the earliest times of European

17. The art of equitation, which began in Renaissance Italy, had as an offshoot the circus tradition as depicted by Goya in this etching of a rope-walking horse. (*The Queen of the Circus*, from *Proverbios* No. 20)

horsemanship and may indeed have been the first purpose for which the horse in the West was taken out from under the chariot-yoke and ridden: its origins seem to have been religious and probably, like racing, connected with funeral games. For instance, rock carvings of the Bronze Age in Scandinavia show human figures performing handstands and acrobatics on horseback and as late as the times of Procopius there is evidence for displays of such non-functional horsemanship among the Goths—significantly, perhaps, by royal persons (page 97). The end-product of this horsemanship is, of course, the circus ring. The modern heirs of Newcastle and Pluvinel (see Chapter 7), practitioners of the classical High School, may refuse to acknowledge any relationship to their distant kinsmen of the rosin and the sawdust, but it is real enough; both have their origin in the same religious aspect of equitation in the dawn of our history.

The quasi-religious origins of horse-racing are almost too well known, from Homeric example (see page 60), to need mention here. The equine connection with funeral rites was long-lasting and its last vestiges, again, are to be seen in the full-scale *pompes funèbres* of exalted personages in a dwindling number of countries, east and west. The 'mortuary' bequeathment of a great man's best horse to the church, vestige of its original dedication to some pagan god by way of funerary sacrifice, was a feature of English wills down to the Reformation and later. In some countries the horse-race was a device whereby the estate of the deceased was divided up, not necessarily among the kinsmen, as King Alfred's account of contemporary customs in the Baltic (page 117) bears witness.

The horse-race survived the coming of Christianity solely by retreating to the field of 'amusement only'. It was long before it again assumed the solemnity with which the Jockey Club has endowed it in our day, all over the world, and the very existence of bodies with titles such as *El Turf-Club de Guatemala* reminds us, first of the concentration and synthetizing, in England, of certain strains of horse which became the universal race-horse, and then of the re-diffusion of what we call the thoroughbred, and other nations call the English thoroughbred, through every continent.

This is a long and copiously documented story, some essential parts of which however are missing and will now never be recovered. It begins with the gradual collapse of Turkish power and its retreat to a very much shallower European bridgehead at the beginning of the eighteenth century. The Turks were the last of the mounted bowmen to come out of Asia, the heirs of a long series of mounted invaders reaching back at least to the times of the Scythian raiders in the first millennium BC. Nothing is more misleading than to suppose that all these mounted bowmen were racially or even linguistically akin. For instance the well-preserved human remains in the barrows of the Altai mountains at Pazyrik, monument to a totally horse-centred culture of the fifth century BC, show the greatest physical diversity of ethnic type: while the more numerous remains of horses there are all of one stamp, though of varying quality. It was simply that a common way of life—that of the mounted pastoralist—imposed a common social structure on all the tribes who fell under its spell. Their members all struck the outsider, for centuries on end, with the same image: trouser-wearers, with long, greasy, licked-back hair and walrus moustaches, begotten and born in a waggon, dressed in expensive if somewhat greasy furs, addicted to narcotics and smelling of sour mare's milk. Broad in the shoulders, with powerful arms and deep chest, narrow-hipped and bandy, unable or unwilling to walk from one tent to the next, dismounted they seemed crippled. Whether they called themselves Sarmatians or Petchenegs was all one: they were just another lash on the Scourge of God. Two things only they feared: the smell of mountain air and the taste of sea water.

The last of these manifestations, the Osmanli Turks, differed from their predecessors in two ways. The disastrous visitations of the Mongols, the Tartars, the Huns, had all ended in one way, whether the invaded were totally defeated or not. When they had had enough —enough gold, enough wine, enough fair-haired women, enough power even—they had simply gone away. But the Turks seemed bent on staying. Moreover, they brought with them something more lethal than rapid-fire archery from the saddle. At the time when they took Constantinople their artillery was slightly better than any European ordnance. Not until they came to the gates of Vienna more than two hundred years later did they meet western guns and gunners better than theirs.

The only Turkish possession that the West really envied was their horses, and these were hard to come by through barter or purchase since the Turks were not commercially inclined. Turkish horses could only be acquired by way of ransom or booty, which was not possible so long as the Turks had the upper hand in the seemingly endless war along the Danube. But in the last quarter of the seventeenth and the first decade of the eighteenth century a thaw set in with the repulse of the Turks before Vienna. And as victory followed victory for the Imperial forces all the way to Belgrade, so the flow of captured Turkish horses westward increased. The whole attitude of the Turkish authorities in the Near East became slightly less exclusive and obstructive.

It became not too difficult to buy, through the medium of consuls at such places as Aleppo and Algiers, Arabian, Barb and Turkish horses. Of these the Barb had been longest established in Europe, infiltrating by way of Spain. The Turkish horse on the other hand, which really came from Turkestan rather than Asia Minor, had previously been obtainable, if at all, solely through Hungarian or Turkish intermediaries who were not too keen to pass on their valuable prizes of war. To these elements, which corresponded in the main to variants of Type III (see page 8), was now added the *kehilan* horse of Arabia which for many centuries had been cut off from Europe by the Turkish iron curtain. The Arab was almost purely Type IV. From the blending of these races with an added catalytic, some native British element which becomes more elusive to the historian the more we discover about the Royal Mares (and that is

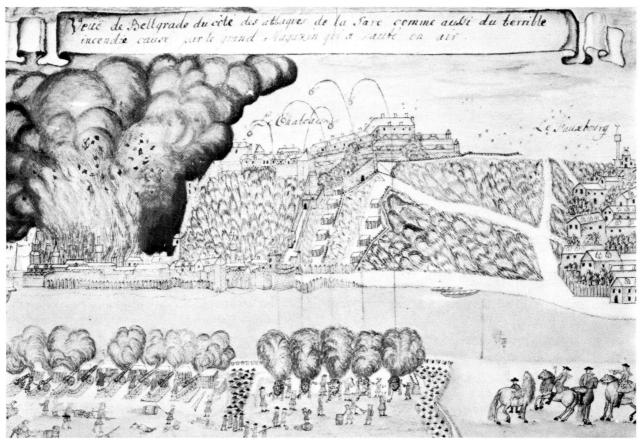

18. *The Siege of Belgrade*, showing the explosion of the Turkish ammunition dump by a lucky hit from the Imperial batteries in the foreground. After this battle, as in other Western victories since the relief of Vienna by Prince Eugene in 1683, large numbers of Turkish horses were taken as booty, thus beginning the flow of Oriental horses westward which induced the genesis of the thoroughbred and various Continental hot-blooded breeds. If the European officers' chargers shown here are typical and realistically drawn it is understandable how welcome the acquisition of Turkish horses was.

19–22. Four of the breeds and types of horse illustrated in Thomas Bewick's *History of Quadrupeds*, 1790: (*top, left*) Arab, (*top, right*) hunter, (*bottom, left*) race-horse, (*bottom, right*) black horse.

little enough), the English 'bred horse', alias thorough-bred, was empirically compounded.

Every major power in Europe, and some minor ones, now set up state studs for the improvement of native stock by up-grading with oriental sires. In every continental case the immediate objective was the improvement of cavalry horses. But the sublime selfishness of the English landowners and an absence of governmental direction enabled them by the middle of the eighteenth century to achieve, for their own use and amusement, without regard to public utility, the perfect race-horse, the perfect hunter, and later the perfect carriage horse.

A military revolution based on the use of the fast horse of largely oriental blood, ridden by hussars and ulans whose technique was, like that of the Cossacks, borrowed from the warcraft of the Asiatic nomad, swept through the armies of Europe in imitation of Frederick the Great's Prussian cavalry; and the dragoon, merely a mounted musketeer, who had dominated the European

cavalry scene since the mid-seventeenth century, took second place, with his slow pace and avoidance of shock tactics. In this field the English hardly competed, much less modified their horse-breeding policy to that end. But then, of course, they had the Navy.

The scene was set for the English-style horse-race and the English-style fox-hunt and its imitations. Hunting is something which, utterly divorced from reality as it may seem under modern sophisticated conditions of agriculture, let alone urban life, yet preserves as a kind of historical drama an essential fact, not of man's past as a 'pure' hunter, but of his early days as a pastoralist and crop-raiser. The unmixed hunting economy of Old Stone Age and Mesolithic times was 'subsistence' hunting in which man was the rival on equal terms with other predators who had twice the number of feet and no fingers. From Neolithic times onward, human hunting was 'defensive'. Herdsmen had to hunt the carnivores which would harry their herds. But they also had

23, 24. The hackney and the cart-horse, from a series of engravings on types and breeds of English horses after Ben Marshall. Both the hackney and the coach-horse now carried a high proportion of thoroughbred blood, but the hackney was still more often ridden than driven. The carthorse in this series is the same breed as Bewick's 'black horse', the ancestor of the modern Shire. In the background to this picture are a pair of Suffolk horses, then hardly known outside the eastern counties of England. The other British heavy breed, the Clydesdale, then scarcely existed.

to hunt herbivores which would eat the grass from under the cow. Venison and bearskins became by-products, not the main objective. Early crop-farmers were also 'defensive' hunters of those herbivores which would raid their cultivated plots; among these latter the horse was numbered.

The modern English fox-hunt, deer-hunt, hare-hunt and the French boar-hunt are a charade or parable presenting a long phase of human existence in which man stood on the defensive against flesh-eaters and grass-eaters alike, and in which it was not only the privilege but the duty of armigerous, equestrian persons to be active on behalf of the poorer, less mobile, worse

armed and more mundanely occupied members of the community who were charged with the truly 'aggressive' function of despoiling the environment of food, both animal and vegetable. The fact that in Britain today the armigerous equestrian hunting person may be from Monday to Friday inclusive a typist or a stockbroker or a hospital nurse or an auctioneer is neither here nor there. The form of hunting today coalesced in England in the eighteenth century after the process of agricultural enclosure was virtually completed, when scrubland had given place to grass or arable fields all bounded by (more or less) jumpable fences. Elsewhere, it is an imitation, more or less faithful, of this state of rural economy.

25. The beginning of the great tradition of English sporting art showing the climax of a foxhunt while greyhounds course a hare in another plane. There are so few people present not because the run has been a gruelling one but because the meet is still attended only by the landlord, his family, servants and friends. Note the docking of tails, a custom most widespread at this period and having no utilitarian purpose. (*A Kill at Ashdown Park* by James Seymour)

THE ROAD

Elizabethan England lived in the horse-borne culture, rather than the horse-drawn culture, still. Despite the wide publicity that the coach enjoyed on its first introduction to the country, its numbers were few during Shakespeare's lifetime, nor was it widely distributed. Whatever coaches were owned in England were all concentrated where they would do least good—in London and its immediate environs, certainly no farther out than Windsor or Hampton Court—and despite their relatively small numbers they were already creating an intolerable traffic problem. Neither the nobility nor the gentry in the remoter provinces owned coaches.

Even the ninth Earl Percy, in about 1632, did not possess such a vehicle, either in Northumberland or on his Sussex property. His will's inventory lists sixteen horses in his stable at Petworth, which sold for £90 in all, and there was also a building that went by the grand new-fangled name of Coache House, beside the older Sadle House; but all it contained was 'one horse litour with two sadles and furniture thereunto' and the accounts for the last year of the Earl's abundantly money-spending life, though they show the same order of disbursements on account of horses as they did for the year 1586 in which year indeed his lordship bought 'ii paire of coache harness' for £1 a set, show no expenses for a coach at the country houses. In all those years a Percy coach and four had been trundling about the town, but hardly ever further out than the yards at Charing Cross and Smithfield for which the scandalously high rent of over £6 a year was paid out, chiefly for the purpose of housing the coach and its team. But for serious travel, just to cross the North Downs, the Weald and the South Downs to Petworth, my lord must ride, and my lady, if indisposed, take the 'horse litour'. Not only was there no coachable Great North Road: there was no coachable Brighton Road either. It is a fact that computerized textual criticism, as shown in concordances to the two poets, shows no more frequent reference to harness horses in Shakespeare than in Chaucer.

The same is also true of baser commercial traffic. Shakespeare's carriers, such as those that were robbed by Falstaff's gang, operate packhorses, not carts. It is true that large wool dealers had begun, at any rate in the South Country, to move their goods by waggon, but

26. The agricultural vehicle of real life. It is thought by some that the 'traditional' English farm waggon is derived from a seventeenth-century copy of the Dutch four-wheeled examples shown here.

27. The horse as weapon. Uccello's enormously corpulent war-horses remind us that the selection of outsize animals was not so much due to their supposed capacity for carrying weight as to the fact that they were themselves a weapon comparable to a battering-ram, and the more weight behind the spear point the better. Note the functionless bells round the root of the tail, which itself is docked, possibly to prevent an enemy getting hold of it.

28. *Mares and Foals Under
an Oak Tree* by George
Stubbs, the incomparable
painter of horses at work
and at rest.

these waggons were still ox-drawn, not horse-drawn. Elizabethan brewers indeed owned dray horses, but the dray was exclusively for town use; it was not a waggon but a kind of sled, taking only one barrel of beer at a time, behind one horse.

And yet there had been carriages, of some kind, in England for more than two centuries before Queen Elizabeth came to the throne. (Even she did not come to it, in a literal sense, in a coach, but in a horse litter.) The word 'carriage' in English usage down to about the Reformation is an abstract noun signifying transport of goods by packhorse. We simply do not know how the first privately owned passenger carriages were designated in England: probably 'chariot', which is appropriate enough since nothing of the kind had been seen in the country or in Western Europe since Roman days. But we do know from Latin account books of 1326 that King Edward II owned a four-wheeled, six-horse passenger vehicle that could travel along the relatively

flat stretch of the Great North Road from London to York but could not ascend the escarpment of the North York Moors on which the King wished to hunt. It was drawn by horses of exactly the same stamp as carried armoured knights, and they ate the same inordinate rations of fodder and forage. This theme will recur, and on a more significant scale, three hundred years later.

The picture is the same throughout Western Europe except that in Spain with its difficult communications system across the sierras the carriage was much slower to gain ground from the mule-litter, and when it finally gained currency it too was drawn by mules. The pictures of early English carriages as well as those of such western countries as France and Burgundy all tell a similar kind of story. It is not derived from the local pattern of agricultural waggon, but from some Central European or Danubian prototype, most likely that in use among the Czech farmers, which in turn was an imitation of a Hungarian pattern of the twelfth century.

In England more Central European carriages came with the train of Anne of Bohemia when she married Richard II in 1382, but these were still long and narrow with the tubular tilt reminiscent of what English gypsies still call an 'open lot'. It was not until the sixteenth century that the definitive Hungarian model, named *coach* after the Hungarian town of Kocs, famous for its wheelwrights, reached the West, and in such numbers as no longer to be restricted to royal households.

In the wide open spaces of the Danubian plain the low standard of roadmaking was of no significance, nor were there any steep gradients. It was not possible to travel by coach during certain seasons, such as those of the autumn and spring rains; between these two the coach was redundant because long journeys by sleigh were possible once the snow was established. Everyone accepted these limitations, but a further one had to be accepted in the humid climate of insular Britain. No wheeled traffic was possible between November and April except for short suburban distances. This was the rule, for traders and travellers alike, until well into the seventeenth century.

This had two direct influences on horse-breeding and on the breaking of horses to work. If the whole country was not to be immobilized during the no-wheels half of the year, all draught horses must be able to double as pack-horses, and as many horses as possible must be at least rideable, if not a *comfortable* ride. Too great specialization beyond a certain point reduced the practical value of the horse or restricted its sale to the very rich who could afford a large string of various single-purpose horses. Thus all draught horses were bred long in the back, not because this was of any service in harness, but because it allowed the packsaddle to accommodate a larger load. Nor were they bred too tall, since this made loading and unloading more difficult. To be done with any speed this was a two-man job anyhow.

The end of the Civil War in England, like the end of the Thirty Years War in Central Europe at the same time, marked a turning point in equestrian history. The situation which some had foreseen since the first hand-guns spat lead at the cuirassier before he could come to close grips with the enemy could no longer be ignored. The Great Horse as a mount for lancers had become

31. An Andalusian horse as the mobile throne for a heroic part. The Isabella-yellow variety with black legs was very typical of the old-style Andalusian. This breed had the capacity to look bigger than it was. Charles I was only 5 feet 2 inches and in proportion to his height this horse is in fact somewhat under 15 hands. (Equestrian portrait of Charles I by Sir Anthony van Dyck)

30. A Paris diligence and cabriolet. The grotesque and rigid bucket-like postilion's boots were also worn in England. Though of earlier origin (*c.* 1575) than any English public coach, the diligence never quite achieved the speed and precision of the English mail-coach services.

obsolete by the end of Queen Elizabeth's reign. By the end of the Civil War it had also become obsolete under the half-armoured cuirassier and the buff-coated dragoon.

But England, like many of the warring states between Austria and Sweden, had become grossly over-horsed during the course of the war. What was to become of these oat-devouring monsters? Both breeding and importation of 'horses meet for service' had been greatly stepped up since Charles I's troubles with the Scots began in 1639. Now in 1651 after the abortive Royalist *putsch* had ended at Worcester with the flight of Charles II in disguise (as a groom, on a falconer's hackney) there were a great many surplus warhorses. Of these, the top layer were generals' and staff officers' chargers, Andalusians or Andalusian crosses, of quality; there would always be employment for them, since the career of this breed, as the nobleman's horse *par excellence* of all Christendom, had yet many years to run. But of the generality, ridden by regimental officers and troopers, there was a great surplus. For the most part country-bred, these tended to be of the stamp for which east central England from Lincolnshire to Cromwell's country about Huntingdon had long been famous: the Old English Black. It had a stately presence, its best pace was a trot, it had great pulling power in the shafts—and by modern standards it was slower than the Mills of God.

From the beginning, carriage teams had consisted of great horses, partly because of the enormous unloaded weight of early 'chariots'. The original *kocsi* was of much lighter construction when it left the Hungarian wainwright's hands, but most English coaches before they came to be built in this country were of German construction and much heavier than the prototype. The coach horse therefore continued to be a heavy horse—heavy enough to pull a waggon or a plough; hence the inroads made by the horse on the domain of the English draught-ox in this period of re-settlement. There were, however, cogent economic reasons that were to keep the plough-ox under the yoke for another century and more. The Great Horse could barely exist, let alone work, on the ration of good straw and indifferent hay which kept the draught-ox pulling away. Moreover it could not work in ox harness, though the converse was possible. In some regions therefore the plough-ox held its ground almost until the coming of the tractor. But in general English landlords, more willing than most to inject capital into their landed properties, made it possible for their tenants to turn over to horse ploughing, and by implication to the horse-drawn waggon. At the same time more and more of them began to equip themselves with coaches. Thus the surplus warhorses were absorbed into the economy at about the same rate as the military establishment was reduced after the Restoration of 1661, and a distinctive type of coach-horse began to emerge, though still more distinguished for pulling-power than for speed, let alone elegance.

Public coaches had already begun to run under the Commonwealth—called 'stage' coaches because every journey of more than about fifty miles entailed spending a night on the road, so that advertisements contained such phrases as 'the Coach sleeps at Reading', and it was not until 1669 that the Oxford coach, for instance, did the journey from London in one day, leaving at six in the morning. No coach, public or private, had glass windows until 1680. This is what the 'glass coach' of the Cinderella story means. Even so, there was no winter coach travelling in England before about 1706, at which time the journey from London to York took seven days, and to Edinburgh ten. When coach travel reached its peak of perfection at the end of the eighteenth century the London–Edinburgh run took forty hours, during which nobody slept, except those of the inside passengers who dozed off out of sheer exhaustion.

The great period of coaching lasted at most sixty years. In 1780 it had barely begun: by 1840 it was all over. It was not until 1784 that English coaches were considered fast enough or safe enough to carry the mails which up to then had been entrusted to post boys (riders), whose speed on the road averaged five miles an hour and who were notorious for their hard drinking. The great acceleration in coach speeds in the second half of the eighteenth century came about by improvements none of which were peculiar to Britain but occurred only there in combination at the same time. There was first of all an improvement in road-building, almost entirely due to capitalistic enterprise on the part of the Turnpike

Trusts, without Government action other than the passing of private Acts of Parliament which merely permitted the improvement or the laying out anew of a given stretch of road and the collection of a toll for its maintenance. Secondly a great advance was made in the design and construction of coaches, beginning with steel-leaf springs instead of leather slings, which resulted in greater stability; better patterns of harness were also developed. These joined with a uniquely English phenomenon, the inundation of thoroughbreds which now overstepped the bounds of the racing establishment and were to be seen in all sorts of employment, both under saddle and in harness. The old heavy stamp of coach-horse disappeared and in its place were found blood horses, either half-bred or wholly thoroughbred. The latter especially were all, one way or another, rejects—from the race-course and the hunting field, as well as from the privately-owned carriage team. They

must have been, at an average price of twenty-five pounds a time. We know a great deal about the performance of mail coaches because detailed statistics are available. No such complete records survive for private turn-outs, but the performance of some of these must have been even more impressive than that of the mail coaches, because though the standard of driving overall, despite the undoubted existence of brilliant amateurs, would not have been quite as high as that of the professionals, the quality of horses employed was much higher, and the loads carried not nearly so great.

One of the factors, perhaps after all the greatest single one, that drove the coach off the road was the cost of coach travel compared with that of the railway. Economies and rationalization became, in the end, impossible. Rationalization had reached its optimum by about 1790, since in addition to technical improvements to the vehicle and the road surface, the harness and the teams,

32. *Scenes on the Road, or a Trip to Epsom*. A possibly somewhat exaggerated print of a nineteenth-century traffic jam.

it was above all organization that had brought the coach services to the peak of efficiency: the split-second timings (one minute to change a team of four horses) and the absolute reliability in the ancillary services. This all cost money in manpower and accommodation, which was reflected in the scale of fares. Even so, before the railway challenge, contracting companies operated on a very large profit margin. At the very end, the surviving services committed themselves to a ruinous price-cutting war which only hastened their demise; when they got to the stage of saving money by cutting down quantity and quality of oats, they were doomed. The more expensive, and more comfortable, post-chaise service which had become efficient earlier than the public coaches, used the same ancillary services. But once the coaches were

gone, it was not worth while to the innkeeper, whose function was similar to that of the modern service station, to maintain his establishment for the sake of the chaise traffic alone, and it became a mere pothouse.

The traditions of the English mail-coach were continued overseas until the railways caught up there too, half a century later; for the American or Australian stage-coach had nothing in common with the lumbering, labouring English stage-coach, of the three-mile-an-hour pre-1780 period. It ran just as fast as the old English mail, commonly on much worse roads. With the demise of the English system there passed much glamour and glory; also much squalor, avarice, ruthlessness and downright brutality. The average life of a horse in a mail-coach team was reckoned at three years.

33. *In Time for the Train.* The railway age did not mean the end of the age of the horse, which continued until the invention of the internal combustion engine.

THE HORSE IN THE RAILWAY AGE

This is the last phase in the relationship of man and horse during which, over the greater part of the earth's land surface, the horse was indispensable for the every-day economic activities carried on by mankind as well as some very uneconomic activities such as war, both in the country and in the towns, and in the most sophisticated of towns at that. The indispensable function and all-pervading urban presence of the horse is perhaps best symbolized in the typically Victorian figure of the crossing-sweeper. He was not sweeping up mud, most of the time, but horse manure. The horse had a profound effect on the town planning of nineteenth-century London. With the rapid expansion of the middle class the carriage-keeping sector of society assumed enormous

34. Regent Street, London, in about 1900. The state of the roads was such as to keep crossing-sweepers continually busy.

proportions, if by carriage we mean any privately main-tained vehicle drawn by one or more horses for passenger purposes. These ranged from the ducal coach-and-four down through an infinitely elaborate scale of vehicles, some of whose details we shall explore later, to the pri-vately owned hansom that was identical in design with those that plied for hire as taxis do today. Thus to the miles and miles of late Georgian and Victorian residen-tial streets and squares and gardens and crescents are added, at the rear, corresponding miles and miles of mewses. A mews had once been a rare urban pheno-menon, in the days when the word meant what it said: a place to keep falcons in. All but a few of the nobility and gentry who spent a part of the year in London had kept their falcons at home in the country, so that the word came loosely, in a town context, to mean the stable-yard.

Almost at the time when the first railways began, what

in Elizabethan times had been called a 'street nag' ceased to exist as part of the London scene; that is to say, a saddle-horse kept exclusively for getting about the town. It was succeeded by the park hack, the function of which was not so much utility as recreation: middle-class Londoners above a certain standard of affluence ceased to go shopping or pay business calls on horseback. Instead, they 'set up a carriage'. This made enormous demands on building space. Quite apart from the fact that a one-horse vehicle requires a space to house it equal to that occupied by at least four horses in stalls, the yard outside the stable-cum-coachhouse must be large enough to manoeuvre in and out without turning nearly as sharply as had been the case when the ridden horse was performing these town functions. Similar developments took place in every city of the western world.

These mewses, in London at least, had a life that was all their own. There was a graded social hierarchy of fascinating interest, from the back premises of mansions in Belgravia (before 'mansions' came to mean blocks of flats/apartments) to cobbled courtyards in Islington where the liveliest activity was going on all day as the turnouts of various trades began and ended their rounds at different hours according to the nature of the business, beginning with the milkmen's and bakers' floats before

dawn. In provincial towns there were still people, mostly in late middle age, who stuck to the custom of their youth and still rode to their shops and offices from their homes in the suburbs, on horseback: like the Norwich printer and publisher Samuel Jarrold, who was still maintaining this daily routine in the 1860s. This meant that the backs of business premises, here and there in the 'downtown' as opposed to the residential quarters, had also to provide stabling space or a mini-mews of sorts.

To understand what this mews-life was like, halfway through the Railway Age, which for our purposes we are going to place between 1825 and 1925, one can do no better than read *Black Beauty*, begun in 1871 and completed and published in 1877, a few months before the death of the author. For indeed this chapter might just as well have been entitled *The Age of Black Beauty*. Anna Sewell, who wrote this, her only published work, died early in 1878, and before that year was out the book had been reprinted five times. It tells the life story of a horse up to the age of fifteen, in the hands of ten different owners, in London and Bath and various unidentifiable country places. Though inimitable, the work has had a host of imitators, almost all of unredeemed badness. No other book exists which demonstrates at every turn how dependent all classes of traveller were on the horse, once

35. A photograph of Hyde Park Corner, London, in about 1901, showing the various types of horse-drawn vehicle.

36. The London street scene of the 1890s. Here are the carthorses, the cab horses, and the omnibus horses that went to make up the 300,000-strong horse population of London.

they emerged from the railway station. From it we also learn what a large sector of the population still worked with horses, whether as grooms in great houses, drivers for hire, commercial travellers, draymen, or butchers' boys.

Butchers' boys had a quite special niche in the English Victorian street scene. Some sign boards over the shop-fronts of certain old-established purveyors still bear the legend '*Families waited on daily*'. What this meant in urban practice was that early in the morning the butcher's errand boy, who had to be a 'scholard', able to read and write, made the round of the regular customers on a pony, taking the day's orders from the cook or the housekeeper or whoever did the marketing but did not care to visit the butcher's personally, and never ordered by the week. Returning to the shop he handed in the order book and when the customers' requirements were made up he sallied forth again on the same pony, at the trot, carrying the joints on a special type of wooden tray which now no longer exists. With such dispatch did he make his round that every household received its order in time for it to be cooked for dinner—and dinner was much earlier than it is now, and the recipes in vogue in Victorian middle-class households all took longer to prepare than any cook of our day would tolerate outside the higher branches of the catering trade. Well patronized retail butchers vied with each other in putting a really good class of pony on the street; in fact it may be said that the nearest approach in the 1870s to the quality riding pony of today was more often seen under the butcher-boy's saddle than bestridden by the children of the rich, on the choice of whose mounts less care was spent, less money was laid out and less prestige depended than is the case in the 1970s. The chief difference was that the best pace of the butcher-boy's pony was of necessity a trot, the fastest possible, and it was not necessarily a comfortable ride, though it was a showy

one. The reason for this lay in the traffic regulations of the pre-motor age; a trot was the permitted pace for travel in the streets, and though in practice some horses and many ponies might gallop slower than they trotted, galloping in town was forbidden, in the eyes of most police authorities.

There were many others directly dependent for their living on riding or driving horses, in town and country alike, and behind them stood rank on rank of other trades ancillary to that of the horseman; first and foremost the shoeing smith, but also the harness-maker, the wheelwright, the coach-builder, the saddler, the cornchandler, the forage merchant. Right down to the

37. Cab horses photographed in London in 1902.

38. Edwardian gamekeeper at the kitchen door with his pony, an original photograph by Frank Meadow Sutcliffe.

beginning of this century hay and straw for the use of urban horse-keepers took up an enormous space in cities. Note the great width of the street near Piccadilly still called Haymarket; actually this market was moved three times, each time further east, before its closure in the 1930s, but to the end the parking of enormous hay-wains with high loads which stopped them passing under certain bridges and thus tied them to certain routes into (but not out of) the town constituted a special traffic problem. Large quantities of hay and straw were brought into London by barge, even by coastal steamer, until the First World War, but other cities were not so fortunate. Again, what goes into the urban stable must come out again, enriched in the process, and the one surviving Laystall Street, in E.C.1., serves to remind us of the vast tonnage of soiled litter and droppings that had to be accommodated somehow until the enterprising market gardeners of the suburbs had time and transport to take it away. That nowadays theatrical thoroughfare, Haymarket W.1., can be matched not merely with Edinburgh's Grassmarket but by scores and hundreds of *Marchés au Foin* and *Heumarktgassen* up and down the cities of Europe. Horses and all that

pertained to them took up an enormous amount of space in cities of the Railway Age. So too did even the buying and selling of them—the Horse Repositories of Knightsbridge and St Martin's Lane and the Elephant and Castle and Islington, successors in function of that Friday horse market at Smithfield which had been doing business without interruption since the twelfth century, more or less on the old stand. These weekly markets still, until the end of the nineteenth century, took place in the centre of London. Only the seasonal fairs, successors of the old Bartholomew Fair at Southwark and others, were pushed outwards. Thus the great North London autumn horse mart had by the turn of the century been pushed out to a field on the edge of the built-up area which is now High Barnet Underground Station. When this was built the fair moved to some fields behind the Old Red Lion at the foot of Barnet Hill, since when in recent years it has moved only a little way across the Dollis Brook, nearer to Totteridge.

The author lived at Hadley in the 1950s, and witnessed one of the last manifestations of the horse–railway symbiosis: in the form of special trains of horse-boxes unloading ponies from Wales for sale at Barnet

39. The brewer's dray horse, probably indispensable in Victorian times, remains in ours as the most prized prestige symbol of the British beer industry.

Fair. Once these ponies had walked in droves all the way from Montgomeryshire to such fairs as Barnet. Now they are moved exclusively by road-going horsebox.

It had been confidently predicted, long before the accession of Queen Victoria, that the coming of the railways would sound the death knell of the harness horse, if not the horse altogether. This prediction proved utterly wrong. While it is true that, for instance, about a thousand coach horses were made redundant by the opening in 1830 of the Liverpool and Manchester line alone, long-distance transport was the only field in which horses were displaced by Mr Stephenson's steam kettle. And it is significant that though in coaching terms Liverpool to Manchester was 'long-distance', in terms of the railway, almost at the outset, it was practically local. By the time the railway became the most considerable goods carrier over long routes, the business of the pack train had been swallowed up, over large areas of England and Europe, by the canals. But still the barge was horse-drawn. Otherwise, throughout the western world, the expanding railway network brought with it an unparalleled expansion in horse-drawn traffic. The railway terminus automatically implied the omnibus to take passengers to and from it, and in due course the omnibus was invented—in Paris.

Revolutions have a way of overtaking each other, sometimes so fast that they nip each other in the bud. In terms of European agriculture, north of a certain latitude the replacement of oxpower by horsepower which had been going on slowly since the Middle Ages was greatly accelerated—virtually completed—in England in the half-century during which steam power came to fruition, so that in the lifetime of George Stephenson a great variety of improved agricultural machinery came into use, to be drawn by horses of the 'improved' heavy breeds such as the Clydesdale, the Shire, the Percheron and the Belgian Ardennais which were now seen at work far and wide outside the narrow circle of the regions whose name they bear. The period when the first railway passenger coaches were being built is the same in which the majestic English harvest waggons of varying regional design reached their ultimate functional and aesthetic perfection. Steam ploughing with static traction engines at either end of the field had a great vogue in the mid-nineteenth century, but entirely failed to displace the agricultural horse anywhere.

That era in which the highroads were temporarily eclipsed by the iron track also saw a new flowering of the long-neglected byroads. The fast smart light post-chaises of the well-to-do now had their counterparts on country roads in the shape of the farmer's gig, not only in England but in such regions as Normandy and Friesland, where local traffic previously had consisted solely of the ridden horse. This is the great period of the coach-builder, of the elegant equipage in all its forms, in which the harness horse almost became supreme; so much so that many breeds which had once been pre-eminently riding horses or of general utility became specialized as coach-horses, like the Yorkshire coach horse which was bred up from the original multi-purpose Cleveland Bay, or the hackney, first employed solely as a riding-horse but now, as a result of nineteenth-century specialization, regarded as the light harness horse *par excellence*. The whirligig of time brings in his revenges; as a result of the revived interest in riding in our own day and the impossibility of putting any sort of horse-drawn vehicle on the road with safety or comfort late in the Petrol Age, many amateurs of this stamp of horse are busy trying to breed out the very characteristics which made them eminently saleable in the 1850s, and to replace them by the conformation of the riding horse.

Not only was the final expansion of the English thoroughbred race-horse completed within this period, so that the genealogical guidelines of the General Stud Book and the code of conduct imposed by the Jockey Club became valid from Seville to Siam, but the railways brought the masses as well as the upper classes to the race-course. The vast expansion of racing, not only in the number of countries where it was indulged in, but also in the scale on which it took place, was largely the result of easy transport by rail, of horses, jockeys, bookmakers, owners and spectators alike. Not only flat racing and steeplechasing enjoyed this fashionable vogue but also its secondary derivative, harness-racing, which is largely the product of an American adaptation. The standard-bred racing trotter, almost entirely descended from the English galloping thoroughbred Mambrino through his trotting son Messenger who was imported to the United States in 1788, is now found in great numbers in many European countries. The breeding of race-horses was greatly facilitated by the possibility of sending mares to stud by rail.

The Napoleonic Wars were the last great armed conflict in which the means of transport and communication by land of the warring powers were essentially those available to Julius Caesar. No mechanical aids

40. *Their Majesties' Return from Ascot* by Sir Alfred Munnings. The familiar Windsor greys taking George V and Queen Mary home from the races.

were present, orders and information were passed by mounted messenger (at most by carrier pigeon and semaphore; both unworkable in stormy weather or bad visibility), and the pace of an army was, if not that of marching infantry, at most that of the artillery teams without whose support a cavalry force was unlikely to be effective against an opponent equipped with all arms. Already in these wars the greater proportion of artillery to infantry in all European armies, forced on them by the Corsican genius who had begun his career as a gunner, meant that greater numbers of horses were employed. Now this proportion was greatly increased in the series of wars which broke out in mid-century: 1848, 1861, 1866, 1870, drawing even greater numbers into the maelstrom of war. But these wars of the mid-nineteenth century, including the catastrophic American Civil War of the 1860s, were also the first railway wars. The railway factor did nothing to discourage the employment of cavalry. On the contrary, mounted units could now achieve strategic moves, as opposed to tactical marches, by rail like any other arm of the service, as shown by the equation 'Hommes 40, chevaux 8' proclaimed until recently on every cattle truck of the French State Railways.

That British Vietnam, the Second South African War, fought in the teeth of European and American disapproval from radical and conservative quarters alike, at great cost in manpower, in shipping, in money, in horseflesh out of all proportion to the political results achieved, was such a horse-and-railway war. In it, British cavalry of the traditional type, whose whole training and equipment were designed to enable them to close with the sword at the earliest possible moment, proved ineffective against a hard-riding, straight-shooting enemy who simply declined to be closed with. This dearly-bought experience gave rise to the 'new' concept of mounted infantry, not differing essentially in function from the Cromwellian invention of dragoons: mounted units organized like infantry and primarily equipped with infantry weapons, whose role was to ride to some position tactically suitable for infantry action in attack or defence, and thereafter fight as infantry. Though the establishment was modified in this sense, the opportunity to profit by these lessons never arose,

simply because never again was a British force to be confronted with an enemy so well provided with campaigning horses, so organized, so equipped and so endowed with tactical sense and small-arms skill as the mounted Boer commandos. In 1914 the other European powers on both sides were practically unaffected by this South African syndrome; all had massive cavalry components equipped either as lancers or swordsmen primarily, as mounted riflemen only secondarily, and intended for a tactical role that was essentially Napoleonic. On the Western Front the cavalry of both schools was alike impotent and frustrated by the combination of barbed wire and machine-guns, and later on the same front by the omnipresent aerial reconnaissance; for of all arms cavalry is the most difficult to hide from the spotting aircraft, though its capacity for dispersal into open order while continuing the advance or retreat makes it less vulnerable to actual attack from the air than one might suppose. On the Eastern Front with its great open spaces and often thinly-held sectors of the line there was more opportunity for the cavalry, and vast masses of horsemen of the German, Russian and Austrian armies did in fact get to grips with each other.

After 1917, in the Russian Civil War, in the Nationalist risings in the Ukraine and in the war of the revitalized Polish State against the new-born Soviet regime, cavalry played a large part, and for the last time in European affairs: here were entire armies composed almost solely of mounted troops, quite in the Jenghis Khan tradition. Their tactics were 'pure' cavalry tactics, with no nonsense about mounted infantry. There was a faint echo of this old tradition during the winters of the Second World War on the Eastern Front, when Russian cavalry formations rode over the frozen snow which the frozen-up German tanks could not cross, to wreak havoc among German reserve units in 'back areas'.

Competitions in horsemanship at international level, Olympic or otherwise, began in the late nineteenth century, the first such event being the long-distance Vienna–Berlin ride, open to officers of the German and Austro-Hungarian armies, in 1892. On a vast scale (580 km) it resembled the road-and-tracks phase of the modern three-day event, known in every country but

41. *Forward the Guns.* Lucy Kemp Welch, who died in 1958, was the English Rosa Bonheur. She was at the height of her powers during the First World War, when she worked in a remount depot. The picture, painted in 1917, reminds us that almost all the artillery of both sides in that war was moved solely by horses, as in the days of Napoleon.

England by the English word 'Military'. When the modern Olympic Games began in 1912 the ridden events were almost entirely confined to officers of the cavalry or other mounted arms. A study of these results shows how remote in practice the technique of horsemanship is from the true business of war. The performance of its select mounted representatives bears no relation at all to the effectiveness of an army. In terms of both individual performance and of national teams, many of the top performers over the years represented armies whose military virtues were quite untried, since they had never fired a shot in anger for as long as a century before the modern Games began; or else armies of deplorable professional calibre; or else armies whose entire function is to support some junta of generals.

All of this has nothing to do with the U.S. Cavalry, without whose existence so many Hollywood producers would not know where to turn for their daily bread. The story would be a remarkable one in any case, since the Hollywood concept is right in at least one respect: most of the active service of American cavalry units was in fact spent in the wars against the Red Indians. And these, in their equestrian capacity, present an almost unique picture. How does it happen that a people, so late in their history, and confronted with the horse (equally late in its history, counting from its first domestication) could have become so skilled in horsemanship so quickly, and have come so soon to depend so utterly on the horse in furtherance of their way of life? Except in the very barest essentials, Amerindian horsemanship owed nothing at all to the equestrian technique of either the North American frontiersman or the Mexican *vaquero* with his Spanish traditions. From the beginning, the Amerindian seat on a horse was something all its own. For one thing, it was stirrupless, as the Eurasian

had been in the beginning. Some authorities have put the natural, spontaneous, instant success of the red man as a horseman down to the forest background of certain tribes, accustomed to climbing high trees from early youth and thereby acquiring a unique sense of balance, which has put a premium on their services in such capacities as steeplejacks and steel erectors in the concrete jungle of New York. But not all, not the majority, and not the most formidable of the mounted Indians were forest dwellers. A parallel case can be sought perhaps in the Bushmen of South Africa, and in the Australian aborigine. Both these races revealed themselves in due course as supremely effective natural horsemen with a technique that owed virtually nothing

to that of the Europeans, before whose coming there had been no horses in the land. Both utterly lacked an agricultural background, both were 'pure' hunters in the same sense as were Europeans of the Old and Middle Stone Ages. So also were certain North American tribes, though others who subsequently took to the horse had practised horticulture at a quite sophisticated level. In an environment where man is just another species of raptor competing on equal terms with other raptorial species like the wolf and the lynx, his relationship to the grass-eaters that are his quarry (including the horse) is something unique; it is also strange and passing unpalatable to the urban humanitarian of today with his conscientious objection to hunting in all its forms. The

42. *Dismounted : the Fourth Troopers Moving the Lead Horses* by Frederic Remington. The US cavalry at the time of the Indian wars. Once again the cavalry are being used as mounted infantry and the horses moved to the rear while their riders take up firing positions. This means that one man in four is ineffective.

43. Painted Attic drinking-bowl showing the chariot team of Achilles.

44. Laconian kylix or cup with a painting of a horseman on the inside.

hunting man whether in Stone Age Europe or in pre-Columbian America was not really on equal terms with competing carnivores. He had not the keen scent of the wolf nor the hearing of the lynx; beside the keen sight of the eagle he was as if purblind; his strength of arm and of jaw were by comparison contemptible, nor was he equipped with anything but an apology for tooth and claw. For these deficiencies the weapons he fashioned did not really compensate—not even the bow. What he had to do, and what he did, was to understand and infiltrate and conquer the mind and the soul of the quarry. Perhaps that is what the animal portraits of the painted caves are all about: not about some vaguely-defined 'magic'. Certainly it was this inherited skill (which had been present also in the hunters of the Eurasian steppe, but not among the peasants of the Fertile Crescent or their priests and rulers in the Old World who are the undoubted ancestors of our urban civilization) that made the Red Indian a 'natural' horseman as soon as he set eyes on a horse. All he needed to learn from the Paleface was the fact that the Medicine Dog actually could be ridden: the rest he did for himself.

The rise and fall of the Red Indian's equestrian culture lasted but two centuries at most, of which the second coincided at least over the greater part with the Railway Age of Europe. It brought him inevitably into ever more bitter conflict with the white American, whose westward expansion was gathering its greatest momentum early in the nineteenth century. And the western pioneer riding his horse in front of the ox-drawn waggon train or guarding its flanks or protecting its vulnerable rear was taking part in the final expansion of the horseman's world. The closest that horses had got to America, after their great migration across the Bering Strait into Siberia, was Greenland, to which the Norse settlers took horses soon after AD 1000. But the last of these, Green-land white man and Greenland horse, were dead long before Columbus set sail. The post-Columbian colonizers, English, Scots, French, Portuguese, Spaniards, all took horses to the New World, but in general these horses made but the shallowest bridgeheads for the first two or three centuries. When the Americans burst out into the enormous spaces beyond the Mississippi, all the stages of European transport history—first the waggon, then the coach—were acted out all over again: but on a gigantic scale. The route traversed by the famous Pony Express in the two years of its existence in 1860 and 1861 was duplicated, most of the way, by the Wells-Fargo coaches, and the distance was almost exactly ten times that of the most famous English mail-coach route—York to London.

Since the seventeenth century when the Dutch had brought the horse to the Cape of Good Hope by sea, thus by-passing the lethal belt of tsetse fly country which had barred its progress down the continent of Africa, there had been no more worlds for the horse to conquer, until Captain Cook found a new one. The very high cost of transportation, which the British Government stinted not to disburse in the process of removing its least desirable subjects to Botany Bay, had the opposite effect in the equine sphere. Nothing but the best was worth the exorbitant passage money. This is the reason why the Australian stock horse, equivalent in function to the western American range pony, is so very nearly thoroughbred. For similar reasons New Zealand horse stock as a whole shows a higher percentage of 'blood' than that of any other horse population in the world. Here in the Antipodes the wheel has gone full circle and the horse is still found in partnership with mankind, in the same employment that led to its first taming on the steppes of Asia; herding livestock on grasslands so great in extent that the task, on foot, is beyond the power of human endurance.

2. The age of the chariots

CHARIOT TRAINING

It has often been stated that the domestication of the horse is younger, as an element in civilization, than the practice of writing: but such is not the case. The horse was first tamed by people who could neither read nor write and who lived a long way from the nucleus of culture where writing was later invented. For this reason we are totally dependent, for the record of the equestrian arts, on archaeological evidence until a fairly late stage. It is purely and literally a matter of bits and bones up till the point where the path of the penman crosses the path of the horseman. The document reproduced below represents that moment, at least in the light of discoveries so far.

In the reign of King Sepululiumas of the Hittites,

about 1360 BC, this training manual was composed for the instruction of the very formidable corps of chariotry which the Hittite empire, then a major Near Eastern power, maintained. It is not the first written mention of horses, but the first book about horses and nothing else. The author's name was Kikkulis, and he was not a Hittite but a Mittannian, a member of that people known to later history as Medes, employed as Master of the Horse by the Hittite king.

One need not be surprised at the lack of 'literary' quality. In the first place, the author was not writing, or dictating, in his native language; and indeed some of the concepts he needed to express had no words in Hittite, so that he is forced to employ some technical terms in the related but different Indo-European language of the Mittanni, which is more like Sanskrit in form. His object was not to please or to entertain but to record a set of standing orders. It is even doubtful

46. Egyptian bronze axe-head of the Eighteenth Dynasty (*c.* 1450 BC), the earliest known Egyptian figure of a horse; not ridden, but led in hand by a method assumed to be that of charioteers and not riders. The reins (bridle not shown) are held over the withers.

45. The eight-spoke, sixty-inch, iron-shod Assyrian chariot wheel drawn by very large horses, probably of Central Asiatic origin, corn-fed, their musculature being the result of systematic training such as that described by Kikkulis.

whether those who would see to their execution, the thickear squadron-leaders of the Hittite Chariot Corps, could read. Quite likely the manual was read out to them by the regimental scribe. It is extremely repetitive, but that is inherent in the nature of the subject.

Allowing for the fact that barley, not oats, is the normal grain fed to horses in the Near East today, and that hay as we know it does not exist there, the dieting aspect of this regime would cause few raised eyebrows at Epsom today. What seems alien is the abundant use of water externally; but we are dealing here with the very hot and dusty summer of eastern Anatolia.

Training begins in March, and the horses, already greatly removed from the conditions of the wild, have become fat, instead of lean, during the winter.

※These are the words of Kikkulis, master horseman from the land of the Mittanni.

When the groom takes the horses to pasture in the spring, he harnesses them and makes them pace three leagues and gallop two furlongs. On the way back they are to run three furlongs. He unharnesses them, rubs them down, and waters them, then leads them into the stable and gives them each a handful of clover, two handfuls of barley, and one handful of chopped green grass, mixed together. When they have eaten all up, they are to be picketed.

Then at evening he leads them out of the stable, harnesses them, and drives them at the pace one league and makes them run two furlongs. On return he un-

harnesses them, rubs them down and waters them. He leads them into the stable and gives them three handfuls of green chaff. When they have eaten this he muzzles them.

The muzzling at night is to prevent the horses eating the bedding or chewing the manger, since they will have a craving for bulk, coming off grass to this sparse if concentrated diet.

Regime for subsequent days is given below mostly in summarized form, save where one differs totally from the rest, regarding work or diet.

Day 2. Pace one league, run two furlongs. Feed two handfuls grass, one of clover, four handfuls barley. Graze all night.

Day 3. Pace $2\frac{1}{2}$ leagues, run two furlongs out. Run three furlongs, pace half a league home. Green grass at midday, followed by watering. Pace one league in evening. Feed grass and straw at night.

Day 4. Pace two leagues, in morning, one at night. No water all day. Grass at night.

Day 5. Pace two leagues, run twenty furlongs out and thirty furlongs home. Put rugs on. After sweating, give one pail of salted water and one pail of malt-water. Take to river and wash down. Swim horses. Take to stable and give further pail of malted water and pail of salted water. Wash and swim again. Give handful grass. Wash and swim again. Feed at night one bushel boiled grain with chaff.

Day 6. Wash five times in morning, graze in afternoon and wash once.

Repeat for 4 days

Day 11. Anoint all over with butter.

Day 12. Keep in stable all day. Feed only grain and cut grass.

Repeat for 10 days

Day 23. Wash in warm water. Feed grass.

Repeat 7 days

Day 31. Same for 3 days but anoint with butter.

Day 34. Picketed outside stable all day without feed or water. Race three furlongs in evening, graze all night.

Repeat 3 days

Day 38. Swim morning, then pace two leagues. No

day feed or water. Evening, pace nine furlongs. Night feed grass and straw.

Repeat 9 days

Day 48. Stand up all day. One handful of grass midday. Evening, pace half a league. Water and grass at night.

Day 49. Pace half a league. Swim.

Day 50. Pace three leagues, run two furlongs. Grass at night.

Repeat 9 days

Day 60. Pace nine furlongs, run (?) furlongs. Grass at night.

Day 61. Pace seventeen furlongs, morning. Pace seventeen furlongs, run two furlongs, evening.

Day 62. Pace seventeen furlongs, run two furlongs. Wash, swim three times. Feed bushel boiled barley with chaff. Grass at night.

Day 63. Pace four leagues, run two furlongs. Repeat nine days. Bathe in hot water on fifth evening.

Day 73. Two handfuls of barley after morning work, with chaff. Pace half a league, run two furlongs, evening.

Day 74. Pace half a league, morning. Pace seventeen furlongs, evening, run three furlongs.

Day 75. Pace seventeen furlongs, run three furlongs. Wash, swim five times, feed grass after every other swim. Boiled grain with chaff at night.

The Hittite league (*Kas*) is computed to have been about 6 km—the distance a man can walk in one hour (Russian *chas*—hour). The furlongs are computed from so many Hittite *Iku*, the hundredth part of a *Kas*.

The gaits mentioned have caused prolonged crises of interpretation. They differentiate in the original between a travelling speed and a racing speed. The

former cannot, on grounds of etymology, be taken to mean walk, or trot. The consensus of opinion is that what is meant is a lateral pace, in which not the sequence of footfalls but only the length of the stride and the speed of movement varies as between travelling and racing. They have been rendered here as 'pace' and 'run' respectively, and the gait will be that seen in American pacers at sulky races.

The above summarizes the content of the first of five clay tablets on which is detailed, in cuneiform writing, the daily routine for a course of training lasting seven months. The great efforts demanded in the first few days are meant as a trial, to eliminate at the outset those horses which will not be good enough to submit to this long and costly course. The procedure of Day Five is known as a 'sweating gallop' and the long drinks of salted and of malted water are meant to replace the fluid in the body. The amounts of feed given should be considered in the light of the size of the horses—perhaps not much bigger than Welsh mountain ponies and only slightly above the size of the aboriginal wild Type IV of this region. This is a highly sophisticated technique of horse-keeping, based entirely on hand-feeding and housing most of the year, developed, probably over a long period of time, in the general area of Western Iran and Kurdistan. It depends on the availability of abundant labour. The large quantities of cut grass given as a feed to last all night, as hay is today, argue the presence of slaves who do little else but cut grass (the scythe, be it noted, had not been invented) with a reaping-hook. There was a special grade of low-caste labourer employed in Anglo-Indian establishments in this way in Victorian India.

From this text it appears that the whole of the training proceeded by pairs: not only the work in the chariot, but the 'slow' pacing in which the horses were yoked but driven by a groom on foot. The teams were inseparable, and if one horse was a casualty the survivor would only accept another yokefellow after considerable re-training.

This document was recovered from the site of the Hittite capital of Hattusas (Boghazköi in Turkey) in 1917, and it and related material, both textual and pictorial, was studied intermittently but intensively for

47. Egyptian chariots (compare with the photograph of the actual chariot from the tomb of Tutankhamun, Plate 12). The harness is the same in both, but whereas the team in the upper register is two horses of Arab strain of indifferent quality, that in the lower register is either a pair of onagers (Asiatic wild asses) or a pair of mules resulting from the cross of horse and onager or, less likely, horse and ass. Wall painting from Thebes, c. 1400 BC.

thirteen years by the Czech scholar Bedrich Hrozny, who produced, in French, the first rendering of the text into a Western language (in *Archiv orientalni*, 1929–31).

FUNERAL GAMES

Homer's superb description of the chariot-race in the games held at the funeral of Patroclus needs little commentary. One might point out that events of this kind, held during a lull in the fighting, differed materially from contests held in peace-time at Olympia and elsewhere, in that the surface of the track was not prepared but contained natural hazards, nor did the race consist of so many laps round a quite small arena but of a straight run to a goal visible from the starting post, and back again. From the spectators' point of view, it must have been very hard to make out who was leading in the middle of the race, when the chariots were far out 'in the country', and even harder because the horses were nearly all of the same colour—duller or brighter shades of dun. Only one other colour is mentioned throughout the Homeric poems—'phoinix'. Colour adjectives are the hardest words to interpret literally from a dead language, so much so that scholars today vary between 'bay' and 'chestnut' in their rendering of this word. For what it is worth, the name of the umpire in this race is Phoinix (Phoenix), presumably because he was born with hair of this colour: which does not help much. However, the team of Meriones is called 'fair-maned' whereas dun horses normally have black manes; Meriones' pair must have been what we now call palomino.

Three of the teams consist of two stallions; one of two mares; and one of a mare and a stallion: a fact which has aroused surprisingly little comment from scholars, since it seems to run dead contrary to the normal practice of antiquity, even to judge by written sources. As for the evidence of antique art, there is no extant picture or statue which suggests that the chariot team, whether for racing or for war, was ever composed of anything but entire males.

The words of the old trainer, Nestor, to his son on

the importance of the fast tight turn do provide a link between Hellenic and Celtic chariotry. In that region of southern Gaul where the Celts rubbed shoulders with the Massiliot Greeks we may assume that dashing young Provençal drivers practised this hazardous manoeuvre in built-up areas, for the corners of houses on such ancient sites as Entremont (Bouches du Rhône) are protected by slabs that have no architectural function but are striated with the scars of passing hubs.

The first to spring to his feet was Admetus' son Eumelus King of Men, who was an excellent horseman. Next, the mighty Diomedes son of Tydeus, who harnessed the horses of the breed of Tros that he had taken earlier from Aeneas on the occasion when Apollo saved their master's life. Then red-haired Menelaus son of Atreus, scion of Zeus, who yoked a fast pair, Aethe, a mare of Agamemnon's, and his own horse Podargus. Aethe had been presented to Agamemnon by Echepolus son of Anchises, on condition that he need not go with him to windy Ilium but could stay at home in comfort—he happened to be a very rich man, who lived in Sicyon of the broad lawns. This was the mare that Menelaus yoked—she was champing to be off. The fourth man to harness his long-maned horses was Antilochus. He was the noble son of the magnanimous King Nestor son of Neleus, and his chariot-horses were of Pylian breed. His father now went up to him and gave him some useful hints, though he knew his business well enough himself.

'Antilochus,' said Nestor, 'young as you are, you stand well with Zeus and Poseidon and they have taught you the whole art of driving horses. So there is no great need for me to put you right. But expert though you are at wheeling round the turning-post, your horses are very slow, and I am afraid you will find this a great handicap. Yet even if the other pairs are faster, their drivers do not know a single trick that is not known to you. So you must fall back, my friend, on all the skill that you can summon, if you do not wish to say goodbye to the prizes. It is skill, rather than brawn, that makes the best lumberman. Skill, again, enables a steersman to keep a straight course over the wine-dark sea when his good ship is yawing in the wind. And it is by his skill that one driver beats another. The average man, leaving too much to his chariot and pair, is careless at the turn and loses ground to one side or the other; his horses wander off the course and he does not correct them. But the cunning driver, though behind a slower pair, always has his eye on the post, and wheels close in; he is not caught napping when the time comes to use the oxhide reins and stretch his horses; he keeps them firmly in hand and watches the man who is leading.

'Now let me tell you something to look out for. It is obvious enough; you cannot miss it. There is a dead tree-stump, an oak or pine, standing about six feet high. It has not rotted in the rain, and it is flanked by two white stones. The road narrows at this point, but the going is good on both sides of the monument, which either marks an ancient burial or must have been put up as a turning-post by people of an earlier age. In any case it is the turning-post that my lord Achilles has chosen for this race. As you drive round it you must hug it close, and you in your light chariot must lean just a little to the left yourself. Call on your off-side horse, touch him with the whip and give him rein; but make the near horse hug the post so close that anyone might think you were scraping it with the nave of your wheel. And yet you must be careful not to touch the stone, or you may wreck your horses and smash up your car, which would delight the rest but not look well for you. So use your wits, my friend, and be on the lookout; for if you could overtake them at the turning-post, no one could catch you up or pass you with a spurt, not even if he came behind you with Adrestus' thoroughbred, the great Arion, who was sired in heaven, or the famous horses of Laomedon, the best that Troy has bred.'

Having thus expounded the whole art of horsemanship to his son, King Nestor went back to his seat. Meriones was the fifth man to get his horses ready. And now they all mounted their chariots and cast their lots into a helmet, which Achilles shook. The first lot to jump out was that of Antilochus son of Nestor; then came that of King Eumelus, followed by that of Atreus' son, the spearman Menelaus. Meriones drew the fourth

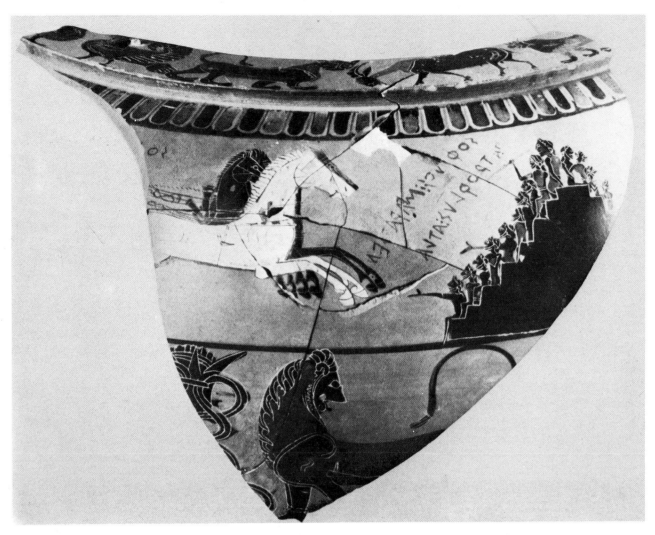

48. Games at the funeral of Patroclus. A fragment of a bowl from Athens, early sixth century BC, showing the grandstand with spectators at the chariot-race.

starting-place, and the last fell to Diomedes, the best man of them all. They drew up side by side and Achilles showed them the turning-point, far away on level ground. He had posted the venerable Phoenix, his father's squire, as an umpire there, to keep an eye on the running and report what happened.

At one and the same moment they all gave their horses the whip, shook the reins on their backs and set them going with a sharp word of command. The horses started off across the plain without a hitch and quickly left the ships behind. The dust that rose from underneath their chests hung in the air like a storm-cloud or a fog, and their manes flew back in the wind. At one moment the chariots were in contact with the fruitful earth and at the next were bounding high in the air. The heart of each driver as he stood in his car and struggled to be first was beating hard. They yelled at their horses, who flew along in a cloud of dust.

But it was not till their galloping teams had rounded the mark and were heading back to the grey sea that each man showed his form and the horses stretched themselves. The fast mares of Eumelus now shot out

of the ruck, and next came Diomedes' stallions of the breed of Tros, close behind, with very little in it. It looked as though at any moment they might leap into Eumelus' car. They were flying along with their heads just over him, warming his back and his broad shoulders with their breath. In fact Diomedes would have overhauled Eumelus then and there or made it a dead heat, if Phoebus Apollo, who was still angry with Tydeus' son, had not knocked the shining whip out of his hand. Diomedes, when he saw Eumelus' mares going better than ever and his own horses slowing down for lack of anything to spur them on, was so angry that the tears poured down his cheeks. But Athene had had her eye on Apollo when he fouled Diomedes. She sped after the great man, gave him back his whip and put fresh spirit in his horses. Moreover she was so enraged that she chased Eumelus too and used her powers as a goddess to break the yoke of his chariot, with the result that his mares ran off on their own and the shaft crumpled up on the ground, while Eumelus himself was flung out of the car and came down by the wheel. The skin was taken off his elbow, mouth and nose; his forehead was bruised; his eyes were filled with tears, and he was robbed of speech. Meanwhile Diomedes swept round the wreckage with his powerful horses, having left the others well behind. Athene filled his pair with strength and let their master triumph.

Next after Diomedes came red-haired Menelaus, Atreus' son; and next again Antilochus, who was shouting at his father's horses and urging them to spurt like Diomedes' pair. 'Show me your best paces now,' he cried. 'I am not asking you to race that pair ahead, the gallant Diomedes' horses, whom Athene has just speeded up so as to make her favourite win. But do catch up Atreides' pair . . . after them full tilt! Trust me to find a way of slipping past them where the track is narrow. I shall not miss my chance.' . . . Very soon Antilochus, that veteran campaigner, saw a place where the sunken road grew narrow. It ran through a gulley:

water piled up by the winter rains had carried part of it away and deepened the whole defile. Menelaus was in occupation of the track, making it difficult for anyone to come abreast of him. But Antilochus did not keep to it. He drove a little off it to one side, and pressed Menelaus hard. Menelaus was alarmed and shouted at him: 'You are driving madly, Antilochus; hold in your horses. The track is narrow here. It soon gets wider—you could pass me there. Be careful you don't hit my chariot and wreck us both.'

But Antilochus, pretending that he had not heard him, plied his lash and drove more recklessly than ever. They both ran on for about the distance that a quoit will carry when a young man casts it with a swing of the arm to test his strength. Then Menelaus' pair gave way and fell behind. He eased the pace himself, on purpose, fearing that the powerful horses might collide

49. Early Greek clay figurines from Tanagra of plough team and chariot both dependent on pairs of draught animals under the yoke, although the yoke is of a different pattern for ox and horse.

in the road and upset the light chariots, in which case their masters, through their eagerness to win, would find themselves rolling in the dust. But red-haired Menelaus managed to give the other a piece of his mind. 'Antilochus,' he cried, 'you are the most appalling driver in the world. We were mistaken when we thought you had some sense. Well, have it your own way; but all the same, you shall not carry off the prize till you have answered on your oath for this affair.'

Then Menelaus turned to his horses. 'Don't stop,' he shouted at them. 'Don't stand and mope. That pair ahead of you will weaken in the leg far sooner than you. They are neither of them as young as they were.' His horses, frightened by their master's reprimand, sped on with a better will and soon were close behind the other pair.

Meanwhile from their seats in the ring the spectators were looking out for the horses, who were rapidly approaching in a cloud of dust.

An argument develops among the spectators over the positions of the drivers.

By now Diomedes was very close. He was driving with the whip, swinging his arm right back for every lash, and making his horses leap high in the air as they sped on to the finish. Showers of dust fell on their driver all the time, and as the fast pair flew over the ground the chariot overlaid with gold and tin came spinning after them and scarcely left a tyre-mark on the fine dust behind.

Diomedes drew up in the middle of the arena, with the sweat pouring to the ground from his horses' necks and chests. He leapt down from his glittering car and leant his whip against the yoke. Sthenelus, his gallant

50. Two chariots confronted. Drawing after a *dinos* (large Greek goblet). Note the harness with knots for quick release in the absence of buckles.

equerry, made short work of the prizes . . . Then he unyoked the horses.

Antilochus son of Nestor was the next man to drive up. He had beaten Menelaus not by any turn of speed but by a trick. Yet even so Menelaus and his fast horses came in close behind. There was no more in it than the space that separates a horse from the wheel of his master's car when he strains in the harness and pulls him along, trotting so close in front that the tip of his tail keeps brushing the tyre and there is hardly any gap, however far he runs. There was no more than that between Menelaus and the peerless Antilochus. It is true that at the time of the incident Menelaus had been left as much as a disk-throw in the rear. But he soon came up with him. Aethe's mettle had begun to tell— she was Agamemnon's lovely mare—and on a longer course Menelaus would have passed him. It would not even have ended in a dead heat.

Meriones, Idomeneus' worthy squire, came in a spear-throw behind the famous Menelaus. His long-maned horses were the slowest pair in the race, and he himself was the poorest racing-driver.

The last of them all to arrive was Admetus' son Eumelus. He was dragging his handsome chariot himself and driving his horses in front of him. When he saw this, the swift and excellent Achilles was sorry for the man. He stood up in the ring and made a suggestion: 'The best driver of the lot has come in last. Let us give him a prize, as is only fair. Make it the second, for of course Diomedes takes the first.'

Antilochus objects to this arrangement, and Achilles agrees to give him the second prize of a mare. This leads to further dissent.

Menelaus had by no means forgiven Antilochus and he now got up in a very ugly mood. A herald handed him the speaker's staff and called for silence. Then Menelaus spoke, looking the king he was. 'Antilochus,' he said, 'you used to be a very sensible fellow. Now see what you have done! By cutting in across me with your own far slower pair, you have made my driving look contemptible and robbed my horses of a win. . . . Come forward here in the proper way; stand in front of your chariot and pair, holding the pliant whip you always

drive with; touch your horses; and swear in the name of the Earthshaker and Girdler of the World that you did not hold up my chariot by a deliberate foul.'

Antilochus apologizes immediately and wholeheartedly; Menelaus, touched, replies magnanimously.

'Antilochus, it is my turn to yield: I cannot be angry with you now. You have never been impulsive or unbalanced, though this was certainly a case where the high spirits of youth got the better of discretion. But another time be careful not to overreach your betters. No other Achaean would have found me so easy to placate. But you have suffered much and laboured hard in my behalf, and so have your noble father and your brother. I therefore accept your apology. And not only that, I will give you the mare though she is mine, to show our countrymen here that there is no pride or malice in me.'

With that, he handed over the mare to Noemon, one of Antilochus' men, and himself took the shining kettle [the third prize].

The Iliad, XXIII, translated by E. V. Rieu

FROM RELIGION TO SPORT

Pausanias, 'the Baedeker of the ancient world', has much to say in his *Itinerary of Greece*, written in the middle of the second century of the Christian era, and the ninth since introduction of harness races into the Olympic programme, about the conduct of the Olympic Games, and about the gods who presided over this festival. Of those mentioned as having temples or shrines at Altis in the Olympian plain, a surprising number have some connection with horses: Hippodamia, a deified princess whose name speaks for itself, to whom a sacred enclosure, an acre in extent, was dedicated; Demeter, worshipped at certain places under the guise of the Mare-Headed Goddess; Artemis, the cold-hearted hunting virgin; Poseidon, Patron of Horses; Ares, Patron of Horses; Hera, Patroness of Horses; Athene, Patroness of Horses; Castor and Pollux, the Divine Charioteers; Apollo, also a charioteer, and others. The influence of Poseidon was symbolized by many points of the race-course. The starting point was marked by a facsimile of the prow (*rostrum*) of a ship, and the start of the race was signalled by means of a model dolphin (sacred to Poseidon) which 'dived' while at the same time a brazen eagle was hoisted in 'flight'.

Pausanias also notes a spot adjacent to the hippodrome that was haunted by an equine ghost which had been the cause of many fatal crashes through horses shying at it. He passes on several explanations given to him about the origins of this intimidating Taraxippus:

such phenomena are well known in modern times, sometimes still in the vicinity of race-courses.

According to Theophrastus, the private owner who entered the most horses, and won the most prizes, was the politician Alcibiades who died in 404 BC. (The most conspicuous prince, as an owner of Olympic race-horses, was Philip II of Macedon, the Aga Khan of his day.) In one event, the first, second, third and fourth prizes were won by the chariots of Alcibiades; but then, he had entered several teams. In any game, then as now, money can bulldoze the opposition flat, if properly laid out. Euripides wrote some verses about the

51. Bronze model of a Roman two-horse chariot (*biga*) recovered from the Tiber. The platform evidently represents woven material of some kind whose pliability is meant to offset the absence of springs. The wheels have eight spokes.

Olympic winners of Alcibiades, thus rendered in North's *Plutarch*:

> For at th'Olympike games, thou hast with chariots wonne
> the first prize, second, third and all, which there in race were ronne.
> With praise and litle payne, thy head hath twise bene crownde,
> with olive boughes for victorie, and twise by trumpets sounde
> The heraulds have proclaimed thee victor by thy name: above all those which ranne with thee, in hope to get the game.

One cannot avoid the uncharitable thought that the front runners owned by Alcibiades may have owed much to the three unplaced teams of the same owner, practising obstructive tactics which left them unplaced themselves, and without actually breaking the rules.

Now both Pausanias and Plutarch regard this matter of racing from the orthodox standpoint of antique paganism. To them the race is a solemn occasion, being either a ceremony in honour of certain gods, or part of the funeral obsequies of some distinguished deceased person.

In the eyes of the early Christians, both these factors together, or one only, were enough utterly to discredit racing, which in the words of the good bishop Tertullian at the beginning of the third century was 'equally tainted with the sin of idolatry'. He maintained, in his 'De Spectaculis', that going to the races was as much an act of homage to the gods of Olympus as going to worship in some temple of Apollo or Jupiter. And of course he was quite right. The *spina* which ran down the centre island of the oval track was one long line of images to pagan gods. His denunciations of race-tracks and racegoers read now like some Ulster Calvinist's denunciation of the Church of Rome, only much better informed: when Tertullian is denouncing idolatry he really does know what the idols represent, and the relationship between the personages who were the subject of the images, and what part they were supposed to play at the race-meeting. He mentions with disapproval because of their pagan religious significance

52. Chariot-race in the late Roman Empire. This leaf of a fourth-century ivory diptych shows the presiding consul seated in his *pulvinar* (state box), while in the arena below four *quadrigas* (four-horse chariots) race round the *spina*, which is a tank of water.

53. Relief carving from Foligno showing a chariot-race, possibly in the Circus Maximus of Rome. The mounted figure on the left with a whip is an umpire. The *spina* with its images of pagan deities, and the presidential box around which centred so much ceremonial connected with the cult of the divine emperor, explain why the races were so repugnant to Christian feeling.

the racing colours worn by the drivers, and these are also mentioned with distaste in the letter of Theodoric the Great, the first barbarian King of Italy to call himself such openly, without maintaining the farce of being the servant of some puppet Emperor. Romulus Augustulus was dead, and so was the Western Empire, and Theodoric the Goth was king. But under him the circus and its races lived on, and much as he disliked it he was sufficient judge of what makes and unmakes a ruler in the public esteem as to write this letter of patronage for the meetings in the Circus Maximus at Rome, recorded in the selection made by his secretary, Cassiodorus, in the late fifth century.

KING THEODORIC TO FAUSTUS, PRAETORIAN PRAEFECT

The sight of a chariot-race drives out morality and invites the most trifling contentions; it is the emptier of honourable conduct, the ever-flowing spring of squabbles: a thing which Antiquity commenced as a matter of religion, but which a quarrelsome posterity has turned into a sport.

He describes the Circus Maximus.

Twelve *Ostia* at the entrance represent the twelve signs of the Zodiac. These are suddenly and equally opened by ropes let down by the *Hermulae* [little pilasters]. The four colours worn by the four parties of charioteers denote the seasons: green for verdant spring, blue for cloudy winter, red for flaming summer, white for frosty autumn. Thus, throughout the spectacle we see a determination to represent the works of Nature. The *Biga* is made in imitation of the moon, the *Quadriga* of the sun. The circus horses, by means of which the servants of the Circus announce the heats that are to be run, imitate the herald-swiftness of the morning star. Thus it came to pass that while they deemed they were worshipping the stars, they profaned their religion by parodying it in their games. . . .

There are always seven circuits round the goals to one heat, in analogy with the days of the week. The goals themselves have, like the decani of the Zodiac, each three pinnacles, round which the swift quadrigae circle like the sun. The wheels indicate the boundaries of East and West. The channel which surrounds the Circus presents us with an image of the glassy sea, whence come the dolphins which swim hither through

the waters. The lofty obelisks lift their height towards heaven; but the upper one is dedicated to the sun, the lower one to the moon: and upon them the sacred rites of the ancients are indicated with Chaldee signs for letters.

The *Spina* [central wall, or backbone] represents the lot of the unhappy captives, inasmuch as the generals of the Romans, marching over the backs of their enemies, reaped that joy which was the reward of their labours. The *Mappa* [napkin], which is still seen to give the signal at the games, came into fashion on this wise. Once when Nero was loitering over his dinner, and the populace, as usual, was impatient for the spectacle to begin, he ordered the napkin which he had used for wiping his fingers to be thrown out of the window, as a signal that he gave the required permission. Hence it became a custom that the display of a napkin gave a certain promise of future *circenses*.

We observe, too, that the rule of this contest is that it be decided in twenty-four heats, an equal number to that of the hours of day and night. Nor let it be accounted meaningless that the number of circuits round the goals is expressed by the putting up of *eggs*, since that emblem, pregnant as it is with many superstitions, indicates that something is about to be born from thence. . . .

We are compelled to support this institution by the necessity of humouring the majority of the people, who are passionately fond of it; for it is always the few who are led by reason, while the many crave excitement and oblivion of their cares. Therefore, as we too must sometimes share the folly of our people, we will freely provide for the expenses of the Circus, however little our judgement approves of this institution.

Cassiodori Variae, Book III

As a Goth, Theodoric admired fine horsemanship (we shall witness, in the next chapter, a notable display of equitation by another Gothic king, Totila). As an Arian, an adherent of one of the most joyless sects ever to have branched off from the main stream of Christianity, he was bound to look askance at such frivolities as race-meetings, quite apart from all the pagan implications of the ceremony of the race-course, of which he was as well aware as Tertullian before him, especially after being briefed by a scholar like Cassiodorus. In writing to the Praetorian Praefect who was a sort of Lord Mayor cum Chief Constable, he feels bound to touch on a problem of public order, the organized partisans of the Blue, Green, Red and White racing stables.

These supporters' clubs were noted for their hooliganism, and in Constantinople where the chariot-racing tradition lived on after it had died on Tiber-side, their mindless brutal violence surpassed anything achieved by the fans of Celtic or Rangers: they became a policeman's nightmare. More, a Special Branch nightmare, for they transferred their interest to affairs of state, and rival politicians jockeyed for the favour of the race-gangs, the Byzantine Rent-a-Crowd, which aspired to make or break emperors.

For many centuries after Theodoric, while Rome declined but Constantinople still prospered, chariot-racing still flourished in the eastern capital, until at least the twelfth century, when the Emperor Alexius Comnenus entertained the Norwegian king Sigurd the Pilgrim in the Hippodrome—called *Padreimr* in Sigurd's biography by the Icelander Snorri son of Sturla. At last there came a day in 1453 when Turkish guns battered a breach in the walls of Constantine's Town, Micklegarth, Byzantium, Istanbul, and the conqueror Mohamed II rode through in triumph. Under the Turks, the buildings around the Hippodrome fell into decay, but the track itself remained an open space, called in Turkish *At-maidan*—'the plain of horses'—now a race-course for ridden horses.

THE DEATH OF CÚCHULAINN

Outside the race-course, the last reference to the chariot in Europe in connection with verifiable historical events is from Ireland. There, St Patrick is given a lift by some of his royal patrons in their chariots. But by this time the vehicle had certainly ceased to have military significance; it was simply used for travelling. In the Irish heroic sagas, the earliest of which depict

Irish society as it was in the last few centuries BC, the chariot figures in the earlier cycles as a fighting vehicle, but in the later cycles it has already been replaced by the mounted warrior. Even in the sequel to Cúchulainn's death, his avenger Conall pursues the slayer not in a chariot but on horseback.

But Cúchulainn's own horses were dual-purpose, ride and drive. The steeds of Irish heroes, like those of Homeric heroes, prophesy, though not in words. Thus the Grey of Macha will not at first be harnessed for the fatal battle, but 'thrice did the horse turn his left side to his master'. Since he was the right-hand member of the team, this made it impossible to put on the yoke. But if the champion had intended to *ride*, then the presentation of the left (near) side would have been appropriate. The Grey's unspoken prophecy runs 'This is a day for riding, not for driving.'

The Grey and his team-mate the Black Sainglend have about them certain attributes which belong to the lowest stratum of the matter of this story—the mythological, extending perhaps as far back in time as the Bronze Age. Eleanor Hull who made the following

English version pointed out that Cúchulainn had certain attributes of a sky-god, and the black horse in his chariot signifies Night, and the grey or white horse Day. In real life, charioteers of the Iron Age laid great stress on the exact matching of the pair, and this included colour. Hence the popularity, in this role, of golden duns with black manes, tails and legs, since it was easy to find horses of this colour to match exactly.

Chariot wheels found in Britain and Eire are without exception made of wood, the hub, felloes and six spokes being made separately and clamped together with an iron tyre. But a more archaic pattern of wheel has been found elsewhere in the Celtic world, in Gaul; also six-spoked, it is cast in one piece of 'white bronze' and its rim has a groove between two flanges, into which a wooden tyre consisting of three or four segments was inserted.

Cúchulainn's manner of driving is described in the *Wooing of Emer*, earlier in the Saga. He 'leaps the hero's salmon-leap into the air, and does many other like swift feats'. This is a memory of the acrobatic style of display described by classical authors as typical of

54. The treasure of Vix: fifth-century BC Greek wine-mixer made in Sicily or Apulia as a present for a Celtic queen in whose tomb it was buried. Greek wine merchants whose pack-horse routes lay through her territory found it worthwhile to buy her favour. The apparently so realistic modelling of the four-horse team is in fact a triumph of impressionism, since the number and position of the legs shown do not nearly correspond with reality. The harness is of a pattern then widespread in Europe and Asia. The chariot with its dashboard is of Mediterranean and not Gallic type.

the Celtic champion, running along the chariot pole and standing on the yoke, and so on.

Let us begin then, with the martial noise of the chariot's onset, that like the twang of the bowstring is heard no more in our world, which prefers sonic bangs and atomic booms.

※When Cúchulainn's foes came for the last time against him, the land was filled with smoke and flame; weapons fell from their racks, and the day of his death drew nigh. . . .

Then he took his shield, and ordered his charioteer, Laegh, to harness his horse, the Grey of Macha. But Laegh said: 'I swear by the God by whom my people swear, that though all the men of Conchobar's fifth were round the Grey of Macha, they could not bring him to the chariot. I never gainsaid thee until today. Come, then, if thou wilt, and speak with the Grey himself.'

Cúchulainn went to him. And thrice did the horse turn his left side to his master. On the night before, the Morrigu had unyoked the chariot, for she liked not Cúchulainn's going to the battle, for she knew that he would not come again to Emain Macha.

Then Cúchulainn reproached his steed, saying that he was not wont to deal thus with his master. Thereat the Grey of Macha came, and let his big round tears of blood fall on Cúchulainn's feet. And Cúchulainn leaped into the chariot, and started southwards along the road of Mid-Luachair. . . .

Then he saw somewhat, the Three Crones [i.e. the daughters of Calatin], blind of the left eye, before him on the road.

They had cooked a hound with poisons and spells on spits of the rowan-tree. Now, one of the things that Cúchulainn was bound not to do, was to go to a cooking-hearth and consume the food. Another of the things that he must not do, was to eat his namesake's flesh. [*Cú-chulainn* means 'Culann's Hound'. *Nevertheless, the Crones persuade him to eat a shoulder-blade.*] Then Cúchulainn ate it out of his [left] hand, and put it under his left thigh. The hand that took it, and the thigh

55. Chariot-race: a fourth-century AD Roman mosaic from the Horkstow Villa, Lincolnshire. At the end of the Roman occupation, a form of racing more like the modern Continental trotting race in sulkies than flat-racing *à la* Newmarket was still flourishing in Britain. The chariots used differed little from those that had been used for this purpose in Homeric Greece. The only thing that marks the passage of time is seen in the outline of the horse led by the race-course official. There are still no stirrups, but the substantial saddle with high wooden arches forming a 'tree', unknown to the classical world, has come to stay.

鹿児嶋英勇傳

篠原國幹

國幹ハ温良
篤實ふーし沈深
勇わり堂々と正く兵
兵と御するふ小懦
熟しー敵の正面り
向ふーるに足りて破るる
丸妙城得伏見の
復德川の兵と大抵
迫逐ひ
夏上野
黒門ー
向ひ敵未だ
解散せらほ小先導ー
黒門に入兵士恐て擁り
門外え七度曳底て乙四ヶ
指所々小戦功つ依らみ
陸軍少将功り拝しー近衛兵
長官と取り明治五年職を

辞も時小種田少將是城
愛ひ斯の如く士官り退小
ハ又慮がふき脈えふと談
論をーふ諸将篠原氏
を一生を誤らざふに又
朋あ乙云めひりせ又
西郷も訊く後賴して疑
を相謀らふゆ其可否
城決さき今回西郷の
爲小誤ーふるりのみ

五其平生業平生の
國幹やと異別人此
云とーと偉聞去云

小林清親

彫銀

画工　相生町三丁目番地
　　　小林清親
版　　吉川町二番地
元版　松木平吉

qui co fuetus erat bn portari
qn stabit sup manu mali por
tatois qm in illo falcone qui
semp male portatus e quado

quacuuq: ille qui male por
tatus e ez tn adeo e bn man
suefactus qp non e timendu
neqp d facie hominis neqp de
aliis rebz supzadcis remediuz

IN THE CHURCH OF MEIGLE Nº 6.

58. The only known British representation of the chariot, from a stone carving now totally defaced in the church of Meigle in Scotland. Executed in the Dark Ages but perhaps as late as the eighth century, it shows the very end of the chariot-driving tradition in Britain, after its latest written mention in the biography of St Patrick. Evidently no longer used for war, but as the conveyance for a royal person, this vehicle with its twelve-spoked wheels and covered top is more like the tinker's tilt-cart of the nineteenth century than anything otherwise recorded in the fragmentary history of Pictish Scotland.

57. Mounted falconers, an illumination from *The Art of Hunting with Birds* by Frederick, King of Sicily.

under which he put it, were stricken from trunk to end, so that their former strength abode not in them.

Then he drove along the road of Mid-Luachair around Sliab Fuad; and his enemy, Erc son of Cairpre, saw him in his chariot, with his sword shining redly in his hand and the light of valour hovering over him, and his three-hued hair like strings of golden thread over an anvil's edge beneath some cunning craftsman's hand.

'That man is coming towards us, O men of Erin!' said Erc. 'Await him.' So they made a fence of their linked shields, and at each corner Erc made them place two of their bravest, feigning to fight each other, and a satirist with each of these pairs; and he told the satirists to ask Cúchulainn for his spear, for the sons of Calatin had prophesied of this spear that a king should be slain thereby unless it were given when demanded.

And he made the men of Erin utter a great cry, and Cúchulainn rushed against him in his chariot, performing his three thunder-feats; and he plied his spear and sword so that the halves of their heads and skulls and hands and feet, and their red bones were scattered broadcast throughout the plain of Muirthemne, in number like unto the sand of the sea, and the stars of heaven; like dewdrops in May, and flakes of snow and hailstones; like leaves of the forests and buttercups on Magh Breagh and grass under the feet of the herds on a summer's day. And grey was that field with their brains after the onslaught and plying of weapons which Cúchulainn dealt out to them.

Then he saw one of the pairs of warriors contending together, and the satirist called on him to intervene, and Cúchulainn leaped at them, and with two blows of his fist dashed out their brains.

59. A more modern tilt-cart of the type used for making deliveries from the breweries at the end of the last century.

'Thy spear to me!' says the satirist.

'I swear by the oath of my people,' said Cúchulainn, 'thou dost not need it more than I myself do. The men of Erin are upon me here, and I too am upon them.'

'I will revile thee if thou givest it not,' says the satirist.

'I have never yet been reviled because of my niggardliness or my churlishness,' said Cúchulainn, and with that he flung the spear at him with its handle foremost; and it passed through his head and killed nine on the other side of him. And Cúchulainn drove through the host, but Lugaid son of Curói got the spear.

'What will fall by this spear, O sons of Calatin?' said Lugaid.

'A king will fall by that spear,' say they.

Then Lugaid flung the spear at Cúchulainn's chariot and it reached the charioteer, Laegh son of Riangabar, and all his bowels came forth on the cushion of the chariot.

Thereupon Cúchulainn drew out the spear and Laegh bade him farewell. Then said Cúchulainn, 'Today I shall be champion and I shall also be charioteer.'

Then he saw the second pair contending. . . .

The sequence of events is repeated; this time Erc takes the spear.

'What shall fall by this spear, O sons of Calatin?' says Erc, son of Cairpre.

'A king falls by that spear,' say the sons of Calatin.

'I heard you say that a king would fall by the spear which Lugaid long since cast,' he replied.

'And that is true,' say the sons of Calatin, 'thereby fell the King of the Charioteers of Erin, namely Cúchulainn's charioteer, Laegh mac Riangabra.'

Thereupon Erc cast the spear at him and it lighted on the Grey of Macha. Cúchulainn snatched out the spear, and each of them bade the other farewell. Thereat the Grey of Macha left him with half the yoke hanging from his neck, and went into Grey's Linn in Sliab Fuad. Then Cúchulainn drove through the host, and saw the third pair contending, and he intervened as he had done before. . . .

Again the same thing happens; this time Cúchulainn kills 'thrice nine other men'.

Then Cúchulainn for the last time drove through the host, and Lugaid took the spear and said, 'What shall fall by this spear, O sons of Calatin?'

'A king will fall thereby,' say the sons of Calatin.

'I heard you say that a king would fall by the spear that Erc cast this morning.'

'That is true,' say they; 'the King of the Steeds of Erin fell by it, namely the Grey of Macha.'

Then Lugaid flung the spear and struck Cúchulainn, and his bowels came forth on the cushion of the chariot, and his only horse, the Black Sainglend, fled away, with half the yoke hanging to him, and left the chariot and his master, the King of the Heroes of Erin, dying alone upon the plain. . . .

Cúchulainn puts his breast-girdle round a pillar, so that he will die standing up.

Then came the men around him, but they durst not go to him, for they thought he was alive.

'It is a shame for you,' said Erc, son of Cairpre, 'not to take that man's head in revenge for my father's head that was taken by him.'

Then came to Cúchulainn the Grey of Macha to protect him, so long as his soul was in him, and the 'hero's light' out of his forehead shone above him. And the Grey of Macha wrought the three red onsets around him. And fifty fell by his teeth and thirty by each of his hoofs. Hence is the saying: 'Not keener were the victorious courses of the Grey of Macha after Cúchulainn's slaughter.'

Then came the birds and settled on his shoulder.

'There were not wont to be birds about that pillar,' said Erc, son of Cairpre. Then Lugaid arranged Cúchulainn's hair over his shoulder, and cut off his head. And the sword fell from Cúchulainn's hand, and it smote off Lugaid's right hand, so that it fell to the ground. And they struck off Cúchulainn's right hand in revenge for this. Then Lugaid and the hosts marched away, carrying with them Cúchulainn's head and his right hand, and they came to Tara, and there is the grave of his head and his right hand. . . .

From Tara they marched southward to the river Liffey. But meanwhile the hosts of Ulster were hurrying to attack their foes, and Conall the Victorious, driving forward in front of them, met the Grey of Macha streaming with blood. Then Conall knew that Cúchulainn had been slain. Together he and the Grey of Macha sought Cúchulainn's body. They saw the corpse of Cúchulainn at the pillar stone. Then went the Grey of Macha and laid his head on Cúchulainn's breast. And Conall said, 'A heavy care is that corpse to the Grey of Macha.'

Then Conall followed the hosts, meditating vengeance, for he was bound to avenge Cúchulainn. . . .

So Conall pursued Lugaid to the Liffey.

There was Lugaid bathing. 'Keep a look-out over the plain,' he said to his charioteer, 'that no one come upon us without being seen.'

The charioteer looked past him.

'A single horseman is coming to us,' said he, 'and great are the speed and swiftness with which he comes. Thou wouldst deem that all the ravens of Erin were above him. Thou wouldst deem that flakes of snow were specking the plain before him.'

'Unbeloved is the horseman that comes there,' says Lugaid. 'It is Conall the Victorious mounted on Dewy-Red. The birds thou sawest above him are the sods from the horse's hoofs. The snow-flakes thou sawest specking the plain before him are the foam from the horse's lips and from the bits of the bridle. Look again,' says Lugaid, 'by what road is he coming?'

'He is coming to the ford, the path that the hosts have taken,' answered the charioteer.

'Let that horse pass us,' said Lugaid; 'we desire not to fight against him.'

But when Conall reached the middle of the ford he spied Lugaid and his charioteer and went to them.

'Welcome is a debtor's face!' said Conall. 'He to whom thou owest debts demands them of thee. I am thy creditor,' continues Conall, 'for the slaying of my comrade Cúchulainn, and here I stand suing thee for it.'

Then it was agreed to fight on the plain of Argetros, and there Conall wounded Lugaid with his javelin. . . .

When Conall found that he prevailed not, he saw his steed the Dewy-Red by Lugaid. And the steed came close to Lugaid and tore a piece out of his side.

'Woe is me!' said Lugaid, 'that is not men's truth [i.e. fair play], O Conall.'

'I gave it thee only on my own behalf,' said Conall; 'I gave it not on behalf of savage beasts and senseless things.'

60. A chariot-race at Batty's Grand National Hippodrome at Kensington, opened in the Exhibition year of 1851 for equestrian displays on the site where De Vere Gardens now lie; its great oval amphitheatre later became a riding school.

'I know now,' said Lugaid, 'that thou wilt not go till thou takest my head with thee, since we took Cúchulainn's head from him. Take therefore my head in addition to thine own, and add my realm to thy realm, and my valour to thy valour. For I prefer that thou shouldst be the best hero in Erin.'

Then Conall the Victorious cut off Lugaid's head. And Conall and his Ulstermen returned to Emain Macha. That week they made no triumphal entry.

But the soul of Cúchulainn appeared there to the thrice fifty queens who had loved him, and they saw him floating in his spirit-chariot over Emain Macha, and they heard him chant a mystic song of the Coming of Christ and the Day of Doom.

The Cúchulainn Saga (trans. 1898)

Much is taken for granted about the actual manner of fighting from the chariot, but it will be obvious that only the spear could be used from the moving vehicle. The sword-play must take place on foot, and the enigmatic 'three thunder-feats' probably have something to do with dismounting and re-mounting to do some damage either with the sword or, as here, with the bare fists. Apart from his javelin-throwing role, the champion was a sort of *panzer-grenadier* or *dragon-porté*, and long-lasting partnerships between him and the charioteer were necessary because of the close and almost instinctive co-operation required in the matter of setting down and picking up. There was another hazard incidental to this manoeuvre. Despite its skilled construction the chariot was rather fragile: there are two instances in Irish heroic stories of a wolf-hound (they were used as auxiliaries in battle, and weighed about as much as a man) leaping into the moving chariot: in both cases the axle broke, as it might well do under the impact of a heavy champion who landed clumsily on the footboard.

Even in the after-life the hero is still chariot-borne (was he not buried in it?). The curious final paragraph about the apotheosis has been described as part of the christianization of the story but apart from the song sung in the spirit-chariot it accords well with pagan Celtic images of the hereafter. If anything, it seems to savour of the Judaic background of Christianity: one cannot help thinking of Elijah and his chariot of fire.

3. From Greeks to Goths

By now there is little new to be said about Xenophon (c. 430–after 355 BC), the Old Master of all masters of horsemanship in all its branches. Except perhaps this: that in the course of a long and varied career he had been a mercenary in the Persian service, during which he will have met a great variety of cavalrymen drawn from Central Asiatic tribes with whom the Greeks had normally no contact whatever; for the armies of the Persian Empire had contingents drawn from subservient tribes in landlocked countries inaccessible to Greeks before the days of Alexander.

It is possible therefore that much of what he says will have been new to his countrymen, such as 'how to put a rider up Persian fashion', which he tantalizingly does not elaborate.

The astonishing thing is that so much of his lore is accepted today in a country and an age very far removed from his own. He deals with the eternal verities of horsemanship, not so much on the physical side but in regard to the psychology of the horse which has remained constant over the centuries, while human practice in riding and driving and horsemastership has varied in response to different demands. Thus much of what he says about the use of the muzzle, and the care to be taken in leading horses out together, is not of general application today, being only a matter that affects stud grooms: whereas around 430 BC the pugnacious stallion was used for all purposes, not just for breeding.

When one has bought a horse that he really admires, and has taken him home, it is a good thing to have his stall in such a part of the establishment that his master shall very often have an eye on the animal; it is well, too, that the stable should be so arranged that the horse's food can no more be stolen out of the manger than his master's out of the storeroom. In my opinion, the man who neglects this matter is neglecting himself; for it is plain that in moments of danger the master gives his own life into the keeping of his horse. A secure stable is a good thing, not only to prevent the stealing of grain, but also because you can easily tell when the horse refuses his feed. Observing this, you may know either that there is too much blood in him, or that he has been overworked and wants rest, or that barley surfeit or some other disease is coming on. In the horse, as in the man, all diseases are easier to cure at the start than after they have become chronic and have been wrongly diagnosed.

The same care which is given to the horse's food and exercise, to make his body grow strong, should also be devoted to keeping his feet in condition. Even naturally sound hoofs get spoiled in stalls with moist, smooth floors. The floors should be sloping, to avoid moisture, and, to prevent smoothness, stones should be sunk close to one another, each about the size of the hoofs. The mere standing on such floors strengthens the feet. Further, of course, the groom should lead the horse out somewhere to rub him down, and should loose him from the manger after breakfast, so that he may go to dinner the more readily. This place outside of the stall would be best suited to the purpose of strengthening the horse's feet if you threw down loosely four or five cartloads of round stones, each big enough to fill your hand and about a pound and a half in weight, surrounding the whole with an iron border to keep them from getting scattered. Standing on these would be as good for him as travelling a stony road for some part of every day; and whether he is being rubbed down or is teased by horseflies, he has to use his hoofs exactly as he does in walking. Stones strewn about in this way strengthen the frogs too. As for his mouth, you must take as much care to make it soft as you take to make his hoofs hard; and the same treatment softens a horse's mouth that softens a man's flesh.

It is also a horseman's duty, I think, to see that his groom is taught the proper way to treat the horse. First of all, he ought to know that he should never make the knot in the halter at the place where the head-piece fits round. The horse often rubs his head against the manger, and it may make sores if the halter is not easy about the ears; and of course when there are sores, then the horse must be somewhat fretful in bridling and grooming. It is well that the groom should have orders to carry out the droppings and the litter every day to a given place; by doing so he may get rid of it in the easiest way for himself, and would be doing the horse good too. The groom must understand that he is to put the muzzle on the horse when he leads him out to be rubbed down or to the place where he rolls; in fact, the horse ought always to be muzzled whenever he is taken anywhere without a bridle. The muzzle, without hindering his breathing, allows no biting, and when it is on, it serves to keep horses from mischievous designs. The horse should by all means be fastened from above his head; for instinct makes him toss his head up when anything is worrying him about his face, and if he is fastened in this way, the tossing slackens the halter instead of pulling it taut.

There follow instructions for grooming.

When a horse is to be led, I certainly do not approve of leading him behind you; for then you have the least chance to look out for yourself, and the horse has the best chance to do whatever he likes. Then again I object to teaching the horse to go on ahead with a long leading-rein. The reason is that the horse can then do mischief on either side he pleases, and can even whirl round and face his leader. Why, only think of several horses led together in this fashion—how in the world could they be kept away from one another? But a horse that is accustomed to be led by the side can do the least mischief to other horses and to men, and would be most convenient and ready for the rider, especially if he should ever have to mount in a hurry.

In order to put the bridle on properly, the groom should first come up on the near side of the horse; then, throwing the reins over the head and letting them drop on the withers, he should take the head-piece in his right hand and offer the bit with his left. If the horse receives it, of course the head-stall is to be put on; but if he does not open his mouth, the bit should be held against his teeth and the thumb of the left hand thrust within his jaw. This makes most horses open the mouth. If he does not receive the bit even then, press his lips hard against the tush; very few horses refuse it on feeling this.

Let your groom be well instructed in the following

points: first, never to lead the horse by one rein, for this makes one side of the mouth harder than the other; secondly, what is the proper distance of the bit from the corners of the mouth: if too close, it makes the mouth callous, so that it has no delicacy of feeling; but if the bit hangs too low down in the mouth, the horse can take it in his teeth and so refuse to mind it.

The following must also be urged strongly upon the groom if any work at all is to be done. Willingness to receive the bit is such an important point that a horse which refuses it is utterly useless. Now if the bridle is put on not only when he is going to be worked, but also when he is led to his food and home after exercise, it would not be at all strange if he should seize the bit of his own accord when you hold it out to him. It is well for the groom to understand how to put a rider up Persian fashion, so that his master, if he gets infirm or has grown oldish, may himself have somebody to mount him handily or may be able to oblige another with a person to mount him.

The one great precept and practice in using a horse

61. Bronze statuette of a mounted warrior from Grumentum, a Greek colony in Lucania, made at least 120 years before the birth of Xenophon (*c.* 550 BC). The human figure is detachable and when the piece first came to the British Museum the group included a female figure seated pillion behind the warrior. Regrettably she has been abducted since then.

62, 63. Details of the Parthenon Frieze, showing a procession of horses in the Panathenaic Festival. This dates from the period immediately before the career of Xenophon.

is this—never deal with him when you are in a fit of passion. A fit of passion is a thing that has no foresight in it, and so we often have to rue the day when we gave way to it. Consequently, when your horse shies at an object and is unwilling to go up to it, he should be shown that there is nothing fearful in it, least of all to a courageous horse like him; but if this fails, touch the object yourself that seems so dreadful to him, and lead him up to it with gentleness. Compulsion and blows inspire only the more fear; for when horses are at all hurt at such a time, they think that what they shied at is the cause of the hurt.

I do not find fault with a horse for knowing how to settle down so as to be mounted easily, when the groom delivers him to the rider; still, I think that the true horseman ought to practise and be able to mount even if the horse does not so offer himself. Different horses fall to one's lot at different times, and the same horse serves you one way at one time and another at another.

The Art of Horsemanship, IV–V

CROWNED BY HIS HORSE

Herodotus died when Xenophon was about six. He was a great traveller in the East: by land as far as Mesopotamia, by sea to the eastern shore of the Black Sea. Much that he has to tell us of the Scyths has been confirmed by the findings of archaeology, especially as regards their horseborne culture. Darius I was chosen king out of the junta of seven generals who had overthrown the tyrant Smerdis in 522 BC. The Persians combined literacy and the mastery of such arts as architecture and sculpture with a standard of horsemanship as high as that of unlettered tent-dwelling nomads like the Scyths. Anything that Herodotus had to tell his countrymen about what made the Persians tick was of practical importance because the King of Kings was a permanent bogey-man to the Hellenic world. Every Greek knew that despite Marathon, despite Salamis and Plataea, there might one day arise another Darius or another Xerxes: and this time his 'enterprise of Hellas' might come off. It was as import-

64. Youth with horse, from a Greek plate of *c.* 510 BC. Though the picture is older by more than a century, it shows the class of young man for whom Xenophon specifically wrote his *Art of Horsemanship*.

ant for Athenians of that day to be well informed about Persia as it was for seventeenth-century Englishmen to know all about Spain; how were they to know there would never be another Philip II?

With regard to the kingdom, they came to the following determination, that he whose horse should first neigh in the suburbs at sunrise, while they were mounted, should have the kingdom.

Darius had a groom, a shrewd man, whose name was Œbares; to this person, when the assembly had broken up, Darius spoke as follows: 'Œbares, we have determined with respect to the kingdom to do in this manner; he whose horse shall neigh first at sunrise, when we ourselves are mounted, is to have the kingdom. Now, therefore, if you have any ingenuity, contrive that I may obtain this honour, and not another.' Œbares answered, 'If, sir, it indeed depends on this, whether you shall be king or not, be confident on this point, and keep up your spirits; for no one else shall be king before you; I have a charm for the occasion.' Darius said, 'If you have any such contrivance, it is time to put it in practice, and not to delay; for tomorrow our trial is to be.' Œbares having heard this, did as follows: as soon as it was night, he led the mare which Darius's horse was most fond of, to the suburbs, tied her up, and led Darius's horse to her; and he led him several times round near the mare, gradually bringing him nearer, and at last let the horse cover her.

At dawn of day, the six, as they had agreed, met together on horseback; and as they were riding round the suburbs, when they came to the spot where the mare had been tied the preceding night, Darius's horse ran forward and neighed; and as the horse did this, lightning and thunder came from a clear sky. These things happening to Darius, consummated the auspices, as if done by appointment. The others, dismounting from their horses, did obeisance to Darius as king.

Some say that Œbares had recourse to the foregoing artifice; others, to the following (for the story is told both ways by the Persians); that having rubbed his hand upon the genital part of the mare, he kept it concealed under his trousers, and at sunrise, when the horses were about to start, Œbares drew out his hand and put it to the nostrils of Darius's horse, and that he, taking the scent, began to snort and neigh.

Accordingly Darius, son of Hystaspes, was declared king.

Thalia III

THE PARTHIANS

Spain excepted, the mounted elements of foreign armies whom the Roman armies encountered during their conquest of Western Europe were not formidable, and they could be neutralized by the numerically small (about two per cent of effectives) mounted wing of the legion under the old establishment, or at worst by a few squadrons of allied or auxiliary cavalry, leaving the field clear for the heavy infantry companies to make mincemeat of the barbarian foot. But as we shall see most clearly from the extract from Arrian, as soon as the empire began to expand outside Europe it met cavalry of a very different quality. Here is a fore-shadowing of what was to come, recounted by Livy from the Italian wars of the late Republic. Berber horsemen from North Africa riding Barb horses and there for the money (but also for the wine, the loot and the women) did not look impressive, nor did their horses, by Roman or other Italic standards, but they could be employed with deadly effect. One is reminded of the Moroccan *goumiers* of General Juin's corps in another Italian campaign, about 1944: they did not look impressive either, but it was better not to stand in their way.

※For a long time, nothing worth recording had occurred in Liguria; but, towards the end of this year, the Roman affairs there were twice brought into great peril; for the consul's camp, being assaulted, was with difficulty preserved; and a short time after, as the Roman army was marching through a defile, the Ligurians seized on the opening through which they were to pass. The consul, when he found that passage stopped up, faced about, resolved to return: but the entrance behind, also, was occupied by a party of the enemy . . . The consul had, among his auxiliary troops, about eight hundred Numidian horsemen, whose commanding officer undertook to force a passage with his troops, on whichever side the consul should choose. He only desired to be told on which part the greater number of villages lay, for on them he meant to make an attack . . . to set fire to the houses, in order that the alarm . . . might induce the Ligurians to quit their posts in the defile, and hasten . . . to carry assistance to their friends. The consul highly commended him, and gave him assurance of ample rewards. The Numidians mounted their horses, and began to ride up to the advanced posts of the enemy, but without making any attack. Nothing could appear, on the first view, more contemptible. Both men and horses were of a small size and thin make, the riders unaccoutred and unarmed, excepting that they carried javelins in their hands; and the horses without bridles, and awkward in their gait, running with their necks stiff and their heads stretched out. The contempt, conceived from their appearance, they took pains to increase; sometimes falling from their horses, and making themselves objects of derision and ridicule. The enemy, who at first had been alert, and ready on their posts, in case of an attack, now, for the most part, laid aside their arms, and sitting down amused themselves with looking at them. The Numidians often rode up, then galloped back, but still contrived to get nearer to the pass, as if they were unable to manage their horses, and were carried away against

65. Bronze equestrian group from Naples, an idealized portrait of Alexander the Great. Alexander became by force the heir of the Persian King of Kings. In terms of horsemanship this meant a penetration of the cavalry of his successors by oriental techniques.

their will. At last, setting spurs to them, they broke out through the midst of the enemy's posts, and getting into the open country, set fire to all the houses near the road. They then set fire to the nearest village, while they ravaged all around with fire and sword. At first the sight of the smoke, then the shouts of the affrighted inhabitants, at last the old people and children, who fled for shelter, created great disorder in the camp. In consequence of which the whole of their army, without plan, and without command, ran off, each to take care of his own.

The History of Rome, Book XXXV

Numidians fought not only for the Romans but also against them in the pay of the Carthaginians, until the Romans outbribed the latter. On their own account they were not so formidable. Far more dangerous were the nomads of the Pontic steppe, among whom were the Parthians who at Carrhae caused the blackest day of the Roman army, when their arrows darkened the sky.

Here Justinus gives a condensed account of the history and culture of the Parthians. What he has to say about the status of women in Parthian society, their system of servitude, and of political dependence based

67. The Persian king Bahram Gur (AD 420–38) fighting lions: in antiquity generally and as late as the last years of the Roman empire when this picture was engraved, horses with much bone and massive body were not so much characteristic of north-west Europe as of certain provinces of the Persian empire. From a silver dish.

66. Macedonian silver and gold staters struck by Philip II, father of Alexander the Great. By acquisition of the most productive gold-mine in the ancient world Philip was able both to issue this impressive currency and to buy cavalry remounts of large size from a source somewhere to the north-east of his kingdom—possibly from Bactria—and also to enter his horses in the equestrian events at the Olympic Games, thus confirming his status as a Greek and not a barbarian.

solely on fear, is strangely reminiscent of Giles Fletcher, in *Of The Russe Commonwealth*, describing the Muscovites just after their liberation from centuries of subjection to the Tartars, the last of the nomad overlords in the Parthian tradition. But socially, the horse nomads of the steppe were not all out of one mould; there were instances, mostly further east towards Mongolia, where the women rode *better* than the men.

※The Parthians, in whose hands the empire of the east now is, having divided the world, as it were, with the Romans, were originally exiles from Scythia. This is apparent from their very name; for in the Scythian language exiles are called *Parthi*. During the time of the Assyrians and Medes, they were the most obscure of all the people of the east. Subsequently, too, when the empire of the east was transferred from the Medes to the Persians, they were but as a herd without a name, and fell under the power of the stronger. At last they became subject to the Macedonians, when they conquered the east; so that it must seem wonderful to everyone, that they should have reached such a height of good fortune as to rule over those nations under whose sway they had been merely slaves. Being assailed by the Romans, also, in three wars, under the conduct of the greatest generals, and at the most flourishing period of the republic, they alone, of all nations, were not only a match for them, but came off victorious; though it may have been a greater glory to them, indeed, to have been able to rise amidst the Assyrian, Median, and Persian empires, so celebrated of old, and the most powerful dominion of Bactria, peopled with a thousand cities, than to have been victorious in war against a people that came from a distance; especially when they were continually harassed by severe wars with the Scythians and other neighbouring nations, and pressed with various other formidable contests. . . .

They have an army, not like other nations, of free men, but chiefly consisting of slaves, the numbers of whom daily increase, the power of manumission being allowed to none, and all their offspring, in consequence, being born slaves. These bondmen they bring up as carefully as their own children, and teach them, with great pains, the arts of riding and shooting with the bow. As anyone is eminent in wealth, so he furnishes the king with a proportionate number of horsemen for war. Indeed when fifty thousand cavalry encountered Antony, as he was making war upon Parthia, only four hundred of them were free men.

Of engaging with the enemy in close fight, and of taking cities by siege, they know nothing. They fight on horseback, either galloping forward or turning their backs. Often, too, they counterfeit flight, that they may throw their pursuers off their guard against being wounded by their arrows. The signal for battle among them is given, not by trumpet, but by drum. Nor are they able to fight long; but they would be irresistible, if their vigour and perseverance were equal to the fury of their onset. In general they retire before the enemy in the very heat of the engagement, and, soon after

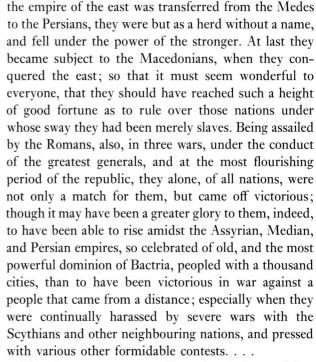

their retreat, return to the battle afresh; so that, when you feel most certain that you have conquered them, you have still to meet the greatest danger from them. Their armour, and that of their horses, is formed of plates, lapping over one another like the feathers of a bird, and covers both man and horse entirely. Of gold and silver, except for adorning their arms, they make no use.

Each man has several wives, for the sake of gratifying desire with different objects. They punish no crime more severely than adultery, and accordingly they not only exclude their women from entertainments, but forbid them the very sight of men. They eat no flesh but that which they take in hunting. They ride on horseback on all occasions; on horses they go to war, and to feasts; on horses they discharge public and private duties; on horses they go abroad, meet together, traffic, and converse. Indeed the difference between slaves and freemen is, that slaves go on foot, but freemen only on horseback.

History of the World, Book XLI

NATURAL HISTORY

Gaius Plinius Secundus always sounds so sane and reasonable that the reader is in danger of believing him even when he is retailing the most outrageous nonsense under the title of what in our day is called science. And when you have said that you have said the worst about him: the *Natural History* which he wrote in the fifties of our era is a splendid work, and that part of Book VIII which deals with the *equidae* is among the most interesting parts of it. He personally was a model of what a Roman of the governing class ought to be; he became a naval officer at the age of forty-nine or so, having previously been a cornet of horse in Africa and a civil servant in Spain. He met his death by asphyxiation while directing rescue operations at an eruption of Vesuvius, being then aged fifty-six and holding a rank approximating, in modern terms, to Commodore.

In the passage which follows, many would quarrel today with his explanation of the name Bucephalus

('Bull-head'), seeing in it only a designation of that characteristic skull-form which we associate with the Arab type. What is here translated 'saddle' does not mean anything like our idea of one, only a sort of luxury-class shabrack or saddle-cloth. The Scythian cavalry regiments referred to are of course those in Roman pay. Horses which carry on racing or hunting even in the absence of a spilt rider or driver are still seen today. The long race-horse career of the chariot-horse is notable; it is *because* they did not race until they were five that they stayed on the track until twenty. There is no modern instance of a stallion getting foals at thirty-three; the record is more like twenty-three. But some of these foals of ancient sires have been in the top class.

Hogging the mane can have no possible effect on the oestrus of mares; but it is still common practice during the breeding season in the very parts of Spain and Portugal where Pliny once served. The reasons are not what he supposed. No mare has foaled in modern times at anything like the age of forty.

Mares do not invariably foal standing up, though a fair number of them do so. It is probable that foals of certain breeds cannot reach the ground with their mouths, as Pliny says, when they are very young. It is noticeable that young foals of part-Arab or part-thoroughbred blood, when they first begin to graze, have to spread the forelegs wider, in order to bring the mouth to the ground, than foals of northern or 'cold blood' (Type II) breeds. But there is no practical reason why a foal should reach the ground with its lips in its early days, since it only goes through the motions of grazing in imitation of its elders.

The belief in wind-begotten foals is an item of folk-lore not confined to Portugal.

The phrase here translated 'shifting of the bladder' probably means what we now call 'twisted gut'.

Chapter 68 of Book VIII is devoted to the ass, especially in the context of mule-breeding; and in regard to hybrids generally, Pliny is a valuable and unique source for the information that in antiquity the domestic (originally African) ass was crossed with the Asiatic wild ass to produce a hybrid that was itself fertile and could be crossed again with a mare to produce a very

68. Parthian mounted
archer, bronze figurine
from the edge of an
Etruscan vase.

superior mule. He points out the great economic importance of mule-breeding by instances from his old province of Iberia. He thought that a mare in foal to an ass would carry the foal twelve months instead of eleven, which is not so. On the other hand he does not mention, and seems to deny, the fact that the she-ass normally goes twelve months with the foal. He notes that foals selected as future mule-getters are taken off their dam at an early age and put on a mare, so that though jackasses they come to look on themselves as 'sons of mares' and in that sense horses. But he and Oppian both interpreted wrongly the practice, still in force today, of shaving the mare's mane if she is to stand to a jackass. The ass can only be persuaded to do his duty by the mare if her mane is shorn down to the proportions common among donkeys. It should have been obvious to Pliny that at the moment of marital embrace the mane occupied the centre of the jackass's field of vision, whereas the mare could not see it. Oppian with his respect for the best classical precedents blindly followed Pliny in this error—but any farmer in

Poitou or Navarre or Valais where mule-breeding is and was then taken seriously could have put him right. Pliny mentions that the surest way to get a she-ass in foal is to cover her on the 'foal-heat' a week after parturition, but has omitted earlier to say that this also holds true for horse-breeding.

It is interesting to learn from him that 'a mule can be checked from kicking by rather frequent drinks of wine'. So can I.

He records certain rare instances of female mules producing live foals, a phenomenon which even now eludes the efforts of science to explain it. One would think the mule is either sterile or fertile: but no; one in so many hundred thousand can breed.

Alexander had the good fortune to own a great rarity in horseflesh. They called the animal Bucephalus, either because of its fierce appearance or from the mark of a bull's head branded on its shoulder. It is said that it was bought for sixteen talents from the herd of Philonicus of Pharsalus while Alexander was

69. Etruscan fresco painting. Etruscans, those mysterious people, were both riders and charioteers. Their art shows only stallions employed in either role. Note the elaborate dressing of the mane and tail.

70. Equestrian statue of the Roman Emperor Marcus Aurelius which, by its very prestige, has done incalculable harm to formal equestrian portraiture of later date as historical evidence. Sculptors ranging from the one who modelled the statue of Charlemagne at Aix-la-Chapelle to the Italian masters of the Renaissance simply modelled their mount on the Aurelian charger without looking at the real-life example. The bridle, which we must presume to be a realistic detail, shows the departure in Roman imperial times from the earlier model seen, for instance, in Greek representations. The headstall is by now of a pattern still common today and is derived ultimately from the head-stalls used on mules. It is difficult to see how the straps are joined because, as was customary, all such joints are covered with rosettes, but probably buckles had by now been invented.

still a boy, as he was taken by its beauty. This horse when adorned with the royal saddle would not allow itself to be mounted by anybody except Alexander, though on other occasions it allowed anybody to mount. It is also celebrated for a memorable feat in battle, not having allowed Alexander during the attack on Thebes to change to another mount when it had been wounded; and a number of occurrences of the same kind are also reported, on account of which when it died the king headed its funeral procession, and built a city round its tomb which he named after it. Also the horse that belonged to Caesar the Dictator is said to have refused to let anyone else mount it; and it is also recorded that its fore feet were like those of a man, as it is represented in the statue that stands in front of the temple of Venus Genetrix. . . .

The Scythian cavalry regiments indeed resound with famous stories of horses: a chieftain was challenged to a duel by an enemy and killed, and when his adversary came to strip his body of its armour, his horse kicked him and bit him till he died; another horse, when its blinkers were removed and it found out that a mare it had covered was its dam, made for a precipice and committed suicide. . . .

The cleverness of horses is beyond description. Mounted javelinmen experience their docility in assisting difficult attempts with the actual swaying of their body; also they gather up the weapons lying on the ground and pass them to their rider. Horses harnessed to chariots in the circus unquestionably show that they understand the shouts of encouragement and applause. . . . In early days a charioteer was thrown at the plebeian circus races and the horses galloped on to the Capitol and raced round the temple three times just the same as if he still stood at the reins. . . .

Some horses live fifty years, but mares live a shorter time; mares stop growing when five years old, the males a year later. The appearance of the horse that ought to be most preferred has been very beautifully described in the poetry of Virgil, but we also have dealt with it in our book on the Use of the Javelin by Cavalry, and I observe that there is almost universal agreement about it. But a different build is required for the circus; and consequently though horses may be broken as two-year-olds to other service, racing in the circus does not claim them before five.

Gestation in this genus lasts eleven months and the foal is born in the twelfth month. Breeding takes place as a rule in the spring equinox when both animals are two-year-olds, but the progeny is stronger if breeding begins at three. A stallion goes on serving to the age of 33, as they are sent from the race-course to the stud at 20. It is recorded that a stallion at Opus even continued to 40, only he needed assistance in lifting his fore-quarters. But few animals are such unfertile sires as the horse; consequently intervals are allowed in breeding, and nevertheless a stallion cannot stand serving fifteen times in the same year. Mares in heat are cooled down by having their manes shorn; they foal yearly up to 40. It is stated that a mare has lived to 75.

In the equine genus the pregnant female is delivered standing up; and she loves her offspring more than all other female animals. And in fact a love-poison called horse-frenzy [hippomane] is found in the forehead of horses at birth, the size of a dried fig, black in colour, which a brood mare as soon as she has dropped her foal eats up, or else she refuses to suckle the foal. If anybody takes it before she gets it, and keeps it, the scent drives him into madness of the kind specified. If a foal loses its dam the other brood mares in the same herd rear the orphan. It is said that a foal is unable to reach the ground with its mouth within the first three days after birth. The greedier it is in drinking the deeper it dips its nostrils into the water. The Scythians prefer mares as chargers, because they can make water without checking their gallop.

It is known that in Lusitania in the neighbourhood of the town of Lisbon and the river Tagus mares when a west wind is blowing stand facing towards it and conceive the breath of life and that this produces a foal, and this is the way to breed a very swift colt, but it does not live more than three years. Also in Spain the Galician and Asturian tribes breed those of the horse kind that we call 'theldones', though when more of a pony type they are designated 'cobs', which have not the usual gaits in running but a smooth pace, straightening the near and off-side legs alternately, from which the horses are taught by training to adopt an ambling pace.

The horse has nearly the same diseases as mankind, and is also liable to shifting of the bladder, as are all beasts of the draught class.

A mare coupled with an ass after twelve months bears a mule, an animal of exceptional strength for agricultural operations. To breed mules they choose mares not less than four or more than ten years old. Also breeders say that females of either genus refuse stallions of the other one unless as foals they were suckled by females of the same genus as the stallions; for this reason they stealthily remove the foals in the dark and put them to mares' or she-asses' udders respectively. But a mule is also got by a horse out of an ass, though it is unmanageable, slow and obstinate. Also all the foals from old mares are sluggish. It causes miscarriage for a mare in foal by a horse to be put to an ass, but not *vice versa*. It has been observed that female asses are best coupled six days after they have borne a foal, and that males couple better when tired.

It is noticed that a female that does not conceive before she casts what are called her milk-teeth is barren, as is one that does not begin to produce foals

71. This picture is near the ultimate in terms of a late-medieval Italian scene masquerading as the antique. Anachronisms abound: the modelling of the horses is superb. (Detail from Piero della Francesca's *Victory of Heraclius over Chosroes*)

73. Clay relief plaque of the third century AD from the southern border of Persia, showing a horse with body armour only. It is either scale-armour or more probably quilting and is what the picture on Trajan's column in the next illustration was trying to represent.

72. This fascinating detail from Francesco del Cossa of Ferrara's picture of the traditional urban horse-race with noble spectators on horseback is remarkable among other things for the presence among the runners of two donkeys ridden in the correct style for donkey and not horse jockeys, one of which is going well, while the other threatens to give the owner apoplexy. (*April*, detail from the *Triumph of Venus* cycle of frescoes)

from the first coupling. Male foals of an ass by a horse were in old days called hinnies, while the term mules was used for the foals of a mare by an ass. It has been noticed that the offspring of two different races of animals belong to a third kind and resemble neither parent; and that such hybrids are not themselves fertile: this is the case with all kinds of animals, and is the reason why mules are barren. A number of cases of reproduction by mules are recorded in our Annals, but these were considered portentous. Theophrastus states that mules breed commonly in Cappadocia, but that the Cappadocian mule is a peculiar species. A mule can be checked from kicking by rather frequent drinks of wine. It is stated in the records of a good many Greeks that a foal has been got from a mare coupled with a mule, called a *ginnus*, which means a small mule. She-mules bred from a mare and tamed wild-asses are swift in pace and have extremely hard hooves, but a lean body and an indomitable spirit. But as a sire the foal of a wild-ass and a domestic she-ass excels all others. The wild-asses in Phrygia and Lycaonia are pre-eminent.

What Pliny means by a hippomane is probably the pad which the foal keeps in its mouth during a great part of its intra-uterine life; among other things, it prevents the foal swallowing its tongue during parturition. It has always played a great part in the folklore of horsemastership and possession of one was a mark of the conscientious stud-groom, since in order to secure this unimpressive bit of gristle it is essential to be

present at the moment of birth, and even then one may often miss it, for it seems to disappear much more readily than the protective pads which shield the sharp rims of the foetal hoof. If you find it at all, you are as likely to find it sticking to the forehead as anywhere else. As a talisman it was invaluable, though different virtues were attributed to it in different countries. In some, it was a lure: the horse would follow the man who carried about him its own hippomane, and him alone. In others, it partook more of the nature of a human baby's caul, to ward off various kinds of evil, conspicuously death by drowning.

ROMAN TACTICS

Flavius Arrianus (*c.* AD 96–*c.* 170) was a Greek, a pupil of the philosopher Epictetus. His great heroes were Alexander and Xenophon: of the former he wrote a history, one half of which he entitled *Anabasis*, in imitation of the latter. He became a Roman citizen at the age of twenty-eight and served the Emperor Hadrian well, both in a civil and a military capacity: as Governor of Cappadocia he defeated the Alani, a roving Indo-European tribe from the Pontic steppe, and the Massagetae, a people of similar habit from further east, beyond the Caspian, who in their time had defeated and killed Cyrus, the great Persian King of Kings. The following fragment, best known by its Latin title (it was written in Greek), describes a projected operation

74. Detail from Trajan's column: Sarmatian 'cataphracts'—armoured horsemen on armoured horses, evidently modelled from an eye-witness description which had not been fully understood. The armour is scale-armour, but not necessarily metal: it could be made up from horse plates. Whatever the material, however, no horse could possibly function in a skin-tight 'diving-suit' like this, and the very making of it to fit, and fasten up, would be an impossible task. In reality most of the 'armour' worn by Asiatic horses was quilted leather, only approximately fitting, and only covering part of the body.

by what must have been the entire garrison of Cappadocia against the Alani. Despite its very precise details no place names are mentioned in this tactical order: this may well be deliberate, as a measure of security, since the non-legionary part of the army was of the most diverse origin (it does not seem to include any inhabitants of the province). As the most important part of the plan was the identity of the spot where Arrian intended to give battle, it might well have been withheld lest some disgruntled 'ally' should be tempted to desert with this valuable intelligence. But it must be within the borders of Cappadocia, which incidentally was a famous horse-breeding province, boasting among other things an imperial stud of horses bred for the chariot-race.

ACIES CONTRA ALANOS

ORDER OF MARCH AND DEPLOYMENT

The whole army will march in one column, with the Scout Cavalry in the van. They will march by squadrons in two ranks each of sixteen troops. The mounted archers will follow under the same command, followed by the Isaurian cavalry. Then the following order:

Advance Guard:

Colonian Squadrons } Cmdr. Daphnes the
Roiian Squadrons } Corinthian

Iturian Squadrons }
Cyrenian Squadrons } Cmdr. Demetrius
Rhaetian Squadrons }

Gallic Cavalry, by squadrons, in two ranks, under their *praefectus castrorum*

Armenian Foot Archers

Half the Allied Infantry, as follows:

Italians, Cyrenians, Bosphorians, commanded by Lamprocles

Numidians commanded by Verus

They will march with colours displayed, by companies four abreast. Achaean Cavalry Regiment will escort the foot, right and left, under the general command of Pulcher the Italian.

Main Body:
The centre of the column will consist of Roman troops headed by the Household Cavalry, then:
Mounted Companies of both Legions
Artillery Train
Light Infantry Companies of both Legions
Heavy Companies of XV Legion, with their eagle, under command of Valens
The second-in-command, battalion commanders of XV Legion, and company commanders of the leading battalion will accompany the General
The Legion will march by battalions four abreast
XII Legion, in the same order
Rear Guard:
This will consist of the other half of the Allied Infantry, viz.:
Armenians
Trapezuntians
Colchians   Cmdr. Siculinus the Aplanian
Rizian Pikemen
Aplanians
Baggage Train
Getae Cavalry Regiment, commanded by their Ilarch. Company Commanders of Infantry will march on right and left flanks. Infantry will be escorted by Italian and Alacian Cavalry Regiments marching in single file right and left.
The Commander-in-chief (code name Xenophon) will have no fixed station, but will move up and down the column to regulate it: when not so engaged he will be found in front of the legionary Eagles.

DEPLOYMENT

On approaching the spot determined on to engage the enemy, the Scout Cavalry will advance and seize such high ground to the front as will enable them to observe enemy movement and report it. All other cavalry will then fall out of the column to take up stations to be indicated by the commander-in-chief, in square formation, to cover the deployment of the infantry.

The signal will then be given for the infantry to dress their ranks and make ready their arms. This will be done in complete silence.

The chosen position has, to right and left, two hills, gently sloping and of medium height. The space between is quite level, and there is flat country all round.

He gives details of the battle-plan.

When all is in order, the troops will hold their fire until the enemy is within javelin range.

On the command 'Utter War Cry', all soldiers will shout their loudest. At the same time the artillery will open fire with bolts and stone balls. Archers and all those armed with missile weapons will shoot, using all available ammunition. Plunging fire will be brought to bear from the peaks of the two hills. The intention is to overwhelm the enemy by fire power; probably the sheer weight of these volleys will throw him into such confusion, causing such losses in horses, that in the event he will not seek to close with us.

If however he does persist, and charge home on our heavy infantry centre, then the second and third ranks of the Legions will close up on the front, until they are actually touching, so as physically to support them under the shock of impact; thus the attacking horsemen will be confronted with an unbroken and immoveable hedge of spear-points at the level of a horse's chest. Spearmen in the fourth rank will thrust at them, and those of the fifth and following will throw their spears overhand. By this means we cannot fail to repulse the enemy and force him to retire in disorder with heavy losses.

When it becomes apparent that the enemy is indeed in retreat, then the Legions will open their ranks for the cavalry to pass through them, reforming in two divisions. As the eight regiments were formed up behind the main body, each in eight troops, the first four troops of each will detach themselves. They will pursue the enemy at whatever speed is necessary, while the second half of each regiment will follow up more deliberately and in tight formation, in order to support the leading squadrons in case the Scyths[1] turn and rally, and in order to relieve the pursuing troops when

---

[1] By this date these people had vanished from the steppes, eclipsed by the Sauromati, of whom the Alani were a sub-tribe, since the third century BC, but Arrian, echoing his master Xenophon, now and again uses the archaic word.

they tire. As soon as the cavalry sets off in pursuit, the Armenians and all other archers will come down off the hills and will march in between the cavalry support squadrons and bring harassing fire to bear on any enemy within range.

The heavy infantry will then advance at a quick pace, following up the light troops, so that if, as is not very probable, the enemy horse rallies sufficiently to bring our light troops to a halt or withdrawal, they may support them until flight is resumed.

After giving instructions on how to cope with a flank attack, the fragment breaks off. But the rest of it cannot have been very long. It probably consisted of paragraphs concerning supply and communications.

Even were it less complete, it would constitute a unique document. It is not a literary work (of which Arrian produced plenty). It is not even a training manual. It is a written operation order, as is evident alone from the fact commanders are designated and units named. No other such order from the whole history of the Roman Army has been preserved. What pass for such are the reconstructions of historians, based on verbal orders as remembered by officers and soldiers many years after the event; or war diaries selectively edited in retrospect by such commanders as Julius Caesar.

It demonstrates most strikingly the changes that had been forced on the Roman armies of the east ever since the disastrous confrontation with the Parthians at Carrhae, in 53 BC, when Crassus, defeated with an almost total loss of 29,000 men, was himself captured and murdered after interrogation by the Parthian leader Surenas. In this order of battle for a force consisting essentially of two legions there are fourteen cavalry units named. Most such *alae* consisted of 500 men, but a few of them were normally a thousand strong. There are therefore some 8,000 cavalrymen in this force, not counting the mounted archers and the small mounted units that formed an intrinsic part of the legions. The emphasis throughout is on the role of the cavalry, offensive and defensive, and on missile weapons of all sorts. The legions alone had a machinery of command, what we should call a staff, that functioned above the regimental level. A force of this nature, even if composed overwhelmingly of cavalry, had to take the form of a 'legion with attached troops' if orders were to be transmitted, either tactical or administrative. The necessary and logical step, the creation of an independent corps of cavalry with an independent staff, was not taken until the next century under the new establishment introduced by the emperor Severus, one of the few really successful campaigners against the Parthians; but even the new-style, cavalry-dominated

75. The hunting scene from the Fourth Book of Virgil's *Aeneid* often brings out, in medieval translations and paraphrases, significant points about the vernacular terms of hunting and horsemanship in different countries and generations: for instance, in the renderings by Chaucer and Gavin Douglas. This mosaic from South Hams in Somerset, of the same period as the Horkstow mosaic of a chariot-race, has no specific British colour: it is derived from a pattern book that might have been used anywhere in Western Europe during the last century of Roman rule. The horses might be Barb, or Camarguais. All are stallions, ridden in a snaffle bridle with a single rein. There is no evidence that British hunting of the fourth century looked like this, except in these last two particulars.

76. Fourth-century glass bowl from Wint Hill, Somerset, which was made and engraved at Cologne. Much more than the South Hams mosaic, however, it shows what hunting was like in North-west Europe under the last Roman emperors. Clothing, equipment and saddlery are very like what might have been seen in Britain or Gaul or Germania Inferior at this time.

Roman army had one more defeat to come, more crushing than any yet sustained, at the hand of the Persian king Sapor.

THE DEFEAT OF TOTILA

The last enemy, and the most deadly, to come out of the steppe before the final submergence of the antique classical culture, were the Huns. Of course such enemies kept on coming after that, but there were no Romans of the West left to face them. The Huns threatened in turn the Chinese, the Persian and the Roman empires, and of all the steppe archers they were the most far-ranging. In so far as the Roman Empire could be said to have been brought down by political and military action rather than (as is more likely) economic and social decay, the Huns were the agents of its fall. But the destruction they wrought was not solely first-hand: even the largest Hunnish expedition was more in the nature of a raid; however prolonged and severe the visitation, it was always certain that once the Huns had had enough of what they wanted, they would go away again.

The secondary effect of the Hunnish horseborne aggression was more serious. Just as in terms of mechanized warfare it is common practice for tank units to

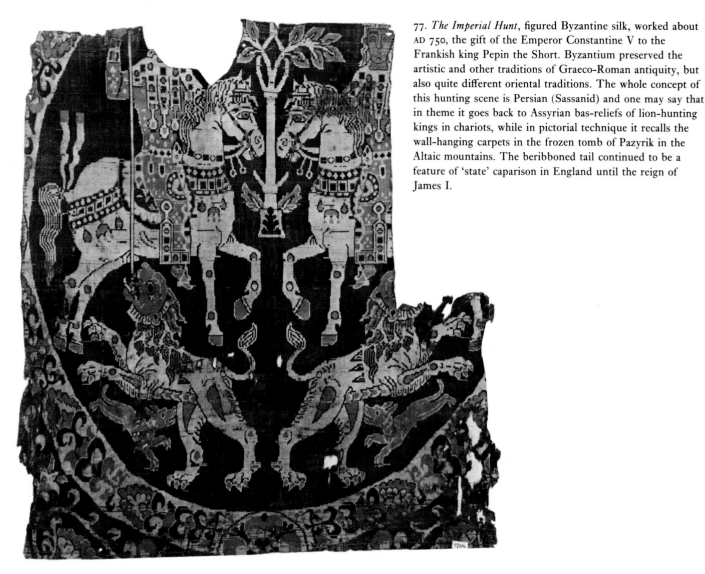

77. *The Imperial Hunt*, figured Byzantine silk, worked about AD 750, the gift of the Emperor Constantine V to the Frankish king Pepin the Short. Byzantium preserved the artistic and other traditions of Graeco-Roman antiquity, but also quite different oriental traditions. The whole concept of this hunting scene is Persian (Sassanid) and one may say that in theme it goes back to Assyrian bas-reliefs of lion-hunting kings in chariots, while in pictorial technique it recalls the wall-hanging carpets in the frozen tomb of Pazyrik in the Altaic mountains. The beribboned tail continued to be a feature of 'state' caparison in England until the reign of James I.

drive before them herds of (other people's) livestock in order to detonate the anti-tank mines, so the Huns in their progress towards the Roman frontiers of the Rhine and Danube swept up and drove before them many tribes (mostly Germanic) who had practised horsemanship on a limited scale, mostly confined to the royal or princely families, before contact with the Huns, but who now began to adopt the full steppe scale of horse-dependence. They blunted the edge of the Roman defences, and they were less hungry for loot than for land. The Byzantine historian Procopius in his *History of the Wars* has much to say about these East Germanic tribes such as the Vandals and Goths, against whom his hero Belisarius fought skilfully, employing, among other troops, Hunnish mercenaries.

In his account in Book VIII of the Gothic King Totila's defeat and death, we seem to see the barbarian king in the grip of one of those premonitions of disaster which are so common in the sagas of the Germanic invaders of Britain.

The armies drew together for battle and arrayed themselves as follows. All the forces in each army took their stand facing the enemy, making the phalanx as deep as possible and the front very long. And the Roman left wing was held by Narses and John near the hill, and with them was the flower of the Roman army; for each of them had, apart from the other soldiers, a great following of spearmen and guards and barbarian Huns, all chosen for their valour; and on the right were arrayed Valerian and John the Glutton along with Dagisthaeus and all the rest of the Romans. Furthermore, they placed on both wings about eight thousand unmounted bowmen from the regular troops. But at the centre of the phalanx Narses had placed the Lombards and the nation of the Eruli and all the other barbarians, causing them to dismount from their horses and making them infantry, in order that, if it should chance that they turned cowards in the engagement or deserted, they might not be too eager to fly. Now Narses had set the extreme left wing of the Roman front at an angle, placing fifteen hundred cavalry there. And the instructions previously given provided that the five hundred, on the one hand, should rush to the rescue the moment that any of the Romans chanced to be driven back, while the thousand, at the moment when the enemy's infantry began action, were to get behind them immediately and thus place them between two forces. And Totila arrayed his army in the same way opposite his enemy. Then going along his own battle-line he kept encouraging his soldiers with voice and expression and urging them to boldness. Narses likewise did the same thing, holding in the air bracelets and necklaces and golden bridles on poles and displaying certain other incentives to bravery in the coming struggle. For some time, however, neither army began battle, but both remained quiet awaiting the assault of their opponents. . . .

But Totila now went alone into the space between the armies, not in order to engage in single combat, but in order to prevent his opponents from using the present opportunity. For he had learned that the two thousand Goths who had been missing were now drawing near, and so he sought to put off the engagement until their arrival by doing as follows. First of all, he was not at all reluctant to make an exhibition to the enemy of what manner of man he was. For the armour in which he was clad was abundantly plated with gold and the ample adornments which hung from his cheekplates as well as from his helmet and spear were not only of purple but in other respects befitting a king, marvellous in their abundance. And he himself, sitting upon a very large horse, began to perform the dance under arms skilfully between the armies. For he wheeled his horse round in a circle and then turned him again to the other side and so made him run round and round. And as he rode he hurled his javelin into the air and caught it again as it quivered above him, then passed it rapidly from hand to hand, shifting it with consummate skill, and he gloried in his practice in such matters, falling back on his shoulders, spreading his legs and leaning from side to side, like one who has been instructed with precision in the art of dancing from childhood. By these tactics he wore away the whole early part of the day. And wishing to prolong

indefinitely the postponement of the battle, he sent to the Roman army saying that he wished to confer with them. But Narses declared that he must be trifling, seeing that he had been set on fighting at the time when there was opportunity to make proposals, but now, upon reaching the battlefield, he came forward to parley.

Meanwhile the two thousand Goths arrived; and when Totila had learned that they had reached the stockade, seeing that it was time for the morning meal, he himself went off to his own tent and the Goths began to break up their formation and retire. And when Totila reached his quarters, he found the two thousand already present. He then commanded all to take their meal, and changing his entire equipment he armed himself with all care with the private soldier's equipment and led the army out straightway against his enemy, thinking that he would fall upon them unexpectedly and thus overwhelm them. But even so he did not find the Romans unprepared. For Narses had feared, as actually happened, that the enemy would fall upon them when they were not expecting it, and so he had given orders that not a single man should either sit down to lunch or go off to sleep or even remove his cuirass, nor yet take his bridle off his horse. However, he did not allow them to be altogether without food, but commanded them to eat a small meal in ranks and with their equipment on, meanwhile maintaining a sharp look-out constantly and expecting the attack of the enemy. However, they were no longer arrayed in the same formation as before, for the Roman wings, in each of which four thousand unmounted horsemen had taken their stand, were moved forward at Narses' command so as to form a crescent. But the Gothic infantry were all placed in a body in the rear of the cavalry, in order that, if the horsemen should be routed, the fugitives might fall back upon them and be saved, and all could then advance immediately together.

Now orders had been given to the entire Gothic army that they would use neither bow nor any other weapon in this battle except their spears. Consequently it came about that Totila was out-generalled by his own folly; for in entering this battle he was led, by what I do not know, to throw against his opponents his own army with inadequate equipment and outflanked and in no respect a match for their antagonists.

The Goths suffer heavy losses from the Roman bowmen, in an effort to come to grips with the enemy.

At this point I cannot admire any of the Romans or of their barbarian allies more than the others. For they all showed a common enthusiasm and displayed the same valour and energy in action, for each of them received the enemy's attack with the utmost vigour and repulsed the assault. And it was now toward evening when each of the two armies suddenly began to move, the Goths in retreat and the Romans in pursuit. For the Goths could no longer hold out against the onslaught of their enemy, but began to give ground before their attack, and finally turned precipitately, terrified by their great numbers and their perfect order. And they gave not a thought to resistance, being as filled with terror as if some apparitions of the air had fallen upon them or as if Heaven were warring against them.

Utterly routed, the Goths kill some of their own men in their panic to escape.

Six thousand of the Goths perished in this battle, while great numbers put themselves into the hands of their opponents. These the Romans for the moment made prisoners, but a little later they slew them. And not Goths alone were destroyed, but also great numbers of the old Roman soldiers who had earlier detached themselves from the Roman army and deserted . . . to Totila and the Goths. But all the soldiers of the Gothic army who had the fortune neither to perish nor to come under the hand of their enemy were able to hide or to flee, according as each could avail himself of horse or foot or good luck so as to find opportunity for the one or a place for the other.

Such was the conclusion of this battle, and complete darkness was already settling down. But Totila was in flight through the night accompanied by not more than five men, one of whom chanced to be Scipuar, pursued by some of the Romans who did not know that he was Totila; among these was Asbadus of the Gepaedes. This man had drawn close to Totila and was charging him with the purpose of thrusting his spear into his back. But a Gothic youth of the household of Totila, who was following his fleeing master, outraged at what was taking place, cried aloud, 'What is this, you dog? Are you rushing to smite your own master?' Then Asbadus thrust his spear with all his strength at Totila, but he himself was wounded in the foot by Scipuar and remained there. And Scipuar was wounded in turn by one of the pursuers and stopped, whereupon those who had been making the pursuit with Asbadus, four in number, gave up the chase in order to save him, and turned back with him. But the escort of Totila, thinking that the enemy were still pursuing them, rode forward without pausing, taking him along with great determination, though mortally wounded and fainting, for necessity compelled them to that headlong flight. So after covering eighty-four stades they came to a place called Caprae. Here they rested from travel and endeavoured to treat the wound of Totila, who not long afterwards completed the term of his life. And there his followers buried him in the earth and departed.

Such was the conclusion of the reign and the life of Totila, who had ruled the Goths eleven years.

DARIUS AND THE SCYTHIANS

The Ister is the Danube: the Tana is the Don. The theatre of operations in this campaign of Darius is about the same as that of the German Army Group South in the 1940s. It extended inwards from the Black Sea coast as far as Transylvania in the west (home of the affluent Agathyrsi) to the region of Voronezh, where lived the black-clad Melanchlaeni and the Sauromatians or Sarmatians, who were later to supplant the Scythians in the hegemony of the steppe.

It is evident from the account of the embassy sent by the three Scythian rulers to the eight nations who dwelt on their borders that they did not live in a state of permanent hostility with them, or of dominance over them, any more than they did with the Greek colonists of the Tauric Cheronese (Crimea) through whose realistic art we have the best visual relics of the Scythian horse-culture. Of these landward neighbours of the Scythians, some resembled them closely in their way of life; others, like the Budini, were forest-dwelling fur-hunters and bee-keepers; others practised 'normal' agriculture; some lived in what passed, to Herodotus, for 'cities'; the Neuri were reputed werewolves; the Androphagi, as their name implies, were cannibals, but probably only for seasonal ritual purposes. None of them were masters, to the same degree as the Scythians, of what Herodotus calls the 'device' of total mobility.

The great rivers of the steppe, which could only be passed by Darius owing to the skill of his sappers in making pontoon bridges, were no obstacle to the nomads, who could not only swim their horses over them, but were able at need to make their light waggons into barges by wrapping hides round the sides and under the floor.

The one horse-like attribute that was a handicap to the Scythians was shyness, sometimes amounting to terror, of the unfamiliar: the mere sound of a donkey braying could upset the tactical performance of their army. The spread of the domestic ass eastwards from its original centre in North Africa to the northern part of the Chinese Empire had taken place before the time of Darius, but by a route south of the Caspian and across the Pamirs, quite out of range of the Scythians and even of their eastern neighbours the Massagetae; and though the horseborne nomads of Western and Central Asia at this time were surrounded by various indigenous species of wild ass, since extinct or become excessively scarce, it never occurred to them that this ungulate might also be domesticated.

The Euxine Sea, to which Darius led an army of all countries, except the Scythians, exhibits the most ignorant nations: for we are unable to mention any one nation of those on this side the Pontus that has any pretensions to intelligence; nor have we ever heard of any learned man among them, except the Scythian nation and Anacharsis. By the Scythian nation one of the most important of human devices has been contrived more wisely than by any others whom we know; their other customs however I do not admire. This most important device has been so contrived, that no one who attacks them can escape; and that, if they do not choose to be found, no one is able to overtake them. For they, who have neither cities nor fortifications, but carry their houses with them, who are all equestrian archers, living not from the cultivation of the earth, but from cattle, and whose dwellings are waggons—how must not such a people be invincible, and difficult to engage with? This device has been contrived by them, as the country is fit for it, and the rivers aid them: for the country, being level, abounds in herbage and is well watered; and rivers flow through it almost as numerous as the canals in Egypt. Such of them as are celebrated and navigable from the sea I will mention: the Ister, that has five mouths; then the Tyres, the Hypanis, the Borysthenes, the Panticapes, the Hypacyris, the Gerrhus, and the Tanais. . . .

The Scythians, considering with themselves that they were not able alone to repel the army of Darius in a pitched battle, sent messengers to the adjoining nations; and the kings of those nations, having met together, consulted, since so great an army was advancing against them. The kings who met together were those of the Tauri, the Agathyrsi, the Neuri, the Androphagi, the Melanchlaeni, the Geloni, the Budini, and the Sauromatae. . . .

The messengers of the Scythians, coming to the assembled kings of the nations above mentioned, informed them that the Persian, when he had subdued all the nations on the other continent, had constructed a bridge over the neck of the Bosphorus, and crossed over to this continent; and having crossed over and subdued the Thracians, he was building a bridge over the river Ister, designing to make all these regions also subject to him: 'Do you, therefore, on no account, sit aloof, and suffer us to be destroyed, but with one accord let us oppose the invader. If you will not do this, we, being pressed, shall either abandon the country, or, if we stay, shall submit to terms; for what would be our condition if you refuse to assist us? Nor will it fall more lightly on you on that account; for the Persian is advancing not more against us than against you; nor will he be content to subdue us and abstain from you: and we will give you a strong proof of what we say, for if the Persian had undertaken this expedition against us only, wishing to revenge his former subjection, he would have abstained from all others, and have marched directly against our territories, and would have made it clear to all, that he was marching against the Scythians, and not against others. But now, as soon as he crossed over to this continent, he subdued all that lay in his way; and holds in subjection the rest of the Thracians, and more particularly our neighbours the Getae.' When the Scythians had made this representation, the kings who had come from the several nations consulted together, and their opinions were divided. The Gelonian, Budinian, and Sauromatian, agreeing together, promised to assist the Scythians; but the Agathyrsian, Neurian, Androphagian, and the Melanchlaenian and Taurian princes gave this answer to the Scythians: 'If you, who make the request that you now do, had not been the first to injure the Persians, and begin war, you would have appeared to us to speak rightly, and we, yielding to your wishes, would have acted in concert with you. But in fact, you having invaded their territory without us, had the mastery of the Persians as long as the god allowed you; and they, when the same god instigates them, repay you like for like. We, however, neither on that occasion injured these men at all, nor will we now be the first to attempt to injure them. Nevertheless, should he invade our territory also, and become the aggressor, we will not submit to it. But until we see that, we will remain quiet at home; for we think that the Persians are not coming against us, but against those who were the authors of wrong.' . . .

When the advanced guard of the Scythians fell in with the Persians, about three days' march from the

78. Fifth-century Attic vase painting of Theseus pursued by an Amazon. Greek legends about the Amazons owed much to the fact that the style of dress affected by the horse nomads in general made it difficult for foreigners to distinguish men from women.

79. Rider, probably belonging to one of the Black Sea tribes, such as the Scythians. From a bronze vase (krater) of about 510–500 BC, found in Bulgaria.

Ister, they, having fallen in with them, kept a day's march in advance, and encamped, and destroyed all the produce of the ground, but the Persians, when they saw the Scythian cavalry before them, followed their track, while they continually retired; and then, for they directed their march after one of the divisions, the Persians pursued towards the east and the Tanais; and when they had crossed the river Tanais, the Persians also crossed over and pursued them, until, having passed through the country of the Sauromatae, they reached that of the Budini. As long as the Persians were marching through the Scythian and Sauromatian regions, they had nothing to ravage, as the country was all barren; but when they entered the territory of the Budini, there meeting with the wooden town, the Budini having abandoned it, and the town being emptied of everything, they set it on fire. Having done this, they continued to follow in the track of the enemy, until, having traversed this region, they reached the desert. . . .

The Scythians pass through the territories of all the nations that had refused to assist them, except those of the Agathyrsi, who threaten them with battle. They then lead the Persians into their own lands.

When this had continued for a considerable time, and did not cease, Darius sent a horseman to Indathyrsus, king of the Scythians, with the following message: 'Most miserable of men, why dost thou continually fly, when it is in thy power to do one of these two other things? For if thou thinkest thou art able to resist my power, stand, and having ceased thy wanderings, fight; but if thou art conscious of thy inferiority, in that case also cease thy hurried march, and bringing earth and water as presents to thy master, come to a conference.' To this Indathyrsus, the king of the Scythians, made answer as follows: 'This is the case with me, O Persian; I never yet fled from any man out of fear, neither before, nor do I now so flee from thee; nor have I done any thing different now from what I am wont to do, even in time of peace; but why I do not forthwith fight thee, I will now explain. We have no cities nor cultivated lands, for which we are under any apprehension lest they should be taken or ravaged, and therefore should hastily offer you battle. Yet if it is by all means necessary to come to this at once, we have the sepulchres of our ancestors, come, find these, and attempt to disturb them, then you will know whether we will fight for our sepulchres or not; but before that, unless we choose, we will not engage with thee. Thus much about fighting. The only masters I acknowledge are Jupiter my progenitor, and Vesta queen of the

Scythians; but to thee, instead of presents of earth and water, I will send such presents as are proper to come to thee. And in answer to thy boast, that thou art my master, I bid thee weep.' (This is a Scythian saying.) The herald therefore departed carrying this answer to Darius.

The kings of the Scythians, when they heard the name of servitude, were filled with indignation; whereupon they . . . resolved no longer to lead the Persians about, but to attack them whenever they were taking their meals; accordingly, observing the soldiers of Darius taking their meals, they put their design in execution. The Scythian cavalry always routed the Persian cavalry, but the Persian horsemen in their flight fell back on the infantry, and the infantry supported them. The Scythians, having beaten back the cavalry, wheeled round through fear of the infantry. The Scythians also made similar attacks at night. A very remarkable circumstance, that was advantageous to the Persians and adverse to the Scythians, when they attacked the camp of Darius, I will now proceed to mention: this was the braying of the asses, and the appearance of the mules; for Scythia produces neither ass nor mule, as I have before observed; nor is there in the whole Scythian territory a single ass or mule, by reason of cold. The asses, then, growing wanton, put the Scythian horse into confusion; and frequently, as they were advancing upon the Persians, when the horses heard, mid-way, the braying of the asses, they wheeled round in confusion, and were greatly amazed, pricking up their ears, as having never before heard such a sound, nor seen such a shape; now this circumstance in some slight degree affected the fortune of the war.

The Scythians, when they saw the Persians in great commotion, in order that they might remain longer in Scythia, and by remaining might be harassed through want of all things necessary, adopted the following expedient: when they had left some of their own cattle in the care of the herdsmen, they themselves withdrew to another spot; and the Persians coming up, took the cattle, and having taken them, exulted in what they had done. When this had happened several times, at last Darius was in a great strait, and the kings of the Scythians, having ascertained this, sent a herald, bear-

ing as gifts to Darius, a bird, a mouse, a frog, and five arrows. The Persians asked the bearer of the gifts the meaning of this present; but he answered, that he had no other orders than to deliver them and return immediately; and he advised the Persians, if they were wise, to discover what the gifts meant. The Persians, having heard this, consulted together. Darius's opinion was, that the Scythians meant to give themselves up to him, as well as earth and water; forming his conjecture thus; since a mouse is bred in the earth, and subsists on the same food as a man; a frog lives in the water; a bird is very like a horse; and the arrows they deliver up as their whole strength. This was the opinion given by Darius. But the opinion of Gobryas, one of the seven who had deposed the magus, did not coincide with this: he conjectured that the presents intimated: 'Unless, O Persians, ye become birds and fly into the air, or become mice and hide yourselves beneath the earth, or become frogs and leap into the lakes, ye shall never return home again, but be stricken by these arrows.' And thus the other Persians interpreted the gifts.

Darius, seeing that the Scythian army treats his force with contempt, agrees that Gobryas's interpretation of the gifts is correct, and asks his advice.

80. Scythian bronze belt plate from the Caucasus, *c.* fifth century BC. The art of the Scythians themselves is all in this fantastic style, so that for an impression of the Scythian horses we have to rely on the more realistic contemporary styles of their neighbours.

'As soon as night draws on, we should light fires, as we are accustomed to do, and having deceived those soldiers who are least able to bear hardships, and having tethered all the asses, should depart . . . ' . Such was the advice of Gobryas. Afterwards night came on, and Darius acted on this opinion: the infirm amongst the soldiers, and those whose loss would be of the least consequence, and all the asses tethered, he left on the spot in the camp. And he left the asses and the sick of his army for the following reason; that the asses might make a noise: and the men were left on this pretext, namely, that he with the strength of his army was about to attack the Scythians, and they, during that time, would defend the camp. Darius, having laid these injunctions on those he was preparing to abandon, and having caused the fires to be lighted, marched away with all speed towards the Ister. The asses, being deserted by the multitude, began to bray much louder than usual; so that the Scythians, hearing the asses, firmly believed that the Persians were still at their station.

Herodotus, *Melpomene* IV

81. Bronze bit with cheek-piece in horse form, of the second or third century BC, from Luristan, a territory bordering on Scythia.

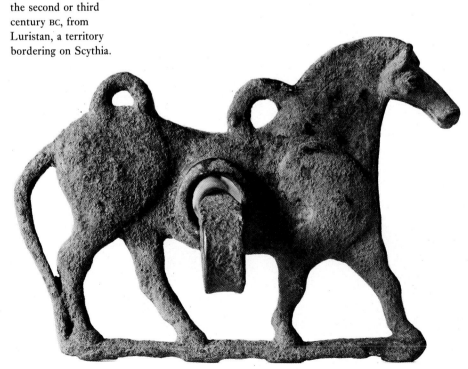

THE TARTAR HORSEMEN

After the Alani, the Parthians, the Huns, and many others, the dominant horse-archers of the steppe in the thirteenth century of our era were the Mongols. They were totally different, ethnically, from the Scythians, but their way of life, their attitude to the surrounding world, was identical with the Scythians', only slightly more aggressive. What matters, in the particular circumstances of nomadic pastoralism and mounted warfare on the great plains, is not 'race' but the mastery of stock-rearing techniques and the total adaptability to life on, with and by the horse. What all these people like Astyages and Ogadai Khan, practitioners of the art of mounted warfare with massed archery, have in common, is not the slant of their eyes or the shape of their noses but greasy leather breeches and a smell of sour mare's milk. When Marco Polo dictated his book *The Diversities and Marvels of the World* he had spent twenty years in Asia, mostly in China but a great deal of it on the way there and back through Tartary and Mongolia.

When one of the great Tartar chiefs proceeds on an expedition, he puts himself at the head of an army of a hundred thousand horse, and organizes them in the following manner. He appoints an officer to the command of every ten men, and others to command an hundred, a thousand, and ten thousand men, respectively. Thus ten of the officers commanding ten men take their orders from him who commands a hundred; of these, each ten, from him who commands a thousand; and each ten of these latter, from him who commands ten thousand. By this arrangement each officer has only to attend to the management of ten men or ten bodies of men; and when the commander of these hundred thousand men has occasion to make a detachment for any particular service, he issues his orders to the commanders of ten thousand to furnish him with a thousand men, each; and these, in like manner, to the commanders of a thousand, who give their orders to those commanding a hundred; until the order reaches those commanding ten, by whom the number required is immediately supplied to their superior officers. A hundred men are in this manner delivered to every officer commanding a thousand, and a thousand men to every officer commanding ten thousand. The drafting takes place without delay, and all are implicitly obedient to their respective superiors. Every company of a hundred men is denominated a *tuc*, and ten of these constitute a *toman*. When the army proceeds on service, a body of men is sent two days' march in advance, and parties are stationed upon each flank and in the rear, in order to prevent its being attacked by surprise. When the service is distant, they carry but little with them, and that, chiefly, what is requisite for their encampment, and utensils for cooking. They subsist for the most part upon milk, as has been said. Each man has, on an average, eighteen horses and mares, and when that which they ride is fatigued, they change it for another. They are provided with small tents made of felt, under which they shelter themselves against rain. Should circumstances render it necessary, in the execution of a duty that requires dispatch, they can march for ten days together without dressing victuals; during which time they subsist upon the blood drawn from their horses, each man opening a vein and drinking from his own cattle. They make provision also of milk, thickened and dried to the state of a hard paste (or curd), which is prepared in the following manner. They boil the milk, and skimming off the rich or creamy part as it rises to the top, put it into a separate vessel as butter; for so long as that remains in the milk, it will not become hard. The latter is then exposed to the sun until it dries. Upon going on service, they carry with them about ten pounds for each man, and of this, half a pound is put, every morning, into a leathern bottle or small *outre*, with as much water as is thought necessary. By their motion in riding the contents are violently shaken, and a thin porridge is produced, upon which they make their dinner. When these Tartars come to engage in battle, they never mix with the enemy, but keep hovering about him, discharging their arrows first from one side and then from the other, occasionally pretending to fly, and during their flight, shooting arrows backwards at their pursuers, killing men and horses, as if they were combating face to face. In this sort of warfare the adversary imagines he has gained a victory, when in fact he has lost the battle; for the Tartars observing the mischief they have done him, wheel about, and renewing the fight overpower his remaining troops and make them prisoners, in spite of their utmost exertions. Their horses are so well broken-in to quick changes of movement, that upon the signal given they instantly turn in every direction: and by these rapid manoeuvres many victories have been obtained. All that has been here related is spoken of the original manners of the Tartar chiefs; but at the present day they are much corrupted. Those who dwell at Ukaka, forsaking their own laws, have adopted the customs of the people who worship idols, and those who inhabit the eastern provinces, have adopted the manners of the Saracens.

THE WESTERN REPLY

European writers of the late Middle Ages usually refer to the Mongols as Tartars or Tatars. Marco Polo at the end of the Mongol Century saw them at their peak of prosperity, on the eve of decline, as the Lords of Cathay. Carpini before the middle of the century saw them as they faced westward, a force that, in the opinion of European rulers, was just containable and might, with adroit management, be used to counterbalance the power of the Muslim Saracens whose power rested in the last resort on the horsemen of the desert, not of the steppe.

That they did not, in the end, achieve the expressed intention of Chingis Chan (Jenghiz Khan) 'to bring the whole world into subjection' is explained by the remark of a Chinese general, Yeh-lu T'su T'sai, who deserted to them at their moment of triumph when they had cracked open the Great Wall and who became a valued technical adviser to succeeding Great Khans. He said, 'The Empire was won on horseback, but you cannot govern on horseback.' The efficiency of their organization, typified by the decimal scale on which their armies were divided into units and leadership delegated, depended on its very simplicity, on the fact

82. Jengis Khan pro-
claiming from the pulpit
of the mosque to the
conquered inhabitants of
Bokhara that he has been
sent by God to punish
them. Persian miniature,
AD 1397–8.

83. Mongol mounted archer, Chinese ink and colour drawing of the Ming Dynasty (1368–1644). Compare with the Parthian archer in Plate 68, whose horse, however, is less hideously ugly than this one.

84. By the time of Froissart in the fifteenth century, mounted armoured combat, as between gentlemen, had become less a form of warfare than a public spectacle. Though mail was of better temper than ever, and plate armour was coming into its own, neither was proof against the best Western missile weapons. It was better to find some sphere where the fighting was exclusively *à l'arme blanche* and everyone adhered to the rules of the game; the stakes, after all, were still worth while. The semi-professional jouster arose; it was just possible to make a knightly living out of forfeited arms, accoutrement and horses, though to do this it was necessary to progress constantly during the season, as our modern knights-errant of the jumping arena do, in order not to miss a single one of the more lucrative meetings. But above all, in the lists one might win the favour of some powerful ruler who was a connoisseur of chivalrous technique, or even better, catch the eye of some fair lady who was a substantial heiress in her own right. (*The Jousts of St Inglevert*, from a Froissart ms)

meulx aduifez et fi remerchies
de voftre deliurance monfeigneur
de bourbon et monfeigneur de
coucy car ilz ont moult fort en
tendu pour vous. Et auffi la
conteffe de fainct pol car la bon

ne dame fen eft moult grande
ment acquittie de vous aydier.
Le feigneur de clary ref
pondy en telle maniere et dift
grans mercis a meffeigneurs
mais ie cuidoie auoir bien fait.

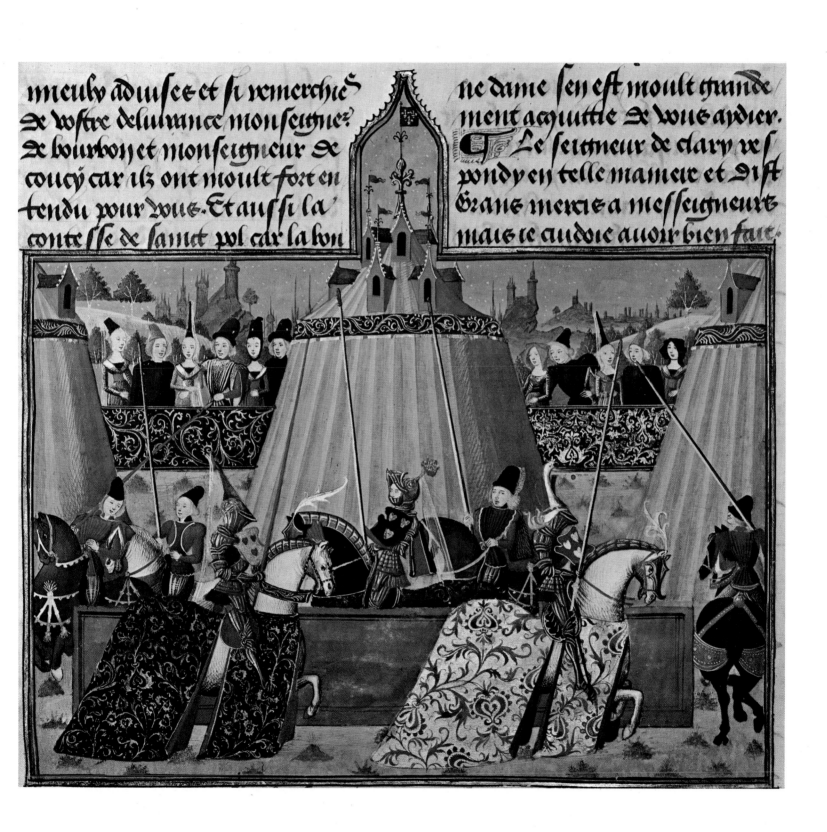

that only a limited variety of problems would have to be resolved by the leadership at every level. Problems of supply for a host perpetually on the move were automatically solved in the manner shown by these two extracts, always provided that the ratio of livestock to people in the 'horde' was maintained at about the level of twenty to one. The logistic system assumed an unlimited supply of grazing and water. When these failed the traditional remedy was simply to move on. In situations where this was not possible the genius of the nomad ruler was at a loss. It was not the measures proposed by Carpini to counter the military power of the Mongols that led to their expulsion from Europe, nor would it have been even if they had been widely and effectively taken. It was simply the inability of the Mongol polity to adapt itself to sedentary conditions in a relatively thickly populated region.

All the empires of the horse-nomads melted away, or in the case of the Turks shrank back within the relatively narrow bounds of Asia Minor, not through 'decadence' (whatever that means) but because the pastures became horse-sick, because there was no more room to ride around.

※HOW TO WAGE WAR AGAINST THE TARTARS

It is the intention of the Tartars to bring the whole world into subjection if they can and . . . on this point they have received a command from Chingis Chan. . . . Since there is no country on earth which they fear with the exception of Christendom, they are preparing to make war on us. Wherefore be it known unto everyone that, while we were in the land of the Tartars, we attended a solemn court, which had been announced several years back and at which, in our presence, they chose Cuyuc as Emperor, or Chan as it is in their language. The said Cuyuc Chan, together with all the princes, raised the standard to proceed against the Church of God and the Roman Empire, and against all Christian kingdoms and nations of the West, unless they carry out the instructions he is sending to the Lord Pope, the rulers and the Christian peoples of the West.

In my opinion, these instructions ought on no

account to be observed, first because of the extreme, nay intolerable, hitherto unheard-of servitude to which they reduce all nations they conquer and which we have seen with our own eyes; then because they are not trustworthy and no nation can rely on their word— they break any promises they make as soon as they see that the tide is turned in their favour, and they are full of deceit in all their deeds and assurances; it is their object to wipe off the face of the earth all princes, nobles, knights and men of gentle birth, as has already been told, and they do this to those in their power in a sly and crafty manner: then because it is unfitting that Christians should be subject to them in view of the abominations they practise and seeing that the worship of God is brought to nought, souls are perishing and bodies are afflicted beyond belief in many ways; it is true at first they speak fair words, but afterwards they sting and hurt like a scorpion; and lastly because they are fewer in number and weaker in body than the Christian peoples.

At the aforementioned court the fighting-men and chiefs of the army were given their appointments. Out of ten men they are sending three with their servants from every country under their sway. One army is to penetrate by way of Hungary, and a second by way of Poland, so we were told. They will come prepared to fight without a break for eighteen years, and they have been assigned their time for setting out. Last March we came upon an army which had been called up from among all the Tartars through whose territory we travelled after leaving Russia. In three or four years' time they will reach Comania. From there they will make an attack on the countries mentioned above; I do not know however whether they will come immediately after the third winter is over, or wait some time longer so that they have a better chance of coming unexpectedly.

All these things are sure and certain, unless God, in his Mercy, places some hindrance in their way as He did when they went into Hungary and Poland. It was their plan to continue fighting for thirty years, but their Emperor was killed by poison and consequently they have rested from battle until the present time. But since an Emperor has been newly appointed, they are

85. Late seventeenth-century reconstruction of the conquistadores and their chief instrument of psychological warfare— the horse. The Aztec emperor, Montezuma, travelled in a man-borne litter. Among the American Indians who had no draught animals except the dog the technique of litter-bearing was developed to the ultimate.

beginning to prepare for the fight once again. It should be known that the Emperor said with his own lips that he wanted to send an army into Livonia and Prussia. Since it is their object to overthrow the whole world and reduce it to slavery—a slavery, as has already been said, unbearable for men of our race—they must therefore be met in battle. . . .

Whoever wishes to fight against the Tartars ought to have the following arms: good strong bows, crossbows, of which they are much afraid, a good supply of arrows, a serviceable axe of strong iron or a battle-axe with a long handle; the heads of the arrows for both bows and crossbows ought to be tempered after the Tartar fashion, in salt water when they are hot, to make them hard enough to pierce the Tartar armour. They should also have swords and lances with a hook to drag the Tartars from their saddle, for they fall off very easily; knives, and cuirasses of a double thickness, for the Tartar arrows do not easily pierce such; a helmet and armour and other things to protect the body and the horses from their weapons and arrows. If there are any men not as well armed as we have described, they ought to do as the Tartars and go behind the others and shoot at the enemy with their bows and crossbows. There ought to be no stinting of money when purchasing weapons for the defence of souls and bodies and liberty and other possessions.

The army should be organized in the same way as the Tartar army, under captains of a thousand, captains of a hundred, captains of ten and the chiefs of the army. The last named ought on no account to take part in the battle, just as the Tartar chiefs take no part, but they should watch the army and direct it. They should make a law that all advance together either to battle or elsewhere in the order appointed. Severe punishment ought to be meted out to anyone who deserts another either going into battle or fighting, or takes flight when they are not retreating as a body, for if this happens a section of the Tartar force follows those fleeing and kills them with arrows while the rest fight with those who have remained on the field, and so both those who stay and those who run away are thrown into confusion and killed. Similarly anyone who turns aside to take plunder before the army of the enemy has been com-

pletely vanquished ought to be punished with a very heavy sentence; among the Tartars such a one is put to death without any mercy. The chiefs of the army should choose their battle ground, if possible a flat plain, every part of which they can watch, and if they can they should have a large forest behind them or on their flank, so situated however that the Tartars cannot come between them and the wood. The army ought not to assemble into one body, but many lines should be formed, separated from each other, only not too far apart. One line ought to be sent to meet the first line of Tartars to approach; if the Tartars feign flight they ought not to pursue them very far, certainly not further than they can see, in case the Tartars lead them into ambushes they have prepared, which is what they usually do. And let another line be in readiness to help the first if occasion require it. . . .

The leaders of the army ought always to be ready to send help to those who are fighting if they need it. Another reason for avoiding too long a pursuit after the Tartars is so as not to tire the horses, for we have not the great quantity which they have. The horses the Tartars ride on one day they do not mount again for the next three or four days, consequently they do not mind if they tire them out seeing they have such a great number of animals. Even if the Tartars retreat our men ought not to separate from each other or be split up, for the Tartars pretend to withdraw in order to divide the army, so that afterwards they can come without any let or hindrance and destroy the whole land. The Christians should also beware of their usual tendency of over-expenditure, lest they be obliged to go home on account of lack of money and the Tartars destroy the whole earth and the name of God be blasphemed on account of their extravagance. They should take care to see that if it come to pass that some fighting men return home, others take their place.

Our leaders ought also to arrange that our army is guarded day and night, so that the Tartars do not make a sudden and unexpected attack upon them for, like the devils, they devise many ways of doing harm. Indeed our men ought to be on the alert as much during the night as in the daytime, they should never undress to lie down, nor sit at table enjoying themselves,

86. In Shunso's *Young Warrior trying to Prevent His Ageing Father from Riding Into Battle* we see a typically romantic and slightly suicidal manifestation of the dashing and curious style of chivalry which grew up at the opposite end of the world from 'Frankish' chivalry once the Japanese warrior class had taken to horsemanship.

so that they cannot be taken unawares, for the Tartars are always on the watch to see how they can inflict some damage. The inhabitants of a country who are apprehensive and fear that the Tartars are coming to attack them should have secret pits in which they should put their corn as well as other things, and this for two reasons: namely so that the Tartars cannot get hold of them and also that, if God shows them His favour, they themselves will be able to find them afterwards. If they have to flee from their country, they ought to burn the hay and straw or hide it away in a safe place so that the horses of the Tartars will find less to eat.

If they wish to fortify cities or fortresses, let them first examine them from the point of view of position, for fortified places ought to be so situated that they cannot be reduced by engines and arrows; they should have a good supply of water and wood and, if possible, it should be impossible to deprive them of an entrance and exit, and they should have sufficient inhabitants for them to take it in turns in fighting. They ought to keep a careful watch to prevent the Tartars from taking the fortress by stealth, by means of cunning. They should have sufficient supplies to last for many years, and let them keep them carefully and eat them in moderation, for they do not know how long they will have to be shut up inside their fortress. When the Tartars once begin, they lay siege to a fortress for many years, for example at the present time in the land of the Alans they have been besieging a hill for the past twelve years, the inhabitants of which have manfully resisted and killed many Tartars and nobles.

Other fortresses and cities which have not the situation described above ought to be strongly protected by means of deep, walled ditches and well-built walls and they should have a good supply of bows and arrows and slings and stones. They must take great care not to allow the Tartars to place their engines in position, but they should drive them off with their own engines. If it happen that the Tartars by some device or cunning erect their engines, then the inhabitants ought to destroy them with theirs if they can; they should also use crossbows, slings and engines against them to prevent them from drawing near to the city. In other respects they ought to be prepared as has already been described. As for fortresses and cities situated on rivers, they should be careful to see that they cannot be flooded out. Moreover, in regard to this point it should be known that the Tartars much prefer men to shut themselves into their cities and fortresses rather than fight with them in the open, for then they say they have got their little pigs shut in their sty, and so they place men to look after them as I have told above.

If any Tartars are thrown from their horse during the battle, they ought to be taken prisoner immediately, for when they are on the ground they shoot vigorously with their arrows, wounding and killing men and horses. If they are kept they can be the means of obtaining uninterrupted peace or a large sum of money would be given for them, for they have great love for each other. As to how Tartars may be recognized, it has been told above in the place where a description is given of their appearance. When they are taken prisoner, a strict guard must be kept over them if they are to be prevented from escaping. There are men of many other nations with them and these can be distinguished from them by means of the description set down above. It is important to know that there are many men in the Tartar army who, if they saw their opportunity and could rely on our men not to kill them, would fight against the Tartars in every part of the army, as they themselves told us, and they would do them worse harm than those who are their declared enemies.

Joannes de Plano Carpini, 'History of the Mongols', in Dawson's *The Mongol Mission*

87. Detail from Dürer's *Adoration of the Magi*, showing a fairly realistic representation of a Turkish mounted archer.

5. Ritual and religion

THUS THEY BURY THEIR KINGS

From at least as early as Neolithic times, from India to Scandinavia, the horse appears to have had special religious significance as the animal most closely connected with the paramount deity, the sun, and as an important fertility symbol; and we have already seen it in a religious context in the description of Greek and Roman chariot-racing. Horse sacrifices were a common practice in the ancient world, whether among the Greeks and Romans or the nomads of the steppes. By far the best account we have of the Scythians and other related horse-nomads is that of Herodotus.

In the whole Crimean/Ukrainian region an abundance of Scythian tombs, systematically plundered since the days of Peter the Great in search of treasure, and latterly excavated with great care in the interests of prehistory, bear out all that Herodotus has to say about the burial rites of the Scyths, especially the role of the horse in funeral practices. The River Borysthenes is the Dniepr.

※ The sepulchres of the kings are in the country of the Gerrhi, as far as which the Borysthenes is navigable. There, when their king dies, they dig a large square hole in the ground; and having prepared this, they take up the corpse, having the body covered with wax, the belly opened and cleaned, filled with bruised cypress, incense, and parsley and anise-seed, and then sewn up again, and carry it in a chariot to another nation: those who receive the corpse brought to them, do the same as the Royal Scythians; they cut off part of their ear, shave off their hair, wound themselves on the arms,

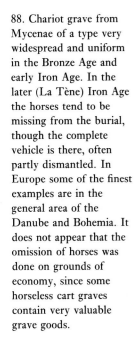

88. Chariot grave from Mycenae of a type very widespread and uniform in the Bronze Age and early Iron Age. In the later (La Tène) Iron Age the horses tend to be missing from the burial, though the complete vehicle is there, often partly dismantled. In Europe some of the finest examples are in the general area of the Danube and Bohemia. It does not appear that the omission of horses was done on grounds of economy, since some horseless cart graves contain very valuable grave goods.

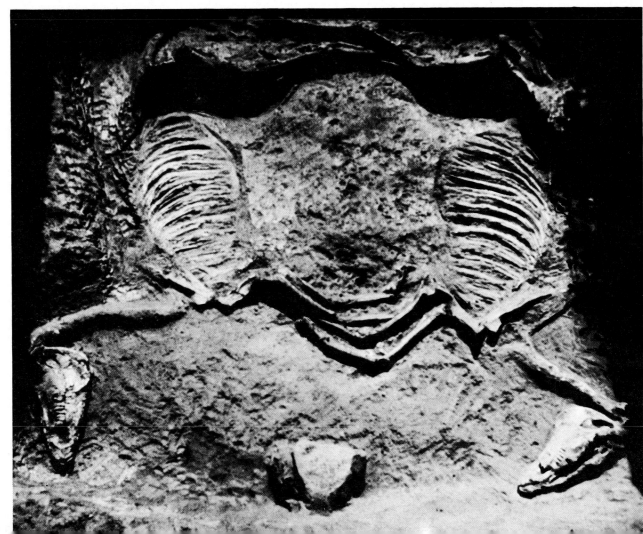

lacerate their forehead and nose, and drive arrows through their left hand. Thence they carry the corpse of the king to another nation whom they govern; and those to whom they first came accompany them. When they have carried the corpse round all the provinces, they arrive among the Gerrhi, who are the most remote of the nations they rule over, and at the sepulchres. Then, when they have placed the corpse in the grave on a bed of leaves, having fixed spears on each side of the dead body, they lay pieces of wood over it, and cover it over with mats. In the remaining space of the grave they bury one of the king's concubines, having strangled her, and his cup-bearer, a cook, a groom, a page, a courier, and horses, and firstlings of every thing else, and golden goblets; they make no use of silver or brass. Having done this, they all heap up a large mound, striving and vying with each other to make it as large as possible. When a year has elapsed, they then do as follows: having taken the most fitting of his remaining servants; they are all native Scythians; for they serve him whomsoever the king may order, and they have no servants bought with money: when therefore they have strangled fifty of these servants, and fifty of the finest horses, having taken out their bowels and cleansed them, they fill them with chaff, and sew them up again. Then having placed the half of a wheel, with its concave side uppermost, on two pieces of wood, and the other half on two other pieces of wood, and having fixed many of these in the same manner, then having thrust thick pieces of wood through the horses lengthwise, up to the neck, they mount them on the half-wheels; and of these the foremost part of the half-wheels supports the shoulders of the horses, and the hinder part supports the belly near

89. Gilt-bronze cult object from Trundholm in Denmark, known as the 'chariot of the sun'. The sacred horse is only shown drawing the sun across the sky very schematically; the wheels are not meant as part of the chariot in which the sun sits but they are part of the structure of what is called a cult-waggon, a toy-sized vehicle carrying statuette groups of religious significance very characteristic of Iron Age ritual from Spain to the Oxus valley. The horse figures in all these cult-waggons one way or another. The four-spoked wheel is not a stylization; it was a real if very archaic method of wheel construction often seen in Scandinavian rock drawing and Greek vase painting.

90. Enigmatic Pictish carving of Dark Age Scotland. In this one there is a Christian symbol central to the whole composition but it is surrounded by other themes redolent of paganism, such as the dragons' heads, the stylized sea monsters and the broken arrows, crescents and mirrors, which taken together have been intercepted as a code expressing the rank and family connections of the deceased. Almost the one unequivocal phrase in this sign language writes that this is the tomb of a skilled farrier, whose tools are shown in the lower register. Between them and the presumably priestly seated figures above is what appears to be an equestrian portrait of the deceased; but in other Pictish carvings the horse appears unridden and without saddle or harness, probably as a religious symbol, not necessarily Christian.

the thighs, but the legs on both sides are suspended in the air: then having put bridles and bits on the horses, they stretch them in front, and fasten them to a stake; they then mount upon a horse each, one of the fifty young men that have been strangled, mounting them in the following manner; when they have driven a straight piece of wood along the spine as far as the neck, but a part of this wood projects from the bottom, they fix it into a hole bored in the other piece of wood that passes through the horse. Having placed such horsemen round the monument, they depart.

Thus they bury their kings. But the other Scythians, when they die, their nearest relations carry about among their friends, laid in chariots; and of these each one receives and entertains the attendants, and sets the same things before the dead body, as before the rest. In this manner private persons are carried about for forty days, and then buried. *Melpomene* IV

The 'chariots' to which this passage refers have little in common with those of the Mediterranean world. They were more like gypsy living waggons, but more lightly constructed, the body consisting of willow hoops covered with felt. In so far as the Scyths in the time of Herodotus had any permanent dwellings, it was these. But the funeral sites show in their construction a harking-back to a time before these people took up the wandering life; before they went in for such extensive horse-breeding. The 'large square hole' is familiar to Russian archaeologists. It was lined with skilfully-joined timbers, in such a way as to form below ground level a substantial wooden house of the kind in which the ancestors of the Scyths had once lived.

Together with their harsh and murderous customs went a highly developed style of art in various media, but this was closely affected by the demands of the horseborne life. There was no pottery or glassware, which would have got smashed on the move. All the art was decorative, literally *art mobilier*, applied to all sorts of portable objects; nothing that could not be stowed in a waggon of about 120 cubic feet capacity, or strapped to a saddle. The Scyths appear, for instance, to have invented the 'Persian' carpet, the oldest extant example of which was made before 430 BC and was

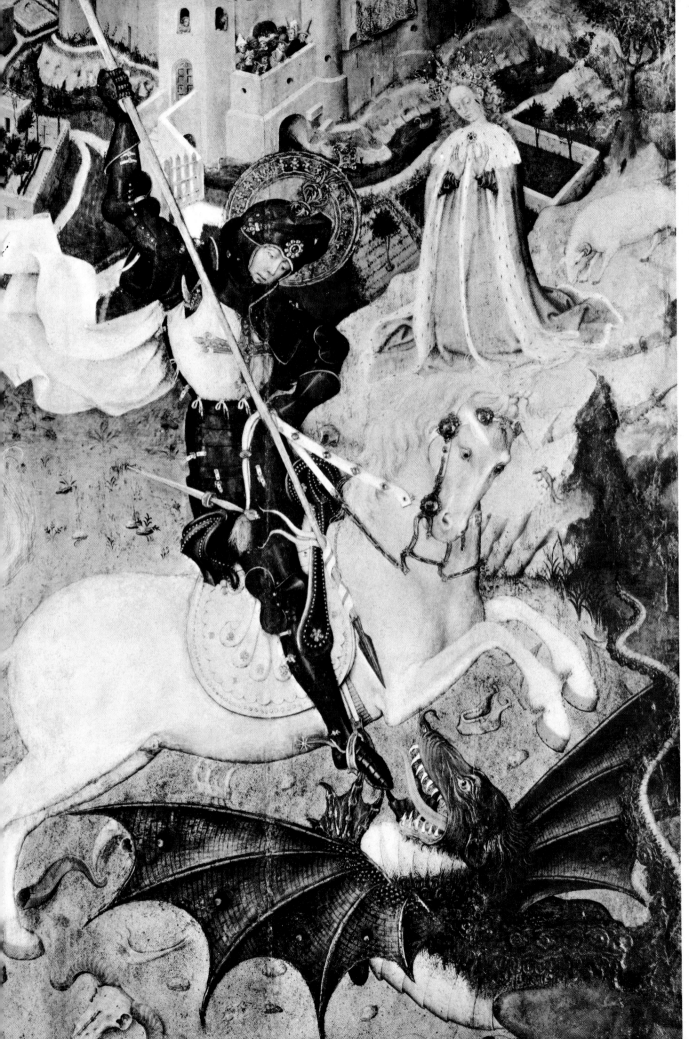

91. As long as patron saints for countries were fashionable St George was by far the most popular, patronizing at least half a dozen and presenting a problem of conflicting loyalties when some of his protégés were at war with each other and their archbishops sending up rival invocations. Official hagiography has endowed St George with a historical identity as a Roman soldier of the second century serving in a unit not identified but stationed in Cappadocia. In fact St George is a take-over from pagan belief, as the resemblance between his iconography and that of several antique cults of monster-slaying gods-on-horseback demonstrates. The most notable of these was the so-called Thracian rider-god whose worship in the late Roman Empire was widespread in the Eastern Mediterranean but also extended to Britain. (*St George and the Dragon*, 1430, by Bernardo Martorel)

92. While the knight was a military reality artists painted St George with contemporary armour, weapons and accoutrements. Thus the fresco in Pickering Church, North Yorkshire, shows the knight armed and equipped as of about Henry V's time, riding a horse such as might have been bred in the royal stud of destriers in Dalby Park outside Pickering. This is one of the few English church frescoes to have survived the Reformation.

found in a tomb such as Herodotus described, far away 'at the back of the North wind' in the Altai Mountains of Western Siberia. Such rugs were woven then on completely portable knock-down looms; and even today the best of such textiles are woven in the borderlands of Persia, Afghanistan and Baluchistan, by people of the same nomadic habit whom 'progressive' westernizing governments are trying by all means to force into a sedentary way of life. When this policy succeeds, the arts of the wandering horse-breeder will die.

DIVIDING THE INHERITANCE

In Homeric Greece horse-races formed an integral part of the funeral games (see Chapter 2). But only in one little country on the south shore of the Baltic have we any record of the division and inheritance of the deceased's estate being decided by such a race. It comes from the Preface which King Alfred wrote to his translation of the classical geography book of Orosius. The information in this opening part of the book was derived from the conversation of certain Norwegian merchant skippers who were in the habit of spending the winter (non-sailing) season at the English King's court. Alfred's Estonia was much larger than the present Russian province of that name; it extended much further inland and it formed the link by which certain customs and techniques of the steppe horsemen reached Scandinavia, though not all of them survived the crossing of the Baltic. Thus the Estonians had

adopted the universal Mongol–Tartar drink, *kumiss*—fermented mare's milk—but this found no favour over the water in Sweden. In the first place, there were not enough mares: besides, the alcohol content is really too low for Scandinavian tastes.

Esthonia (Eastland) is very large, and there are many towns, and in every town there is a king. There is also very much honey and fishing. The king and the richest men drink mare's milk, but the poor and the slaves drink mead. There is very much war among them; and there is no ale brewed by the Esthonians, but there is mead enough.

There is also a custom with the Esthonians, that when a man is dead, he lies, in his house, unburnt with his kindred and friends a month—sometimes two; and the king and other men of high rank, so much longer according to their wealth, remain unburnt sometimes half a year; and lie above ground in their houses. All the while the body is within, there must be drinking and sports to the day, on which he is burned.

Then, the same day, when they wish to bear him to the pile, they divide his property, which is left after the drinking and sports, into five or six parts, sometimes into more, as the amount of his property may be. Then, they lay the largest part of it within one mile from the town, then another, then the third, till it is all laid, within the one mile; and the least part shall be nearest the town in which the dead man lies. All the men, who have the swiftest horses in the land, shall then be assembled, about five or six miles from the property. Then they all run towards the property; and the man, who has the swiftest horse, comes to the first and the largest part, and so each after the other, till it is all taken: and he takes the least part, who runs to the property nearest the town. Then each rides away with the property, and may keep it all; and, therefore, swift horses are there uncommonly dear. When his property is thus all spent, then they carry him out, and burn him with his weapons and clothes. Most commonly they spend all his wealth, with a long lying of the dead within, and what they lay in the way, which the strangers run for and take away.

Alfred, *Whole Works*: Orosius Book 1

93. The most realistic of the better known St Georges from the point of view of practical chivalry is that by Carpaccio. This is the seat adopted by the knight of real life in battle at the moment of contact, this is the way the weight was distributed and this is the way the lance was directed, along the left side of the horse's neck.

SACRED WEDDING

Among the Celts, the earth-goddess had sometimes been personified as a mare, and in his sacred character of the bringer of increase the king had to perform a ritual act of physical union with her. But this custom also seems to have been observed in the Bronze Age outside Celtic territory. There are rock carvings in Sweden which represent this act, or its prelude, quite unmistakably. How long the custom survived in Ireland, the last stronghold of Celtic ritual despite its early conversion to Christianity, we do not know, nor whether all the kings of what are now the Irish provinces performed the sacred drama of fertilization of the earth mare-goddess; we do not know for certain whether any of them did it, but only the High King of Tara. Giraldus Cambrensis of Barry, the Norman-Welsh ecclesiastic who in the late twelfth century made a tour of Ireland and afterwards wrote an intelligence report, the *Topographia Hiberniae*, for the information of the king and Anglo-Norman military leaders, was quite certain that this ceremony still went on in his own day. His Chapter XXV reads as follows.

OF A NEW AND MONSTROUS WAY OF INAUGURATING THEIR KINGS

There are some things which shame would prevent my relating, unless the course of my subject required it. For a filthy story seems to reflect a stain on the author, although it may display his skill. But the severity of history does not allow us either to sacrifice truth or affect modesty; and what is shameful in itself may be related by pure lips in decent words. There is, then, in the northern and most remote part of Ulster, namely, at Kenel Cunil,[1] a nation which practises a most barbarous and abominable rite in creating their king. The whole people of that country being gathered in one place, a white mare is led into the midst of them, and he who is to be inaugurated, not as a prince but as a brute, not as a king but as an outlaw, comes before the people on all fours, confessing himself a beast with no less impudence than imprudence. The mare being immediately killed, and cut in pieces and boiled, a bath is prepared for him from the broth. Sitting in this, he eats of the flesh which is brought to him, the people standing round and partaking of it also. He is also required to drink of the broth in which he is bathed,

[1] See note at end of this extract.

94. *The Four Horsemen of the Apocalypse.* Almost the only passage in the New Testament that affords the equestrian artist scope to make his contribution to religious art is the passage in the Revelation of St John. More numerous than testament illuminations are those to manuscripts of the widely read Commentary on the Apocalypse by Beato de Labiena. Here is one of the earliest examples from the end of the first millennium. Because 'he that sat on a white horse' bore a bow, it was customary to suggest some oriental features (in the case of a Spanish artist, inevitably Moorish), and this is done here simply by the suggestion of an exotic head-dress (*top left*). The swordsman on the red horse (*top right*) is shown like the European mounted warrior of about the year 1000, with the characteristic two-edged sword, knee-length hauberk and chausses of mail.

95. Eight centuries later William Blake's rider and horse are among the most powerful figures he ever drew, though anatomically impossible. (*Death on a Pale Horse*)

not drawing it in any vessel, nor even in his hand, but lapping it with his mouth. These unrighteous rites being duly accomplished, his royal authority and dominion are ratified. (*Tirconnell, now the County of Donegal. Irish antiquaries utterly repudiate the disgusting account here given by Giraldus of the inauguration of the kings of this territory.* [*Editor's note*])

No wonder they repudiated it. Most of them were clergymen. What we have to decide is whether Giraldus fully comprehended what was being told to him, and again to what extent his leg was being pulled anyhow. In the first place, many of his informants were well aware for what purpose he was gathering information, and this was only one of the many reasons they might have for pulling his leg. In the second place, he spoke no Irish, and neither English nor Welsh nor Norman-French were at all widely spoken in Ulster in the 1180s. The most likely informants would be Irish priests, using their version of the international language of intellectuals, Latin. But many fine shades of meaning might go astray when a Latin sentence is uttered by Irish lips and received by Norman-Welsh ears— including the tenses of verbs. Most probably the oral

sources were describing what used to happen, not necessarily in the remote times before the mission of St Patrick, but in the troubled period of the Viking invasions which had ended little more than a century earlier, one symptom of which, in Ireland as in Britain, was a relapse into paganism, involving not only the adoption of Norse cults but, here and there, the revival of indigenous ones that bore some resemblance to them.

MYTHS AND RITES

No English pageant is complete without a representation of Lady Godiva, even in places far remote from Coventry, where the legend survived long enough to be committed to writing. As a slice of pop history the story of the wife of the cruel earl who said he would repeal his unjust taxes only if she rode naked through the streets of Coventry is the most effective turn on the bill, streets ahead of Alfred and the Cakes, well up in the Robin Hood bracket. And like Robin, Godiva is a figure of mythology, not of history. Only her personality has been grafted onto the historical Godiva, Lady of Mercia, aunt of Hereward the Wake, perfectly authentic, identified and described in quite prosaic documents: the wife of Earl Leofric, who in real life was not at all the monster of rapacity painted by legend. An explanation must be sought in pagan tradition, either in the deep layers of Celtic myth along with Epona, the patron goddess of horses, or at the level of Anglo-Saxon heathendom with its sacred white horses figured in the arms of Brunswick and Kent alike, but more probably in the revival of heathendom which the Viking invasion brought to England.

The historical Leofric and Godgifu (Godiva), despite their English names, were of that mixed Anglo-Danish nobility to which even the last two pre-Norman kings belonged, and though Coventry lies west of the old frontier dividing English from Danish Mercia it is very close up to it. Scandinavian religious practice, before Christianity, included the annual spring parade of the image of a goddess, or of a pretty girl impersonating her, either on a sacred waggon or else side-saddle on an equally sacred horse, either white or palomino. Her name was Freya (earlier, Nerthus). No doubt the legend as we now have it was concocted to make respectable in the eyes of the Church a ceremony which the people were loath to abandon. This earth-goddess is seen as the mother of mankind, and the Pluto-Persephone relationship of Leofric and Godiva serves to indicate the original nature of the former. Rationalized as a wicked earl, avaricious and grasping, he stands in the place of some Frost Giant or Winter King, who threatens mankind—and indeed all life, animal or vegetable. Freya on the other hand is spring and summer and autumn by turns.

There is a detailed description of the spring perambulation of Freya in her waggon by Snorri Sturlason in his Saga of Olaf Tryggvason (d. AD 1000) as then practised in Sweden. The waggon was horse-drawn.

The figure of Peeping Tom can best be accounted for in terms of an earlier description of the same ceremony by Tacitus in his *Germania*, about AD 100. At that time the waggon was ox-drawn, and after the ceremony was washed by slaves. They, and anyone who touched the sacred object, were afterwards drowned in a 'lake' (more likely bog) as a sacrifice to the goddess.

96. *Lady Godiva* by Marshall Claxton. An illustration of the legend which is itself probably the remnant of a pagan tradition.

97. The processional vehicle was a special branch of the wain-wright's art. While some of the triumphal cars in the Antwerp Ommeganck (painted by Denis van Alsloot early in the seventeenth century) were plainly built up on the ordinary Low Country farm-waggon of the period, like the second from the left in the second rank, others were specially built to a design, including the wheels, that had no relevance to normal locomotion. Perhaps the nearest equivalent is the pageant waggon on which the mystery cycles of plays at York, Chester, etc. were performed in the streets.

Another Latin history of the twelfth century, dealing not with contemporary events but with those of King Edgar's reign, bears a strong and detailed resemblance to Gerald the Welshman's story about the Irish king, only here it is a West Saxon queen who is involved in what is obviously a pagan rite concerned not so much with fertility in general but with the specific encouragement of breeding, by sympathetic magic, among the herds of what we now call New Forest ponies, which were then royal property, as were the Exmoor pony herds down to the nineteenth century. The following is an excerpt of Chapter 56 of Book II of the Chronicle of Ely. Byrhnoth was Abbot of Ely:

The holy abbot set out for the king's court [*at Winchester*] on church business; as he was journeying on this side of Geldedune [*not now identifiable*] through the woods now called the New Forest, as it is said, he sought some more secluded spot to satisfy the needs of nature: as he was a modest man and of great integrity he took care to look round on every side. By chance under a certain tree he surprised the queen, Aelfthryth, engaged in the preparation of magic potions (for, transformed by her caprice and magic art into an equine animal, she wished to appear as a horse and not as a woman to onlookers, so that she might satisfy the unrestrainable excess of her burning lust), running, leaping hither and thither with horses, and showing herself shamelessly to them; regardless of the fear of

God and the honour of the royal dignity, she thus contemptibly brought reproach upon her fame.

She lamented not without shame and great fear to be seen engaged in such practices: she was indeed most skilled, as it is said, in machinations. But the man of God greatly upset by things of this kind withdrew from the place as quickly as possible, and being honourably received on his arrival at the king's court very speedily transacted his business. So enjoying and stimulated by the king's favour he sought the road for return; and so as not to shun the queen (though abhorring her) he went down to her apartment, which by chance he found deserted. . . .

And that was his undoing: he never came out alive. For well she knew what the abbot had seen. She asked him to hear her confession, which did not include that day's activities but a lurid catalogue of erotic misdemeanours, from which she led on, naturally, to an attempt to seduce her confessor and thus keep his mouth shut. When this failed she summoned her attendants, and while some of her ladies-in-waiting set up a great lamentation to drown the noise of what was actually going on, the rest of them murdered Byrhnoth in a singularly brutal way, reminiscent of the death of Edward II.

Now all this happened about 980. That part of Hampshire had been, at the outset of the Anglo-Saxon Settlement, Jutish territory, and the best-known

Jutish royal family of the Migration Period had been the famous brothers Hengest and Horsa. Now, five centuries later, the original Jutish population had been overlaid by later waves of West Saxon settlers. Yet it would seem that among the men of the forest whose first rulers in the Isle of Britain had been men with names meaning Stallion, most likely signifying their role as hereditary priests of a horse-fertility cult, the emotional necessity for a horse-cult still existed and needed the patronage of a royal person. Not only the emotional necessity but economic survival: to the New Forest commoner of yesterday a bad foaling year might mean his living was cut in half; and since the pony herds of king and churl alike ran in the same forest, their interests were identical. Fertility was indivisible, and the ceremonies the queen performed were for the benefit of her subjects as well as her own in her capacity of stud-owner. It is obvious from two passages in the whole narrative that it was generally known what part

the queen played in the cult. Had the East Anglian abbot been more familiar with West Saxon local custom he could have walked out of the palace alive.

The whole attitude, even to the style and vocabulary employed, is the same in the Ely chronicle as in Giraldus. It was the established way of treating this subject. Among other things the writer must not appear to know about this polluting theme; hence occasional vagueness and apparent contradiction of terms, a foreshadowing in some ways of later medieval writers describing acts of witchcraft which, at least in part, must have been derived from such practices. But from the few analogies that exist we can deduce that the queen at some stage donned ritual costume, probably including a mare's tail and a mask made out of the skull and mane of a foal—'transformed into an equine animal'—took a stiff dose of some drug—'magic potions'—and performed a sort of ballet miming the characteristic behaviour of a mare on heat.

98. *The Funeral of President Lincoln Passing Union Square*, New York, 25 April 1865. 'The magnificent funeral car was drawn by 16 grey horses richly caparisoned with ostrich plumes and cloth of black trimmed with silver bullion.' (A Currier and Ives lithograph.) Over a hundred years later President Eisenhower was carried to interment on a horse-drawn gun carriage.

Whether one ascribes the origins of chivalry to the last traditions of the Roman cataphract (mail-clad lancer) or to the Gothic mounted swordsman in the *comitatus* of those barbarian kings who finally felled the dying oak of Rome, indubitably an embryo-knight was the central figure in the society of western Christendom during what is called in Britain the Saxon heptarchy and in Europe the period of Frankish hegemony. And when, three or four hundred years after everyone had stopped pretending that there was a Western Empire any more, the successor states of the Roman patrimony were threatened by a new (fortunately uncoordinated) threefold assault by external enemies—the Vikings, the Saracens and the Magyars—it was the forces of chivalry which broke the teeth of this attack, and in the process hardened into a military, a political and a social system that was the same everywhere from the March of Spain to the March of Styria and the Dannevirke.

THE CID

'Lady', said the Cid Campeador, 'You see the horse sweating and the sword bloody. That is how one vanquishes Moors in the field.'

And that is essentially what the caballero was for. History is never as simple as that. A large part of the time the caballero was not battling against the infidel, but upholding the 'right' of his feudal lord against the equally inalienable 'right' of some other lord. This was the inevitable consequence of an ideology whose mainspring was the personal loyalty of vassal to suzerain. Situations often arose in which one Christian party in Spain was allied to some Muslim ruler, just as, in the Britain of the heptarchy, a Christian prince of Wales joined the pagan King of Mercia in a sanguinary war against the Christian King of Northumberland, and a dispute between two Irish Christian dynasties was fought out, at Clontarf, by heathen Danish and Norwegian mercenaries. In all European epic, the Poem of the Cid Ruy Díaz de Bivar (c. 1043–99) is the sweatiest, the bloodiest, the dustiest, the most evocative of what

it was like to 'ride with Galician saddles, with our boots over our hose'.

Nowhere else, not even in the *Song of Roland* itself, do we have such a picture of the knight as he really was, grim and gay and occasionally tender, fighting frankly often for booty, sometimes for revenge, very occasionally in genuine self-defence, because there was no other option: but mostly out of the sheer pride of horsemanship, since battle itself was the ultimate test of the destrier, and the only way to display the merit of his most prized possession was to take part in a battle—any battle—just as the Arab cavalier could only prove the virtues of his kehailan mare in the *ghazu*—the inter-tribal raid—which had by Ruy Díaz de Bivar's day become inflated into that super-ghazu, the *jehad* or war of conquest against the Infidel. Only with the aid of such a mare could one attain the status of Ghazi—slayer of infidels.

They clasp the shields
    over their hearts,
they lower the lances
    swathed in their pennons,
they bowed their faces
    over their saddle-trees,
with strong hearts
    they charged to attack them.

He who in good hour was born
    cried with a great voice:
'Attack them, knights
    for the love of the Creator!
I am Ruy Díaz, the Cid
    the Campeador of Bivar!'
All rushed at the rank
    where Pedro Bermúdez was.
They were three hundred spears
    each with its pennon;
all struck blows
    and killed as many Moors;
on the second charge
    they killed three hundred more.

You would have seen so many lances
    lowered and raised,

زه هون رہ کنید نامون نورد

نان کرد کردوں کردان زکرد

99. Prince Humay wounds Princess Humayun in combat, the lovers not having recognized each other. Although this miniature, embellishing the manuscript of a Persian epic, dates from the late fourteenth century of our era, it does serve to remind us that the armoured horse as such is probably a Persian invention going back perhaps to the second century AD.

100. The pageantry of the Renaissance in all its glory, a fresco by Benozzo Gozzoli nominally showing the *Journey of the Magi to Jerusalem* but actually showing the followers and court of Lorenzo the Magnificent coming down the hill from Fiesole to Florence. A good cross-section of Italian Renaissance horses as used for peaceful travelling and war. In the turbulent days of the late fifteenth century a well-organized retinue with first-class mounts was essential to a leader of the Medici's standing.

101. Pieter Bruegel the Elder's depiction of the *Massacre of the Innocents* (detail). Although the historical event took place in Bethlehem, Bruegel, probably for political reasons, set it in a Flemish village.

102. Acquamanile of the late thirteenth century representing an armed knight with characteristic pot-helm and armour still composed of mail rather than plate.

so many bucklers
        pierced and split asunder,
so many coats of mail
        break and darken,
so many white pennons
        drawn out red with blood,
so many good horses
        run without their riders.
The Moors call on Mohamet
        and the Christians on St James.
A thousand three hundred
        of the Moors fall dead
upon the field
        in a little space. . . .

They have killed the horse from under
        Minaya Álvar Fáñez,
hosts of Christians
        charge to his aid.
His lance is broken
        his sword in his hand,
even afoot
        he deals great blows.
Ruy Díaz, the Castillian,
        My Cid, saw him;
he rode up on a Moorish lord
        who had a good horse,
struck so with his sword
        with his right arm,
he cut him through at the belt
        half the body fell to the field.
He took the horse
        to Minaya Álvar Fáñez:
'Mount, Minaya
        you who are my right arm!
This very day
        I shall have need of you;
the Moors stand firm
        they have not yet fled the field,
we must fall upon them
        relentlessly.'
Minaya mounted
        his sword in his hand,
fighting bravely
        through all that host,
delivering of their souls
        all who came near him.
My Cid Ruy Díaz
        who in good hour was born,
has aimed three blows
        at King Fáriz;
two of them missed
        and the third struck home,
the blood ran down
        over the tunic of chain-mail;
he turned his horse
        to flee from the field.
With that blow
        the army was beaten.

Martín Antolínez
        struck Galve a blow,
he broke in pieces
        the rubies of his helmet,
he split the helmet
        cut into the flesh;
the other dared not wait
        you may know, for another.
King Fáriz and King Galve
        and their armies are routed;
it is a great day
        for Christendom,
for the Moors flee
        on either hand.
My Cid's vassals
        ride in pursuit,

103. Close combat between knights, an anonymous Italian
drawing of about 1460.

King Fáriz
        has gone into Terrer,
as for Galve
        they would not receive him;
toward Calatayud
        he rode on at full speed.
The Campeador
        rode in pursuit,
they continued the chase
        as far as Calatayud. . . .

My Cid's men
        have sacked the Moors' encampment
seized shields and arms
        and much else of value;
when they had brought them in
        they found they had taken
five hundred and ten
        Moorish horses.
There was great joy
        among those Christians,
not more than fifteen
        of their men were missing.
They bear so much gold and silver
        they do not know how much there is.
All those Christians
        were made rich
with the spoils
        that had fallen to them.
They have called back the Moors
        who lived in the castle,
my Cid ordered
        that even they should be given something.

The word of it has gone out
        in all directions;
the news has come
        to the Count of Barcelona
that my Cid Ruy Díaz
        overruns all his land!
It troubled him sorely
        he took it as an affront.
The count is a great braggart
        and spoke foolishly:

'My Cid of Bivar
      inflicts great losses on me.
He offended me once
      in my own court:
he struck my nephew
      and gave me reparation;
now he sacks the lands
      under my protection;
I have never affronted him
      nor withdrawn my friendship,
but since he seeks me out
      I shall force him to a reckoning.'

  Great are his armies
      they assemble with speed,
Moors and Christians
      all gather about him
and ride forward
      toward my good Cid of Bivar;
three days and two nights
      still they rode on,
and came to my Cid
      in the pine grove of Tévar;
they come in such numbers
      they think to take him into their hands.

  My Cid Don Rodrigo
      bringing great spoils,
came down from a mountain
      into a valley.
The message arrives
      from Count Ramón;
when my Cid heard it
      he sent back an answer:
'Tell the Count
      not to take it amiss,
I have nothing of his
      tell him to let me alone.'
The Count answered:
      'That is not the truth!
Now he shall pay me all
      from now and from before;
he shall learn, this outcast
      whom he has dishonoured.'

The messenger returned
      at his full speed.
Thereupon my Cid
      of Bivar understood,
that he could not leave that place
      without a battle.

  'Now, knights
      set the spoils to one side;
arm yourselves quickly
      put on your armour;
the Count Don Ramón
      seeks a great battle,
he has with him multitudes
      of Moors and Christians,
without a battle
      on no account will he let us go.
If we go on they will follow us
      let the battle be here;
cinch tight the saddles
      and arm yourselves.
They are coming downhill
      all of them in breeches;
their saddles are flat
      and the girths are loose;
we shall ride with Galician saddles
      with boots over our hose;
with a hundred knights
      we should overcome their host.
Before they reach the plain
      let us greet them with lances;
for every one that you strike
      three saddles will be emptied.
  Ramón Berenguer will see
      whom he has come seeking
to-day in the pine grove of Tévar
      to take back the spoils from me.'

  When my Cid had spoken
      all made ready;
they have taken up their arms
      and mounted their horses.
They saw the Catalans
      descending the slope;

104. Complete war armour for man and horse, not for tournament purposes, as used in the last stages of the faction fight among the English aristocracy known as the Wars of the Roses.

105. *The Italian Joust*, picture of a tournament by Albrecht Dürer showing that the lists, the plank barrier, while they prevented actual head-on collisions between horses did not and were not meant to prevent the gravest injuries to horse and rider.

when they came near the foot of the hill
    where it joins the plain,
my Cid who in good hour was born
    called to his men to attack
his knights charged forward
    with a will
skilfully handling
    their pennons and lances,
wounding some
    and unhorsing the rest.
He who was born in good hour
    has won the battle.
He has taken prisoner
    the Count Ramón;
he has taken the sword Colada
    worth more than a thousand marks.

IN THE CRUSADES

We have no Moorish poem from Islamic Andaluz to match the epic of the Cid. But in the memoirs of Usamah Ibn Munqidh (1095–1188) who was born in the year the Franks took Jerusalem and died in the year that the Muslims won it back, we have an unrivalled picture of 'the other side of the hill'. Apart from his riding a mare where the faranghi would ride a stallion, and his wearing wadded arrow-arresting jerkins instead of mail, Usamah's ideology at the other end of the Mediterranean is strangely like that of the Cid and just as businesslike; and just as unthinkable outside the context of horsemanship.

106. Titian's picture of
the Emperor Charles V
at the Battle of Muhlberg,
1547.

A Frankish ruse on Shayzar foiled. Here is something of men's intrepidity and gallantry in warfare which I saw:

One day we arose early in the morning at the time of the dawn prayer only to find a band of Franks, about ten cavaliers, who had come to the gate of the lower town before it was opened. They asked the gatekeeper, 'What is the name of this town?' The gate was of wood with beams running across, and the gatekeeper was inside of the gate. 'Shayzar', he replied. The Franks thereupon shot an arrow at him through the crack of the door, and they turned back with their horses trotting under them.

So we mounted our horses. My uncle (may Allah's mercy rest upon his soul!) was the first to ride, and I was in his company; while the Franks were marching along unworried. A few of our troops came following us. I said to my uncle, 'Command only, and I shall take our companions, pursue the enemy and dislodge them from their saddles as long as they are not so far away.'

'No', replied my uncle, who was more of an expert in warfare than I was. 'Is there a Frank in Syria who knows not Shayzar? This is a ruse.'

He then called two of our cavaliers riding on two swift mares and said, 'Go and reconnoitre Tell-Milh.' This was the place where the Franks usually laid their ambuscade. As soon as our two men were in a position overlooking the Tell, the army of Antioch set out against them *en masse*. We hastened to the encounter of those who were in the vanguard, desiring to take advantage of them before the battle was over. In our company were Jum'ah al-Numayri and his son, Mahmud. In fact, Jum'ah was our leading cavalier and our sheikh. His son, Mahmud, somehow got into the midst of the ranks of the enemy. And Jum'ah cried, 'O real cavaliers! My boy!' So we went back with him,

numbering sixteen cavaliers, smote with our lances sixteen Frankish knights and carried back our comrade from among them. We got so much mixed up with them in the course of the encounter that the head of Jum'ah was held under the armpit of one of them, but he was soon delivered by those lance blows which we administered. . . .

In flight before the Franks of Antioch. The army of Antioch made an incursion on us. Our comrades met their vanguard and were retreating before them. I posted myself on their route, expecting their arrival and hoping thereby to be able to get an opportunity to attack the enemy. Our comrades began to pass by me in defeat. Among those who thus passed was Mahmud ibn-Jum'ah. I said, 'Halt, O Mahmud!' He stopped for

107. Stradanus included falconry in his series of engravings on modern inventions, meaning thereby things unknown in classical antiquity. In fact falconry was known to the extent that it is mentioned by travel writers of the Graeco-Roman world, but it was something practised only by Scythians and the like and not by civilized people. It is first mentioned in English documents in the year 757, probably as a result of contact with Scandinavia, and appears to have penetrated Europe by this route, through contact with Asiatic nomads on the lower Danube and lastly by the example of the Muslim emirs in Sicily.

an instant; then he spurred his horse and left me. By that time the vanguard of the Frankish horsemen had reached me, so I retired before them, turning back my lance in their direction and my eyes towards them lest some one of their horse should prove too quick for me and pierce me with his lance. In front of me were some of our companions, and we were surrounded by gardens with walls as high as a sitting man. My mare hit with its breast one of our companions, so I turned its head to my left and applied the spurs to its sides; whereupon it leaped over the wall. I so regulated my position until I stood on a level with the Franks. The wall only separated us. One of their horsemen hastened to me, displaying his colours in a green and yellow silk tunic, under which I thought was no coat of mail. I therefore let him alone until he passed me. Then I applied the spurs to my mare, which leaped over the wall, and I smote him with the lance. He bent sideways so much that his head reached his stirrup, his shield and lance fell off his hand, and his helmet off his head. By that time we had reached our infantry. He then resumed his position, erect in the saddle. Having had linked mail under his tunic, my lance did not wound him. His companions caught up with him, all returned together, and the footman recovered his shield, lance and helmet.

108. The fatal tournament in which King Henri II of France was killed in 1559 and which brought jousting into disrepute because of the awkward political consequences attendant on the sudden death of distinguished jousters.

DERISSIM · FECIT · 1570

109. The entrance of the Emperor Charles V into Tunis, from a manuscript illumination. The Spanish counter-attack on the Moors was carried over into Africa by Charles V and this picture of the storming of Tunis demonstrates the limitations of chivalry and indeed all cavalry. Before they could charge into the stronghold somebody on foot had to force the gate for them.

Even Jum'ah flees. When the battle was over and the Franks withdrew, Jum'ah (may Allah's mercy rest upon his soul!) came to me apologizing on behalf of his son, Mahmud, and said, 'This dog fled away while in thy company!' I replied, 'What of it?' He said, 'He flees from thee and what of it?' 'By thy life, O abu-Mahmud,' said I, 'thou wilt also flee away while in my company.' To this he replied, 'O what shame! By Allah, my death would verily be easier for me than to flee away and leave thee.'

Only a few days passed after that when the horsemen of Hamah made an incursion on us. They took a herd of cattle which belonged to us and shut it up in an island under the Jalali Mill. Their archers mounted on the mill in order to defend the herd. I went to them with Jum'ah and Shuja'-al-Dawlah Madi, one of our adopted men who was a man of valour. I said to the two with me, 'We will cross the water to the other side and take our animals.' So we crossed. Madi's mare was hit with an arrow which caused its death. The mare carried him back to his companions with great difficulty. As for me, an arrow struck my mare at the nape of its neck and entered a span deep in it. But by Allah, my mare neither kicked nor was disturbed, but it went on as though it felt no cut. As regards Jum'ah, he went back, fearing for his horse. When we returned I said, 'O abu-Mahmud, did I not tell thee that thou wouldst flee away from me, when thou wert blaming thy son Mahmud?' 'By Allah,' he replied, 'I feared for nothing except for my mare. It is so dear to me.' And he apologized. . . .

Tancred's guarantee of safety proves worthless. Tancred, who was the first lord of Antioch after Bohemond, had previous to this pitched his camp against us. After the fight, we had a reconciliation, and he sent a message requesting that a horse belonging to an attendant of my uncle, 'Izz-al-Din (may Allah's mercy rest upon his soul!), be given him. That was a noble steed. My uncle dispatched it to him mounted by one of our men, a Kurd named Hasanun, one of our valiant cavaliers, young, good-looking and thin, in order to hold races with other horses in the presence of Tancred. Hasanun

ran a race and his horse out-ran all the horses which were in the course. He was brought before Tancred, and the knights began to inspect his arms and wonder at his thin physique and his youth, recognizing in him a valiant cavalier. Tancred bestowed a robe of honour on him. But Hasanun said to him, 'O my lord, I wish that thou wouldst give me thy guarantee of safety to the effect that if I should fall into thy hands at war time thou wouldst favour me and set me free.' Tancred gave him his guarantee of safety—as Hasanun imagined,

110. This vast panoramic sketch gives an impression of the huge numbers of horses and draught animals of all kinds used not only in the fighting echelons of medieval armies but above all in the supply train. (Dürer's *Siege of a Fortress*)

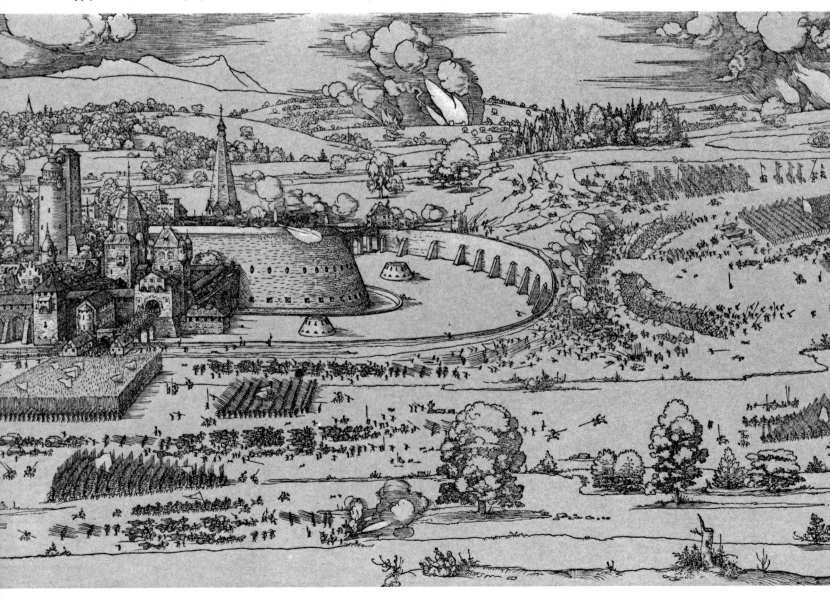

for these people speak nothing but Frankish; we do not understand what they say.

A year or more passed. The period of truce having expired, Tancred advanced anew at the head of the army of Antioch. A battle ensued near the wall of our lower town. Our horsemen had met their vanguard, and one of our men, a Kurd, named Kamil al-Mashtub, had used his lance on them to great effect. Kamil and Hasanun were peers in valour. This took place while Hasanun on his mare was standing near my father (may Allah's mercy rest upon his soul!) and awaiting his charger, which his attendant was bringing to him from the veterinary, and his quilted jerkin. The attendant was late and Hasanun was getting impatient, seeing the lance blows of Kamil al-Mashtub. So he said to my father, 'O my lord, put at my disposal light equipment.' My father replied, 'Here are the mules laden with arms and standing still. Whatever suits thee, put on.' I was at that time standing behind my father. I was a mere lad, and that was the first day in which I saw actual

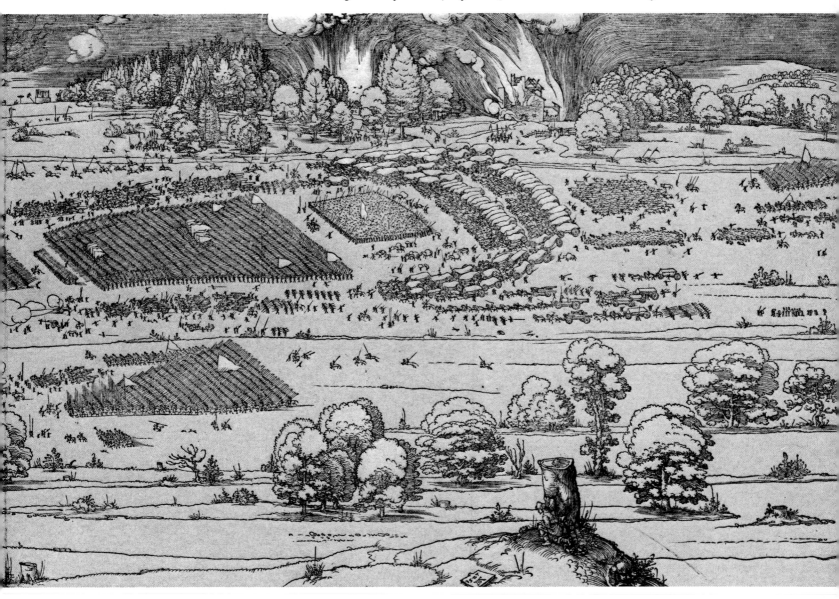

fighting. Hasanun examined the jerkins, in their cases on the backs of the mules, but none of them suited him. In the meantime, he was boiling in his desire to proceed and do what Kamil al-Mashtub was doing. So he charged on horseback, void of arms. A Frankish knight intercepted his way and struck the mare in its croup. The mare, getting the bit in its teeth, rushed with its rider on its back until it threw him off amidst the lines of the Franks. They took him prisoner and inflicted on him all varieties of torture. They even wanted to put out his left eye. But Tancred (may Allah's curse be upon him!) said to them, 'Rather put out his right eye, so that when he carries his shield his left eye will be covered, and he will be no more able to see anything.'

So they put out his right eye in accordance with the orders of Tancred and demanded as a ransom from him one thousand dinars and a black horse, which belonged to my father, of Khafajah breed and one of the most magnificent horses. My father (may Allah's mercy rest upon his soul!) ransomed him for that horse. . . .

Stories of horses: An enduring horse. Having made mention of horses, I might add that there are among them, as among men, those which are enduring and others which are faint-hearted. Here is an illustration of the former kind. Among our troops was a Kurd named Kamil al-Mashtub who was a repository of valour, religion and benevolence (may Allah's mercy

111. The horse in medieval agriculture. While all this mounted warfare was going on the role of the horse in agriculture was limited both geographically and functionally. Thus in England horses were used in harvest waggons and carts only in certain counties, notably Suffolk. Here is a realistic drawing from the Luttrell Psalter of a farm cart with hurdle sides and iron-bound wheels of about the year 1340, drawn by one horse between the shafts and two in the traces. In the majority of English shires at this period all such work, but especially ploughing, was done by oxen.

ertristi testamentum serui tui: pro
iasti in terra sanctuarium eius.
truristi omnes sepes eius: posu

112. Facing the other way, the Turks and the Tartars exercised their influence on Persia and India, especially as regards outdoor pursuits for the upper classes. Here is a picture of falconry as practised by a Sikh rajah of the eighteenth century.

113. Realistic hunting scene by an unknown Florentine of the same period as Uccello. Aristocratic riders at the meet on the handy palfreys that were actually used for hunting. From a Florentine *cassone*.

rest upon his soul!). He possessed a horse of solid black colour as big as a camel. An encounter took place between him and a Frankish knight. The Frank dealt a blow to the horse beside the throatlatch. The violence of the blow made the neck of the horse bend to one side so that the lance came out through the lower part of the neck and hit the thigh of Kamil al-Mashtub, transpiercing it. Neither the horse nor the horseman budged on account of that blow. I have often seen the scar of that wound in the thigh after it was healed and closed up. No wound could have been bigger than it. The horse also survived, and Kamil had occasion to mount it again for a battle in which he had an encounter with a Frankish knight who thrust his lance into the frontal bone of the horse and made the whole bone cave in.

Again the horse did not budge, and survived the second blow. Even after it healed up, one could close his hand and stick it in the frontal of the horse where the wound was inflicted and have room for it.

A horse with its heart cut carries its rider. A horse was wounded under me as we engaged in combat at Hims. The thrust of the lance cut its heart asunder and a number of arrows hit its body. But it, nevertheless, carried me out of the battle with its two nostrils flowing blood like two bucket spouts, and I felt nothing unusual in its conduct. After having reached my companions, it died.

An Arab-Syrian Gentleman and Warrior,
trans. P. K. Hitti (1924)

7. Horsemanship as an art

The first European writer on the art of horsemanship was not Xenophon but Simon whom he quotes, though hardly ever word for word. But of Simon we know nothing except what Xenophon tells us. And that is so little that poor Simon hardly rates a heading in any classical dictionary.

In some versions of the *Hippike* the terms have been translated by words out of the common vocabulary of post-Renaissance horsemanship, and in that thesaurus there is a wide enough choice to find an equivalent for every Greek term used by Xenophon, so that the interpretation remains consistent within itself. But other combinations are possible, and other versions have been constructed, in English and other languages, different and equally consistent renderings from the original. A totally equivalent rendering, in any modern language, is not possible, since though in principle what Xenophon says can be applied in some measure to modern equitation, yet in practice the fact cannot be ignored that Xenophon teaches riding without stirrups, virtually bareback, on a cloth not a saddle, and with the aid of a simple snaffle, on a much smaller horse than is commonly ridden in classical equitation today or has been for some centuries past:

When the rider takes his seat, whether bareback or on the cloth, I do not approve of a seat which is as though the man were on a chair, but rather as though he were standing upright with his legs apart. Thus he would get a better grip with his thighs on the horse, and, being upright, he could hurl his javelin more vigorously and strike a better blow from on horseback, if need be. His foot and leg from the knee down should hang loosely, for if he keeps his leg stiff and should strike it against something, he might get it broken; but a supple leg would yield, if it struck against anything, without at all disturbing the thigh. Then, too, the rider should accustom himself to keep his body above the hips as supple as possible; for this would give him greater power of action, and he would be less liable to a fall if somebody should try to pull or push him off. The horse should be taught to stand still when the rider is taking his seat, and until he has drawn his skirts from under him, if necessary, made the reins even, and taken the most convenient grasp of his spear.

This is not to detract from the abiding value of the work, merely to point out that these differences are of some practical importance. Nor is the aim quite that of Newcastle or Pluvinel or of the Neapolitans. This is in part due to the political background. Renaissance riding-masters and those who derive from them tacitly presuppose a spectator, as is pointed out in another section of this book, in the royal box: *Il Principe*, in Machiavelli's sense, what Xenophon would call a tyrant. It was no part of his intention to entertain or please such patrons. What he is teaching is how to perform a civic duty (unpaid service in the mounted arm of some republic such as Athens) efficiently and with elegance.

114. As well as equitation the anatomy and proportions of the horse became subjects of interest in the Renaissance. This illustration is from Carlo Ruini's *The Anatomy and Diseases of the Horse*, 1598, the earliest series of anatomical plates that exists.

The revival of interest in scientific equitation which came in the sixteenth century was marked by the establishment of Gian Battista Pignatelli's academy of riding in Naples and the publication in 1561 of the first book on equitation of the Renaissance, Federico Grisone's *Gli Ordini de Cavalcare* ('The Rules of Horsemanship').

Grisone's methods were brought to France by Salamon de la Broue and further refined by Louis XIII's riding instructor, Antoine de Pluvinel, whose *Instruction du Roi* was published posthumously in 1629, and by William Cavendish, Duke of Newcastle (1592–1676), whose *Nouvelle Méthode* was first written in French and later translated into English as *A General System of Horsemanship in All Its Branches*. Their emphasis on Haute Ecole, which continued in the work of François Robichon de la Guerinière (1687–1751), dominated the teaching of horsemanship, including the training of cavalry, and continued to do so, with modifications by Count Antoine d'Aure (1799–1863), François Baucher (1796-1873) and James Fillis, until the revolution in riding style brought about by Caprilli in the first years of the twentieth century.

115. Study of the flexion of the hind-limb by Leonardo, from a series of studies of the anatomy and proportions of the horse.

116. The Hall of the Horses in the Palazzo del Té at Mantua. These *trompe l'oeil* equine portraits were the work either of Giulio Romano or of members of his atelier and with their stereoscopic effect are the most realistic representations of the famous horses owned and bred by the Gonzaga dynasty. They obviously owe much to Andalusian ancestry. Henty VIII went to some trouble to buy some of them and they must have contributed much to the ancestry of the original Royal Mares and thus of the thoroughbred.

❋LA GUERINIÈRE ON THE TERMS OF THE ART

Nothing contributes more to the knowledge of an art or science than an understanding of those terms that are proper to it. The art of riding has many such, of a kind peculiar to it; and therefore I have tried to give here clear and precise definitions of them.

Manège, which [in French] has two meanings: the place where horses are exercised, and the exercises which they perform. [In the English of La Guerinière's contemporaries, both these meanings were rendered by the word 'manage'.]

Airs are the handsome carriage a horse ought to have at different paces. It is also the proper measure or cadence of every move that he makes at every pace [= American gait] whether natural or artificial, as we shall explain hereunder.

Changing hands is the action of a horse's legs when he changes, either to lead with the off- or with the near-leg. This term comes from the masters of old time, who were wont to call the parts of the horse after the parts of a man, thus saying nose and not muzzle, chin and not jowls; so they said hand and not forefoot. Thus changing hands means changing feet. (This usage they followed with no other animal.) According

to custom, changing hands means also the track which the horse describes in crossing the manège before changing hands.

Aids are the means the horseman uses to make the horse go, and to help him; they consist of different motions of the hands and the legs.

Appui is the sensation produced by the action of the bridle in the rider's hand, and likewise the sensation produced by the bridle hand on the bars of the mouth. There are horses which have no *appui*, and others which have too much, and yet others that have *appui* to the full. Those that have none are such as fear the bit and cannot suffer any pressure on the bars, which makes them fight the hand, as above. Those that have too much are those that weigh on the hand; *appui* to

the full, which makes the best mouth, is when the horse without weighing on or fighting the hand, is firm, light and tempered on the bit. These three qualities go to make the perfectly-mouthed horse and correspond to those of the rider's hand which must be light, soft and firm.

Collecting a horse, or bringing him together, is to shorten his pace, or the air that he is performing, to bring his haunches under him. This is done by gently restraining the forehand with the bridle-hand, and bringing the haunches under him with the calf of the leg, so as to hold him between the hand and the heel.

Within and without is a figure of speech used sometimes (or outside and inside) instead of near and off, describing the aids to be given with the hand and the leg and

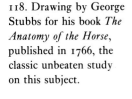

118. Drawing by George Stubbs for his book *The Anatomy of the Horse*, published in 1766, the classic unbeaten study on this subject.

117. The ordinary hay-cart of the Flemish countryside, painted by Rubens (detail from the *Château de Steen*)

119. Heroic equestrian statue of Cosimo de' Medici, one of the foremost warlords of the day. The horse bears a remarkable resemblance to that beneath the statue of Marcus Aurelius (Plate 70), which was an admired prototype.

the heel, as also the movement of the horse's legs, according to which hand he is going on. The better to understand this you should know that formerly trainers [*écuyers*] almost always worked their horses in circles, and the centre of the circle around which they turned determined which hand they were going on; so that in turning a horse to the right on one circle, the bridle-rein, the leg and the heel of the rider, and those legs of the horse which were nearer the centre, were called the 'inside' leg, rein, etc., which is as much as to say the right leg, etc. Then the outside rein, leg, were the left rein, leg; and likewise in turning a horse to the left in a circle, the rein and the leg which are towards the centre are called the inside rein and leg, and they are the left rein and leg; consequently the outside rein and leg are the right rein and leg. But nowadays we have rectangular schools indoors and out, bounded by walls or fences, and it is easy to understand that by 'outside' we mean that side nearest the wall. If the wall is to the left of the rider, this is called going on the right hand, and then the outside rein and leg are towards the wall, being the left rein and leg, and the inside ones are towards the centre of the school. If the wall is on the rider's right this is called working on the left hand; the right rein and leg are the outside rein and leg, and consequently the left rein and leg are the inside ones. I have had to explain this at some length because many people confuse these terms. But to be more explicit one says right and left, which is simpler, whether one is speaking of the horse's or the rider's legs, or the bridle reins.

I have not further complicated this intricate explanation by rendering 'right' as 'off' and 'left' as 'near'. The time when high school horses were worked in circles was, in England, the sixteenth century, though some Jacobean authors still speak of working in a 'ring'. This itself indicates that the traditions of the circus are more conservative than those of 'noble' horsemanship; that is, that they adhere more closely to the ritual of an ancient solar cult, with which horses are closely associated. This is not the place to air my theory that Stonehenge embodies a static representation of a procession of horses (with or without riders?) in honour of the sun, but the circular procession of horses is a common theme of Bronze Age, and Iron Age, ritual art.

120. Pacing horse by Antonio Susini, about 1600–24. Eighteenth-century and later critics familiar only with the trotting and galloping horse have labelled this and similar statues unrealistic, but it is in fact a faithful rendering of a phase of the pacing gait.

AIRS ON THE GROUND

Those 'low' airs which are executed on the ground or close to it are the Passage, the Piaffer, the School Gallop, Changing Hands, the Volte, the Demi-volte, the Passade, the Pirouette and the Terre-à-terre.

Note that most of these terms are derived from Italian, because the Italians were the inventors of the rules and principles of this art.

Passage was formerly called, in French, *passege*, from the Italian *passegio*, which means walk or parade. It is a balanced walk or trot keeping good time. In this movement a horse must keep his feet in the air, one fore and one hind, diagonally, as in the trot; but he must shorten himself and it must be more sustained and precise than the ordinary trot, so that there is not more than one foot distance between every step that he takes; that is, the foot which is in the air should be set down a foot in advance of the one which is on the ground.

Piaffer: when a horse passages in one spot without advancing or retiring or moving to one side, raising high and flexing his legs, with a graceful action, that is *piaffer*. This gait, which is most noble, was most in demand for carousels and fêtes on horseback: it is still highly esteemed in Spain, and the horses of that country, and of Naples, have a great aptitude for it.

School gallop. Very smooth, well-collected, striding short in front, using the hind-legs neatly, that is, not letting them trail out behind, thus producing by the evenness of each bound, that fine rhythm which charms the spectators as much as it pleases the rider.

121. *The Levade*, rearing circus horse by Toulouse-Lautrec.

Volte. This is another Italian expression signifying properly a circle, a ring, or a round track. What the Italians call a volte is the circle described by a horse going simply on one track, but what we in France mean by volte, they call *Radoppio*; but in France the word volte is taken to mean going sideways on two tracks, the horse describing two concentric circles, or a square with rounded corners. . . .

Terre-à-terre. My lord the Duke of Newcastle has neatly defined the terre-à-terre as a gallop in two-time on two tracks. In this action the horse raises both fore-legs together, and puts them down together: the hind-legs follow and accompany the forelegs, which forms as it were a series of short low bounds, very close to the ground, always going forward and sideways.

Though the terre-à-terre is rightly reckoned among the airs on the ground, because it is so close to the ground, nevertheless this is the air which serves as the foundation for all the airs above the ground, because in general all leaps are made in two-time, as in the terre-à-terre.

AIRS ABOVE THE GROUND

All airs are so called in which the horse leaves the ground more than he does in the terre-à-terre. There are seven of them, as follows: the Pesade, the Mezair, the Courbette, the Croupade, the Balotade, the Capriole, the Step and Leap.

Pesade. This is an air in which the horse lifts the fore-hand off the ground in one spot without moving forward, keeping the hind legs on the ground without moving them, so that he does not keep time with his hind legs, as in all the other airs. This lesson is used to prepare a horse for leaping with greater freedom, and to gain control of his forehand. . . .

Courbette. This is a leap in which the horse goes up higher in front, a sustained and heightened version of the mezair, in which the hind legs go forward with a low but smart action, in concert with the forelegs at the moment when they come to the ground.

Croupade. This is a higher leap than the courbette, both in front and behind, in which, while the horse is in the air, he gathers up his hind feet and legs under him, keeping them at the same height as the forefeet.

Balotade. This is a leap in which, while all four feet

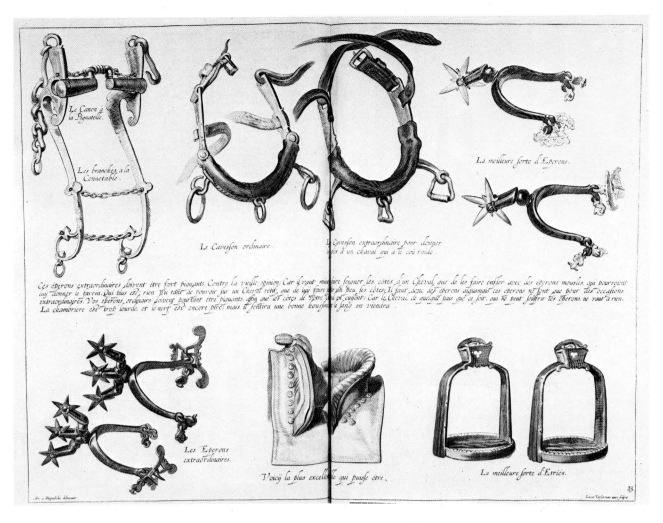

122. 'For a horse of no matter what country if he will not abide the spur is nothing worth.' The type of spur approved by Newcastle and also the pattern of saddle, stirrups and cavesson recommended by him.

are in the air, at an equal height, the horse flexes the hind pasterns so as to show the soles of his feet, as if to kick (without actually doing so, as in the capriole) instead of folding his hind legs under him, as in the croupade.

Capriole. This is the highest and most perfect of all the leaps. While the horse is in the air, and level from front to rear, he launches a kick as if, as it were, to tear himself in two, so that his hind legs shoot out like arrows; formerly this was called 'knotting the aiguillette' [or, tying the shoulder-knot].

Note that these last three airs, the Croupade, the Balotade and the Capriole, differ in as much as the horse in the Croupade does not display the soles of his feet behind at the apex of his leap, but on the contrary draws them up under him; in the Balotade he does show the soles and make as if to kick out behind, but does not actually do so; while in the Capriole he kicks out behind with all his might.

The Step and Leap. This consists of three actions: first, a shortened gallop or terre-à-terre; second, a courbette, and the third, a capriole. And so on, over again. Horses which do not feel strong enough to repeat the Capriole do this of their own volition. And even the strongest leapers, when they are beginning to wear out, do it to relieve the strain and to give themselves more time for the leap.

Ecole de Cavalerie, 1733

THE HIGH SCHOOL OF HORSEMANSHIP

The Cadre Noir of Saumur performs all the exercises described here by La Guerinière, and all over the Western world grave-countenanced devotees of what is now called dressage solemnly perform the essential groundwork of classical equitation; and everywhere, the vocabulary employed is virtually the same as that displayed in La Guerinière's glossary: most of the terms have no English equivalent and the practice of academic equitation in England, from the reign of James I onwards, gave rise to a very considerable body of *franglais* all of which is still current within the charmed circle, which, as this extract has pointed out, is since about 1600 a rectangle.

All over the Western world is an understatement; the

Airs près de terre.

Le Passage.

La Galopade.

La Volte à droite.

La Pirouette à Gauche.

Le Terre à terre.

Le Mezair.

123. From La Guerinière's *Ecole de Cavallerie*.
Artificial gaits: airs on the ground. Passage,
Galopade, Volte, Pirouette, Terre à terre, Mezair.

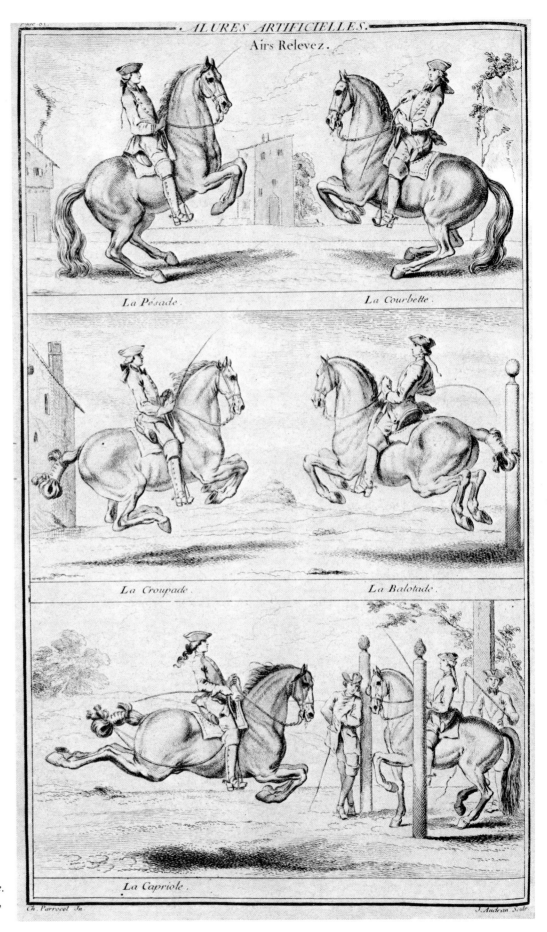

124. From La Guerinière's *Ecole de Cavallerie*.
Artificial gaits: airs above the ground. Pésade,
Courbette, Croupade, Balotade, Capriole.

125, 126. Pluvinel, riding-master to Louis XIII, is the French master who corresponds most closely to the Duke of Newcastle among English instructors. In the first of these two pictures he is shown giving instruction. He is the figure behind and immediately to the right of the pupil. In the second, the horse on the left is wearing the blind-fold hoods described as useful by La Guerinière. The figure in the extreme right corner is the sixteen-year-old king.

art is practised in Japan as well as in Eastern Europe to which it was long foreign: but wherever it is, the vocabulary itself is this essentially French one, which bears traces, as La Guerinière shows, of Italianate fashion because the art as such was derived from Naples. And in their turn, these Neapolitanisms are Italian of a somewhat Hispanic tinge, because the school of equitation of Naples only came to its flowering under the tutelage of the Spanish monarchy. The first professors in Naples were Spaniards, and the Neapolitan horse working in the schools was nothing other than the old reliable Andalusian model, fitted with a governor.

'Charms the spectators as much as it pleases the rider', says the Master, and we are to understand that the *passade*, for instance, is a passing to and fro in front of the Royal Box, opposite the mid-point of the arena. The *reprise* is the eternal rehearsal for the grand gala performance in the presence of the Most Christian King or the Most Catholic Prince or the Most Lutheran Queen, or at least before some peer of some realm. And

yet today there are Soviet citizens who excel internationally in this art. The performance does presuppose a distinguished audience, ideally also a knowledgeable one. When the Marxist exponent of the High School is demonstrating his own and the horse's skill at home, he does so in theory before an audience of the Sovereign People but more especially, one presumes, for the admiration of high-grade *apparatchiks* in the once-Imperial box. For patronage, just as much as in music or authorship or painting, was ever an essential adjunct of this art.

LADY'S SEAT

The French term both for a woman riding side-saddle and for the habit worn for the purpose was *Amazones*. Semantically it could not be more inappropriate, since the Greek source which described the original Amazons does not imply that they rode in any way other than men did except rather better. In the abundant Victorian

(or Second Empire, or Wilhelmine, according to country) literature of instruction in this art, the most tortured attitudes are adopted rather by the writer than by the rider. Archness reigns supreme, especially in English.

The words 'woman' and 'girl' occur but rarely; most of the time it is 'lady', 'fair equestrienne', 'gentler sex' and so on. This is also by many lengths the most class-conscious branch of writing about equitation, and largely reflects the fact that by the mid-nineteenth century riding (which in effect meant side-saddling only) had become something exclusively for upper-class females or those who considered themselves such; the husbandman's and tradesman's womenfolk were less and less seen in the saddle because the introduction of light vehicles such as the trap and the gig had made it possible for them to get about locally, automatically solving also the problem of what to do with the shopping basket.

The tone is set by an early passage in *The Horse and How to Ride Him* by John Butler, 1861, which is for 'young equestrians' but does not pretend to be for children:

> There cannot be a more favourable argument as to the popularity of the art of riding and the essential part it forms in the education of a gentleman, than the well-known fact that His Royal Highness the Prince of Wales is one of the most skilful and graceful horsemen of the present day.

Turning to the section of Butler's work entitled 'Ladies' Riding' we read that ' . . . when carried to extremes it ceases to be an accomplishment in a lady; for instance, the hunting field is scarcely the place for a young lady.'

The reason for this was the still-remembered antics of the mistresses (in some cases, for instance Lady Lade, the wives) of Regency Corinthians and Meltonians out hunting, but also the presence, still in the 'sixties and 'seventies, of that type of open-air *poule de luxe* typified in fiction by Surtees' Lucy Glitters and in real life by 'Skittles' (Catherine Walters), who lived on until 1922, having in her time shared a pillow with

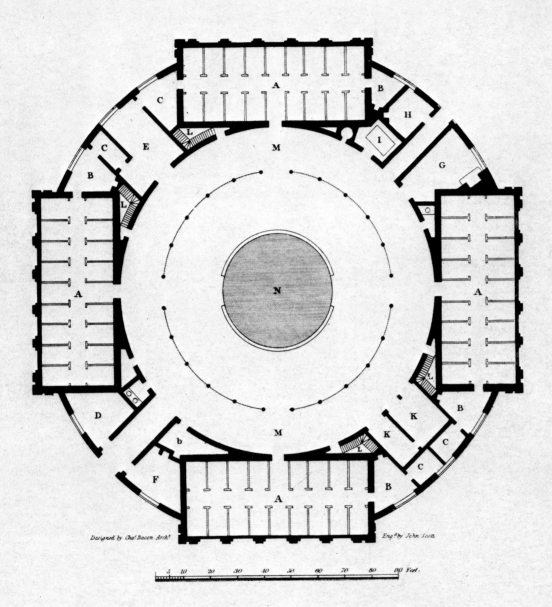

ELEVATION AND GROUND PLAN OF A STABLE.

A. *Stables containing Boxes for 68 Horses* _ B. *Rooms for Bridles, Saddles &c* _ b. *Coach Harness* _ C. *Corn Rooms*
D. *Hay Room* _ E. *Granary* _ F. *Store Room* _ G. *Smiths Forge* _ H. *Surgery* _ I. *Warm Bath* _ K. *Coach House, for 6 Carriages*
L. *Staircase leading to the Lodging Rooms, for the Grooms &c. over the Stables* _ M. *Covered Ride* _ N. *Wash Pond.*

Published Jan.1.1810. by James Candee & John Scott London.

127. Eighteenth-century stable in the grand manner, including instead of a separate riding-house a circular covered arcade.

the above-named 'skilful and graceful horseman', with the future Napoleon III and with Wilfrid Scawen Blunt.

At no point is class distinction so apparent as in mounting and dismounting from the side-saddle:

There are few gentlemen who, having moved much in society, have not at some time been called on to assist a lady into her saddle: and I know nothing so mortifying to a gentleman as to stand by. . . . Whenever a gentleman is able to perform with ease and grace this, at all times, agreeable duty, his services are always highly appreciated by a lady; and they are services to which any gentleman can very easily and becomingly aspire . . .

The trouble was that, except for the very athletic and practised, long-legged woman, getting into the side-saddle entailed close physical contact with a servant, and a male servant at that. Therefore:

Two persons should be in attendance to assist a lady in mounting: one (generally the groom) to stand by the horse's head, while the gentleman performs the more agreeable office of *cavaliere servente* or that of assisting her to vault into the saddle . . . the gentleman arranges the reins of the bridoon, and places them in her right hand; he then stands with his left shoulder in front, but close to the horse's shoulder; when, if the fair one be a weighty or inactive personage, he will probably require the use of both hands to lift her; in which case he should join his hands by uniting his fingers one within the other, so as to receive the lady's foot within the palms of both hands.

128. All the exercises described by La Guerinière are illustrated in the magnificent plates to the Duke of Newcastle's *Nouvelle Méthode*. La Guerinière had as much respect for Newcastle as it was possible for a French practitioner to entertain towards an English one. The first of these two engravings after Diepenbeke for Newcastle's manual shows the duke instructing Captain Mazin in the *volte*.

Pour travailler avec la rêne du
cavesson dedans la volte et dans
la main et la jambe hors la volte
sur le terre à terre à droite et
à gauche.

Le Capitaine Mazin étant à Cheval.

Monseigneur le Marquis donne leçon.

Terre à terre, à Main droite.

Terre à terre, à Main gauche.

Monseigneur le Marquis.

Terre à terre la teste contre la muraille
à Main gauche.

Terre à terre la teste contre la muraille
à Main droite.

129. The second engraving for Newcastle's manual shows the *terre à terre* on either hand with the head to the wall. The riding house in which the drawings were made stood behind Rubens's old house in Antwerp which the exiled Newcastle rented from the widow of the artist.

Instruction on the whole was not very good, whether in print or practice, because few of the male instructors had ever ridden side-saddle themselves. The best book on the subject (*The Horsewoman*, 1893) was written by Alice Hayes, and contains absolutely no nonsense whatsoever. Her approach to hunting for women is positive and practical:

> Until she is well able to manage her horse, she should limit her attention to hare hunting, if possible; for 'puss' generally runs in circles and will not take the field far from her form. When the tyro begins to aspire to riding with foxhounds, she should be content to join in mildly at first, and work gradually on, until she has the ability and confidence to take her own part in the sport. By that time she will have recognized the paramount importance of getting well away, of taking her own line, and of avoiding any interference with the hounds.

She also advocated little girls being taught to ride astride before being introduced to the side-saddle. She made sensible remarks like 'Almost all women like light-hearted showy horses, though they generally desire the fire and gaiety to be well under control' or, what no male contemporary in her line of business saw fit to admit, 'A young lady with a slight pretty figure will look best on a horse that is all blood and quality; though a portly and dignified matron will be best suited with one of the weight-carrying hunter stamp, or with a clever cob.' 'Women who have had the same opportunities as men, of learning to ride, ride quite as well as they. But as a rule they do not *get* the chance of excelling, nor are they "set right" by unpalatable home truths being told them without favour or affection . . .' '. . . a girl who has a nice slim figure will, other things being equal, ride better than one who is stout'—a reminder that despite the aesthetic ideal prevalent throughout most of the nineteenth century, the majority of English women in Victorian days who could afford enough food more or less ran to fat.

But then, Alice was a remarkable woman. She had been a 'fair horsebreaker' in a literal and legitimate sense towards the end of that period when the phrase meant, in common usage, 'mounted tart'. Before she

130. Queen Margherita of Austria side-saddle on a piebald Andalusian, painted by Velasquez. The piebald colour has now been bred out of the Andalusian race.

131. Side-saddle riding in the nineteenth century: *Riding in the Bois de Boulogne* by Renoir.

married Captain Horace Hayes, a veterinary officer who was also a successful and prolific author on practical equitation and horsemastership, she was a medical missionary serving in Indian leper hospitals. She was the only woman, then or since, to have been photographed riding side-saddle on a zebra, and we regret this vintage photograph is now too murky, in its eighty-year-old half-tone form, to be reproduced here.

James Fillis, who is an important link in the apostolic succession of riding masters at the highest level, was for long a riding instructor in the Imperial Russian Army: besides the Cossacks, who owed their riding technique as well as their tactical methods and skill-at-arms to Tartar models, the Tsarist army had a complete range of 'European-style' cavalry—hussars, dragoons, lancers, cuirassiers, and it was in the training of these that Fillis was employed. The frontispiece of his best-known work, *Principes de Dressage et d'Equitation* (published in Paris in 1890 and translated into English as *Breaking and Riding*), from which the following passage is taken, shows him in Russian uniform.

※Except as regards the legs, a lady should sit on a saddle exactly like a man. For some time there has been talk of ladies riding astride, which practice would deprive her of all feminine grace, and would afford no useful result. The great want in a man's seat is firmness,

which would be still more difficult for a woman to acquire if she rode in a cross-saddle, because her thighs are rounder and weaker than those of a man. Discussion of this subject is therefore useless. Ladies who ride astride get such bad falls that they soon give up this practice.

At all paces the shoulders should be parallel to the ears of the horse, which is possible only when the hips occupy a similar position. Therefore the position of the lady depends entirely on that of the hips. The two legs being on the left, the right leg is hooked round the upper crutch, and is more advanced and higher than the left leg, which presses against the leaping-head, a little above the knee, and the foot rests in the stirrup.

132. By English convention, ladies rode side-saddle on the near side, as the left-hand figure does here. But it was better for the horse to alternate with riding on the off-side, like the right-hand figure here. A few ladies, among them the future Queen Alexandra of England, however, always rode on the off-side. (*La Promenade au Bois*, watercolour by Constantin Guys)

It has been proposed that ladies should sit on the right side of the saddle. English and American journals have dwelt on the bad effects of girls on only one side of the horse, and they have tried to make out that this practice causes curvature of the spine. As I judge only by practical observations, I cannot say how it would affect children of five or six years old; but as I have often taught beginners of twelve or thirteen years old, I can certify most positively that girls of that age have nothing to fear on that score. . . .

The position of a lady on the left side of a saddle, causes almost all the weight of her body to be carried to the right side; consequently, the left hip being freer from weight, is apt to be stuck out behind the right hip, which is a fault that ought to be avoided. The weight of the body ought to be equally distributed on both sides. Like a man in his saddle, she ought to sit in her saddle exactly as she sits in a chair, namely, with the hips and shoulders parallel to the ears of the horse. This is a question not only of correct attitude, but also of strength of seat, which is the main thing. . . .

She should keep her body well under her when rising at the trot. The upper part of the body makes no effort, but allows itself to be raised by the movement of the horse. The foot rests in the stirrup iron without stiffness, and the ankle and knees act only as hinges. The slightest muscular contraction, or the least effort made by the ankle, knees or loins will give the rider a stiff and ungraceful appearance, and will cause fatigue. If the lady will carry out these rules, she will ride in two-time, namely, one on the saddle and one in the air. Otherwise she will come down too quickly, and will mark two-times on the saddle, which will give her a useless and fatiguing shock. . . .

A horsewoman should have great pliability of body, which she will acquire by practice in riding and other

133. The advent of the lady show-jumper, still in the side-saddle. Miss Helen Prentice in the United States, 1922.

134. François Clouet's portrait of Francis I, King of France, mounted on the Isabella-coloured (yellow with black points) Andalusian mobile throne, which was *de rigueur* for all European monarchs for many centuries.

135. Goya the unromantic tackles from imagination a theme of the Napoleonic adventure in Egypt, which was treated less realistically by French romantic painters who had actually witnessed such events without recording the blood and guts. (Detail from *The Second of May 1808: The Charge of the Mamelukes*)

preliminary exercises, of which dancing is the best. It also depends on certain small details of dress, about which I may give the following advice.

A lady on horseback is apt to cut herself. The slightest crease in her clothes may cause an abrasion. For a long ride, and still more for hunting, she should wear a short chemisette, made of very fine material, and fitting close to the body. The collar and cuffs ought to be strongly connected to this chemisette, and not fixed to it merely by pins, which are liable to fall out or hurt the wearer. I strongly advise that she should wear socks instead of stockings; because a garter is always inconvenient and may cause serious wounds. The socks should be furnished with a close-fitting collar of some soft and elastic material, such as knitting or jersey, lined with silk, or, still better, very fine doeskin. The trousers should be strapped with india-rubber and should fit rather closely, so that they may not wrinkle. The boots should have elastic sides and not buttons, which might cause wounds. I prefer ordinary boots to long boots, which are too hard, and are consequently apt to cut the wearer under the knee, and to prevent her feeling the horse with her leg. The corset should be very short and low. A long busk is not only inconvenient but is also dangerous. I would not have touched on these details but for the fact that the dress of the horse-woman is closely connected with her strength of seat and ease in the saddle. I have seen so many ladies returning from a ride in pain, and condemned to spend many days in a long chair, that I am certain the points to which I have drawn attention are important.

The head-dress of the lady should be firmly arranged, so that it may not occupy her attention, in which case she will think too little of her horse. Then, if she loses her hat, she will probably lose her head.

CAPRILLI AND THE FORWARD SEAT

Federico Caprilli (1868–1907) comes next in succession after Fillis; and between them comes a turning-point. Competitive equitation at the present day, apart from the ceremonial High School, is of the school of Caprilli,

and no longer of Fillis. The annotations to this extract from Caprilli's work are by Piero Santini, his pupil and principal disciple, who died only a few years ago. 'Accompanying with the body the forward thrust of the centre of gravity' is the key phrase in the whole Caprilli–Santini doctrine, and this work is the definitive statement of the principle of the 'forward seat' dominant today in competitive show-jumping at every level throughout the world.

Let us observe a riderless horse jumping. Approaching the obstacle he will extend his neck the better to look at and measure it—an important detail even from the purely mechanical point of view; at the same time he thrusts his forefeet into the ground so as to throw his weight on to the quarters. By this movement he brings his centre of gravity back so that the quarters next receive most of the weight of his body, which is then thrown forward again by the rebound of the quarters themselves. This movement is accomplished by retracting head and neck and contracting the muscles of the trunk, which throw back the centre of gravity, thereby allowing, with the aid of the forefeet's counterthrust, the forehand to rise. The horse thus attains the desired height by adding the impulse of the quarters to the momentum of the whole mass of his body accumulated in the last strides.

This movement, by means of which the horse is projected off the ground, is of the greatest importance. Having reached the desired height the horse again throws his centre of gravity ahead of him by thrusting his forelegs which have, as we have seen, contributed to the upward thrust of the centre of gravity, aided by the contraction of the muscles of the trunk from back to forward. As soon as the forefeet touch the ground the hind ones are brought forward, ready to receive the horse's landing weight and permitting him to get into his stride again.

The principal lesson that the rider should learn from these remarks is that he should be at pains to allow the horse to jump in the way I have described *and in no other*.

The jump must always be approached at right angles, at a regular cadence, with the horse's head perfectly straight, the rider's hands quiet and just above the withers. The body should be inclined forward but without exaggeration. . . .

Systematically to signal to the horse when he is to jump, as some people advocate, is extremely difficult and, even if perfectly timed, does as a rule more harm than good, for the horse may learn to fear these signs, and, by anticipating, seriously compromise the result of the jump itself.

A capable jumper should not be thus interfered with, because the moment he has measured his obstacle he has already instinctively made up his mind regarding the strength he needs to clear it without the rider requiring to add any more. The mediocre and inexperi-

enced jumper, on the other hand, can only be improved by rational and continuous practice and not through the aids, or violent and sudden means. It is only exceptionally that the aids can be of any use in the last two or three strides or at the instant the horse is about to jump—in cases, for example, where he hangs back or seems to be about to 'put in a short one'. One must in any case act prudently, and in the right measure.

Caprilli disapproved on principle of 'giving the office' because he maintained that a horse should approach his jumps at a regular cadence and take them in his normal stride, whereas nowadays in the show-ring 'putting in' one or several 'short ones' appears to be more encouraged than condemned—Piero Santini.

136. The hunter: Duncombe, the property of George Treacher Esq. By Ben Marshall, 1809.

A horse schooled on my principles knows enough, when jumping, to realize that he is about to need extra energy and therefore acts accordingly; any interference on the part of the rider can only be harmful. If you were putting a foot wrong when descending a stair and someone attempted to assist you by jerking you under the chin you would probably resent it, for he would have interfered with natural co-ordination between head and leg. . . .

I have always found that my hand may have had some influence *before* a jump, but *during* it it has never prevented but, in fact, *rather contributed to*, a fall. It is axiomatic that a horse should be under control; it is precisely for this reason that he should be freed of it in

time. If the rider's heart is in the right place, his seat will be independent of his hands. I should like someone to quote a single case in which it would have been better that the horse be less free. The more violent the nature of the horse, the better Nature prompts him to extend his neck. A horse ridden without reins is as elastic as if there was a puppet in the saddle. Even the donkey and the mule are excellent in the mountainous country because no human hand interferes with them. The Sardinian horse is particularly sure-footed because he is used to climbing about freely from his earliest years.

I ask anyone who has done much jumping whether or not, when they feel their horse taking off badly, there is

137. 'Young gentlemen amusing themselves by what is called riding *at* one another.' From a series of plates by Sir Robert Frankland, 1815.

Young Gentlemen amusing themselves with what is called riding at one another.

any reason why they should not relinquish their reins completely so that the horse may recover as Nature has taught him to do. Furthermore, if the horse's head is free he will look where he puts his feet; try and scatter a few stones on the landing side and notice how cleverly he will avoid them.

In this belief Caprilli had a predecessor in the Englishman, 'Flying Childe', of Kinlet Hall, Shropshire (born 1750), supposed to be 'the first to introduce the present spirited method of riding to hounds' and who 'not seeming to care what he did on a horse, amazed the local people by galloping down a very steep boulder-strewn part of the Clee Hills known as Titterstones, assuring them that "as long as a horse was allowed his head, so that he could see the ground he was alright"'. Thus J. R. Young in his book Fox Hunting—Piero Santini.

It is not true that the rider's presence on his back inevitably prevents the mounted horse from arching his backbone; if head and neck are free nothing can prevent it. Neither is it true that by leaning forward and leaving the neck free the centre of gravity is shifted towards the horse's shoulder; as a matter of fact, it is, on the contrary, thrown lower, thereby lightening the rider's weight by added elasticity. . . .

As the horse's centre of gravity is behind and below the shoulder, with our system the man on his back does not receive the counterblow of the horse's movements on the ilium, but on the soft muscles of the thighs by which, even in trotting, the weight of the rider returning to the saddle is rendered hardly noticeable to the horse.

The rider's bust swung backwards, or held perpendicularly, describes in jumping a much greater arc than if leant forward, thereby causing those harmful shiftings

138. King George III hunting in Windsor Park, 1820, by James Pollard Junior. The latter end of the buck-hunting tradition in Windsor Park, continuous since the reign of Queen Elizabeth I. The royal buck-hounds were kept on until Queen Victoria's reign.

in the saddle that are of no advantage and result in useless expenditure of energy.

All we have said in conjunction with jumping applies also to the various paces. As riding with the body inclined forward at the gallop forms part of natural equitation, if we insist on leaning back we shall be forced in jumping suddenly to assume an unfamiliar attitude. (The forward inclination of the body is not permitted in school equitation; this is, in a sense, right, because the empirical application of such a principle would do more harm than good.)

As in natural equitation the body is always inclined forward, it must especially be so in the landing stage of the jump because otherwise, at the instant in which the horse's quarters are above the obstacle, they are prevented from rising sufficiently to clear it.

The Forward Impulse, 1936

139. A meet of the Duke of Beaufort's hounds: entraining horses at Badminton in the second decade of this century. These must have been among the last rail-borne fox-hunters.

RULES FOR BAD HORSEMEN

The 'Country' school of equitation in England faded away about the end of Queen Anne's reign and its passing is closely connected with the improvement of horse-drawn vehicles on the one hand, and on the other with the extinction of the sport of falconry, when fowling pieces that could 'shoot flying' came in.

But travel by coach between towns was still very expensive and inefficient. For the middle classes, one must be able to ride in order to get on in the world, or one's activities would be limited to the home town, or worse still, country parish. There was absolutely no question of liking, or not liking, to ride. It was as mandatory, for most business and professional men of

any aspiration, as it still was for candidates for the Indian Civil Service up to 1939, who might be observed enduring agonies under the eye of the riding master at an approved establishment in South London right up to that date.

Few writers on equitation deigned to notice this mundane fact. *Rules for Bad Horsemen*, written in 1762 by Charles Thompson, is almost unique. Now that everybody had to conform, in some degree, to the former knightly style of riding the 'great and rough' horse, in particular to sit it at the trot, this was an ingenious treatise on How to Get By. It was intended (and no doubt succeeded) for the many people of Dr Johnson's class and equestrian capacities, to take the agony out of utility equitation: riding not as an art but as an indispensable accomplishment, not just the equivalent of driving a car, but of riding a bicycle.

It is often said with emphasis, that such a one [a bad horseman] has no *seat* on horseback; and it means, not only that he does not ride well, but that he does not sit on the right part of the horse. To have a *good seat*, is to sit on that part of the horse, which, as he springs, is the center of motion; and from which of course, any weight would be with most difficulty shaken. As in the rising and falling of a board placed in aequilibrio, the center will always be most at rest; the true seat will be found in that part of your saddle, into which your body would naturally slide, if you rode without stirrups; and is only to be preserved by a proper poise of the body, though the generality of riders imagine it is to be done by the grasp of the thighs and knees. The rider should consider himself as united to his horse in this point, and when shaken from it, endeavour to restore the balance. . . .

Stretch not out your legs before you: this will push you against the back of the saddle; neither gather up your knees, like a man riding on a pack, this throws your thighs upwards: each practice unseats you. Keep your legs straight down, and sit not on the most fleshy part of the thighs, but turn them inwards, so as to bring in your knees and toes; and it is more safe to ride with the ball of the foot pressing on the stirrup, than with the stirrup as far back as the heel; for the pressure of the heel being in that case behind the stirrup, keeps the thighs down. . . .

When you want your horse to move forward, raise his head a little, and touch him gently with your whip; or else, press the calves of your legs against his sides. If he does not move fast enough, press them with more force, and so, till the spur just touches him. By this practice, he will (if he has any spirit) move upon the least pressure of the leg. Never spur him by a kick; but if it be necessary to spur him briskly, keep your heels close to his sides, and slacken their force, as he becomes obedient.

When your horse attempts to be vicious, take each rein separate, one in each hand, and advancing your arms forward, hold him very short. In this case, it is common for the rider to pull him hard, with his arms low; but the horse by this means having his head low too, has it more in his power to throw out his heels: whereas, if his head be raised very high, and his nose thrown out a little, which is consequent, he can neither rise before, nor behind; because he can give himself neither of those motions, without having his head at liberty. A plank placed in aequilibrio, cannot rise at one end, unless it sinks at the other.

If your horse is headstrong, pull not with one continued pull, but stop, and back him often, just shaking the reins, and making little repeated pulls till he obeys. Horses are so accustomed to bear on the bit, when they go forward, that they are discouraged if the rider will not let them do so.

If a horse is loose-necked, he will throw up his head at a continued pull; in which situation, the rider seeing the front of his face, can have no power over him. When your horse does thus, drop your hand, and give the bridle play, and he will of course drop his head again into its proper place: while it is coming down, make a second gentle pull, and you will find his mouth. With a little practice, this is done almost instantaneously; and this method will stop, in the distance of a few yards, a horse, which will run away with those who pull at him with all their might. Almost every one must have observed, that when a horse feels himself pulled with the bridle, even when he is going gently; he often mistakes what was designed to *stop* him, as a direction to bear on the bit, and to *go faster*.

140. Utility equitation.

When a horse starts at any thing on one side, most riders turn him out of the road, to make him go up to what he starts at: if he does not get the better of his fear, or readily comply, he generally goes past the object, making with his hinder parts, or croup, a great circle out of the road; whereas, he should learn to keep strait on, without minding objects on either side.

If he starts at any thing on the left, hold his head high, and keep it strait in the road, pulling it *from* looking at the thing he starts at, and keeping your right leg hard pressed against his side, towards his flank: he will then go strait along the road. By this method, and by turning his head a little more, he may be forced with his croup close up to what frighted him; for as his head is pulled one way, his croup necessarily turns the other. Always avoid a quarrel with your horse, if you can; if he is apt to start, you will find occasions enough to exercise his obedience, when what he starts at lies directly in his way, and you *must* make him pass: If he is not subject to start, you should not contend with him about a trifle.

8. Dealing and stealing

BUYING HORSES

The earliest cash price that we can quote for a horse was made in a society that had no coinage as yet, but a monetary system based on the value of silver. In a code of the Hittite kings that may have been current at the time when the manual on training chariot teams was written by the mercenary Master of the Horse, Kikkulis, the price of an unbroken horse appears as fourteen shekels and that of a trained horse thirty shekels. It does not help us very much to know that a shekel was about five grammes of silver at that time, since we do not know how much silver was in circulation. More significant is the value of other domestic animals and commodities in the same tariff. One shekel equals one sheep; a cow is priced at seven shekels, and a plough ox at fifteen.

About three centuries later we learn from the second Book of Chronicles that King Solomon, who was only the second Israelite king to employ chariots, bought horses and chariots from, among other sources, 'all the kings of the Hittites'. But now a chariot team was worth 150 shekels, or 75 per horse. The chariot itself, if of the finest Egyptian make, cost 600. Inflation had been brought about partly by the increased scale of warfare with chariots, partly by the greater abundance of precious metals—'the king made silver and gold as common in Jerusalem as stones'. But something must be allowed for the fact that Solomon never bought direct, dealing always through Tyrian merchants.

At its height, the Solomonian establishment numbered (II Chron. 1:14) fourteen hundred chariots and twelve thousand horses. According to the same book (9:25) these twelve thousand horses have nothing to do with the chariots, but are chargers and troop-horses. The teams for the chariots amounted to four thousand,

141. Rajah examining the points of a horse by torchlight, c. 1750. The white screen shows up the profile.

142. *The Great Summer Horse Fair*, Japanese print by Ando Hiroshige (1795–1858).

that is, fourteen hundred pairs for immediate action and six hundred pairs or 'yokes' for replacements. But we are not to suppose that all these had been bought, whether by Tyrian agents or otherwise. Many were prizes of war. Others were tribute, others again were taken as ransom. It may be that some were given as pledges, in the same way that hostages were taken from partners to a treaty. The last form of acquisition is often disguised, in chronicles, by the euphemism 'gift', and no doubt a high proportion of the best quality horses in Solomon's vast stables at Megiddo were gifts from other rulers; though it is significant that the Queen of Sheba did not give him any, because South Arabia at that time was not noted either for the quantity or the quality of horses bred there. This element of royal present-giving has ever since then been important in the top flight of horse ownership: and not only as between hereditary monarchs. Gamal Abdel Nasser made gifts of horses from the State stud to prominent political figures in countries whose friendship he desired; and Nikita Khruschev had a magnificent sleigh team of five Arab mares presented to him by the vassal rulers of Hungary in 1964. Nor is there any reason to believe that the steady flow of gift horses from oriental potentates in the direction of Sandringham and Windsor will dry up even when the sheikhdoms have been replaced by People's Republics of Ras-el-Some-where. This is after all the channel by which a majority of the foundation sires of the General Stud Book reached Europe, and the custom was observed among the ancestors of the English before they left the Continent, as we read in Beowulf of King Hrothgar's gift to the hero of eight horses with gold-ornamented bridles.

The earliest extant account of the classic situation of capture of horses in war is the night raid on the enemy horse-lines in the tenth book of the *Iliad*, which is also remarkable as being almost the only episode in the entire Homeric cycle in which horses are ridden rather than driven. A modern description of one of the many societies in which the most honourable means of acquiring a horse has been deemed to be by robbery, with or without violence, can be found in Carl Raswan's book on his stay with the Bedouin, *The Black Tents of Arabia*. Other such societies were that of the Cossacks before about 1700, and of the English-Scottish border, on both sides, before 1603. Xenophon on buying a horse is so explicit that he requires little commentary.

❊His youth once made sure of, the way in which he lets you put the bit into his mouth, and the head-piece about his ears, should not escape you. This would be least likely to pass unnoticed if the bridle were put on and taken off in the sight of the purchaser. Next we ought to observe how he receives the rider upon his back; a good many horses hardly let come near them things whose very approach is a sign that there is work to be done. This, too, must be observed,—whether, when mounted, he is willing to leave other horses, or whether, when ridden near horses that are standing still, he runs away towards them. Some horses, also, from bad training take flight towards home from the riding-grounds. The exercise called the Volte shows up a hard mouth, and even more the practice of changing the direction. Many horses do not try to run away unless the mouth is hard on the same side with the road for a bolt towards home. Then you must know

143. *Eston Horse Fair*, about 1909, in Yorkshire, the home county of the Cleveland Bay. By J. Atkinson.

144. *The Fair of Barnet* in the early years of this century. By Jack Yeats.

whether, when let out at full speed, he will come to the poise and be willing to turn round. . . .

You must learn, too, whether the horse has any particular vice, shown towards other horses or towards men, and whether he is very skittish. These are all troublesome matters for his owner. You could much better discover objections to being bridled and mounted and other vices, by trying to do over again, after the horse has finished his work, just what you did before beginning your ride. Horses that are ready to submit to a task the second time, after having done it once, give proof enough of high spirit.

What we know little about, and what tempts to speculation, is the position of the horse-dealer in Athenian society, and the extent to which dealing was a specialized matter or merely just another part of the exchange of surplus products between land-owning citizens. But probably the majority of horses ridden by Athenians were not locally bred but came either from Thessaly or Thrace or even from barbarian lands over towards the Danube: in which case we may assume the existence of a class of horse-dealers who were either foreigners from the North or Hellenes who made regular seasonal trips in the direction of the Black Sea to buy stock.

The *Qabus Nama* ('A Mirror for Princes') of the Persian Kai-Kaus ibn Iskander (AD 1082) is a kind of manual of gentlemanly behaviour and savoir-faire that has its counterpart in many European medieval works such as the Norwegian *Konungs-Skuggsja* or *Speculum Regale*. All of them contain something about horsemanship—not about how to ride but such matters as the choice of dress, saddlery and accoutrements; in this case, some hints on buying horses. Kai-Kaus assumes his reader will only be buying stallions, but less with a view to breeding than to cutting 'a goodly figure' on horseback. Note his aversion to 'broken colours' such as piebald and roan, and to the 'glass eye' which is most often seen in parti-coloured horses.

The curious thing is that among Chinese pictures of the 'Heavenly' Bactrian horses which were the most renowned breed of Persia in antiquity, piebald and other odd-coloured animals are frequently seen. The sense of the passage about places that should be black is that the horse should have a black skin all over. There are two kinds of cream horse, one with black skin and one with pink: and it is this second kind of cream (which usually has blue eyes) that Kai-Kaus would reject, as he would anything approximating to albinism.

When you buy horses, be on your guard against making any mistakes. In essence horses and human beings are alike in that you may value a good horse or a good human being at as high a price as you like, in the same way that you may depreciate a bad horse or man to any extent possible. There is a saying that the world persists through mankind and mankind through animals; and the horse is the best of all animals because its maintenance is required both by husbandry and knightly duty. It is proverbial that you must keep horses and garments in good condition if you wish them to maintain *you* in good condition.

It is more difficult to judge horses than men, because something of the true significance of men can be obtained from what they claim, whereas all the horse's pretensions lie in his external appearance. In order to discover what its claims are, first consider its external aspect, because in general a good horse has a good appearance and a bad one the reverse. The teeth must be without gaps, thin and white, the lower lip longer than the upper, the nose high, wide and straight, the forehead broad, the lower part of the ears smooth, the ears long with the upper part pointed and raised, the middle of the ear being straight, the neck well extended, the barrel [lit. 'place of the girth'], the base of the neck and of the ear fine, the cannon heavy, with the upper bone shorter than the lower, the hair scanty, the hoof long and black, the sole round, the back arched [lit. 'high'], the part between flank and belly short, the chest broad, the space between fore and hind leg well open, the tail bushy and long, the root of the tail fine and short, the scrotum black, eyes and lashes black also. On the road it should move with caution.

Further, its shin should be smooth, the quarters well-suspended, the crupper wide, the inner side of the thigh fleshy and well-knit. As the man riding it moves, it should be aware of his movement.

These good points which I have detailed should be present without fail in every horse. There are others which may be present in one horse but not in another. Amongst colours, bay is reputed best, but date-colour is good too. The horse should be able to tolerate both heat and cold, and be a willing worker. It is a good quality if the scrotum, the middle of the thighs, stifle, tail, fore and hind legs, breast and forehead are black. A dun-coloured horse is good too, especially if the colour is deep, the face flecked with black, and it is black in the breast, forehead, tail, scrotum, stifle, the middle of the thighs, the eyes and the lips.

A cream horse should be similarly variegated, but a light bay should be all of one colour, without any contrasting flecks. The black horse must be shining black. Horses must not have red eyes; generally a red-eyed horse is unmanageable and vicious. The ash-grey with black legs and possessing the qualities I have described for the dun is good, but the piebald is of small worth and not well regarded, being generally bad-tempered.

Now that you know the good points of the horse, you must also learn the bad ones. There is a particular fault which is damaging to a horse's capacity for work and has an ugly appearance but only means that the animal is on heat; but there are also faults due to defects and ugly qualities of which some can be tolerated and others not. Each blemish and defect has a name by which it is identified, as I shall set out.

Of the defects in a horse, one is dumbness; the dumb horse has very little value. The sign of it is that when it sees a mare, although it may erect the penis, it fails to neigh. Then there is a half-blind horse, which is night-blind. The sign of it is that it has no fear at night of those things which horses usually fear and will not shy, and it will venture on to any ground however bad on to which you ride. A deaf horse also is bad. The sign of it is that it does not hear the neighing of other horses and never answers although it always has its ears forward and open. A 'left-legged' horse is bad also, constantly stumbling. The mark of it is that when you lead it into a passageway it puts forward first its left foreleg. Furthermore it cannot swim. The pur-blind horse is bad because it cannot see in the daytime. The mark of it is that the pupil of the eye is black verging on green, it keeps its eye always open so that the lids never touch. This may occur in one eye or both. . . . The 'stockinged' horse has a white fore or hind-leg; if the left fore and hind-legs are white it is ill-omened.

If the horse is blue in both eyes, that may pass; but if it is so in one only, then it is defective, particularly if

145. *On the Stones*—the Cattle Market, Caledonian Road, selling cheap nags. Gone with the wind; the last vestiges of this tradition in the London area are to be seen at Barnet Fair: faces like this, horses like this. Another Yeats picture.

it is the left eye. The wall-eyed horse is bad, that is, the horse that has a white eye; and the blue roan is bad too, so is the long-necked horse, that is, the one which has its neck stretched out straight. No regard should be paid to a horse of that description. The (?) 'crab' horse is bad because both its hind legs are crooked; in Persian it is called 'bow-legged'. It frequently falls down. The hairy-backed horse is bad, having hair on top of its back and round its hind legs. The hair-ringed horse is similarly bad because it has hair round its legs and under its hoofs. It is worst if the hair grows on both sides, but it is bad if the hair is about the legs above the hoof on the inner side. If it is on the outer side, it is tolerable. . . .

Buy large horses, because even though a man may be fat and of goodly figure he has an insignificant appearance on a contemptibly small mount. Another thing to know is that there may be a bone more in the left side than in the right; count them, and if the bones on either side balance in number, then buy the horse for more even than it is worth, for no horse could be better. Whatever you buy, whether it be animals or lands, let it be such that you will enjoy the benefits of it during your lifetime and your friends and heirs will do so after you.

BASE VILLANY

The horse-stealing business in Shakespeare's England was just as widespread, and much better organized, than the car-stealing business is in ours. It had its wholesalers, its middlemen, its retailers, as well as those who procured the stock and processed it beyond all recognition. Besides the outright criminals, the priggers and lancemen and trailers, there was a quasi-criminal fringe of ancillaries, farriers, innkeepers and the like, who did a job, took their money and asked no questions. The trade was well equipped to deal with the legal side of its affairs. This was important because the Elizabethan act which Greene mentions was only part of a great body of legislation concerning the marketing of horses, the impounding and eventual sale of strays, etc., then in force and dating from the first Tudor reigns or earlier. Indeed the law mentioned here was only a re-enactment of a comprehensive law concerning the sale of horses passed in 1555 under Philip and Mary. Mention of the tricks used to alter the horse's appearance recalls that even the respectable Gervase Markham, the prolific seventeenth-century veterinary writer, has a recipe for making an indelible artificial white star in the forehead.

✳To the effecting of this base villany of Prigging or horse-stealing, there must of necessity be two at the least, and that is the Priggar and the Martar. The Priggar is he that steales the horse, and the Martar is he that receives him, and chops and changeth him away in any Faire, Mart, or other place where any good rent for horses is: and their method is thus. The Priggar if he be a Launce-man, that is, one that is already horst, then he hath more followers with him, and they ride like Gentlemen, and commonly in the form of Drovers, and so comming into pasture grounds, or inclosures, as if they ment to survey for Cattell, doe take an especiall and perfect view, where prankers or horses be, that are of worth, & whether they have horse-locks or no, then lie they hovering about till fit opertunitie serve, & in the night they take him or them away, and are skilfull in the blacke Art, for picking open the tramels or lockes, and so make hast till they be out of those quarters. Now if the Priggars steale a horse in Yorke-shire, commonly they have vent for him in Surrey, Kent, or Sussex, and their Martars that receive them at his hand, chops them away in some blind Faires after they have kept them a moneth or two, till the hue and crie be ceast and past over. Now if their horse be of any great value, and sore sought after, and so branded or eare-markt, that they can hardly sell him without extreame daunger, either they brand him with a crosse brand upon the former, or take away his eare-marke, & so keep him at hard-meat till he be whole, or els sel him in Corne-wall or Wales, if he be in Cumberland, Lincoln-shire, North-folke or Suffolke: but this is, if the horse bee of great valour & worthie the keeping: Mary if hee be onely coloured and without brands, they will straight spotte him by sundry pollicies, and in a blacke horse, marke saddle spots, or star him in the forehead, and change his taile, which secrets I omit, least I shuld give too great a light to others to practise such leud villanies. But againe to our Launce-men Priggars, who as before I saide, cry with the Lapwing farthest from their nest, and from their place of residence, where their most abode is, furthest from thence

they steal their horses, and then in another quarter as far of they make sale of them by the Martars means, without it be some base Priggar that steales of meere necessity, and beside is a Trailer. The Trailer is one that goeth on foot, but meanely attired like some plaine gran of the Countrey, walking in a paire of boots without spurs, or else without boots, having a long staffe on his necke, and a blacke buckram bag at his back, like some poore client that had some writing in it, and there he hath his saddle, bridle and spurs, stirhops & stirhop-leathers, so quaintly and artificially made, that it may bee put in ye slop of a mans hose: for his sadle is made without any tree, yet hath it cantle and bolsters, only wrought arteficially of cloth and bombast, with foldes to wrap up in a short roome: his stirhops are made with vices and gins, that one may put them in a paire of glooves, and so are his spurs, & then a little white leather headstal and rains, with a small scotish brake or snaffle, all so featlie formed, that as I said before, they may be put in a buckram bag. Now, this Trailer he bestrides the horse which he priggeth, and saddles and bridles him as orderly as if he were his own, and then carieth him far from the place of his breed, and ther sels him.

Robert Greene, *A notable discovery of coosnage*

THE DISCOVERY OF SEVERAL TRICKS AND CHEATS USED BY JOCKEYS

The word jockey did not acquire its meaning of a professional rider of race-horses until some time in the eighteenth century. In Ben Jonson's time it meant most often a man in the service of a horse-dealer who 'ran' the horses up and down (sometimes rode them) at such markets as Smithfield. To Gervase Markham, jockey meant dealer, especially low-class dealer, in horses; as a nickname, the word has a Northern flavour, and its use in the context of horse-dealing probably goes back to the North Country and Scottish dealers and drovers who dominated the metropolitan livestock markets of the sixteenth and seventeenth centuries.

146. *Showing at Tattersall's*, by Robert Bevan. Tattersall's was at Knightsbridge Green, where it still has an office, but nothing more. 'Tattersall's is usually looked upon as the head-quarters of horsey London. It is certainly the headquarters of the horse of pleasure . . . The yard is under cover, a lofty glass-roofed hall, which cost 30,000*l.* to build, and which is as big as many a railway station . . . If you want riding horses or carriage horses you go to Tattersall's' (W. J. Gordon, *The Horse World of London*, 1893).

First then, to make a dull Jade both kick, wince and fling, without either Whip or Spur, they use this device; in the fore-part of a Saddle made for that purpose, they have an Iron Plate, through which is drilled three holes, through which with a spring come three sharp wires, the which as long as the Rider sits upright do not prick the horse, but when he leans forward and presses the Bow of the Saddle, they torment him so that he capers and dances though never so dull, which the ignorant Buyer often supposes to proceed from the height of his Mettle which the Jockey spares not to avouch with Oaths.

The Second is, if any Gentleman have set up a horse in a Stable at Livery, the Jockey either by bribing the Hostler, or privately by taking an opportunity in his absence, will with a hair take up the vein on the inside of the Horses Leg, or by cramping him in the Fet-lock with a small Wyer (neither of which can be observed without a curious search) either of which, will cause the Horse after a quarter of an hours Riding to halt down-right Lame, then is the owner sent for, whose coming

the Jockey having notice of, pretends some Business in the Stable, and whilst the Gentleman is admiring the sudden mischance befallen his Horse, he puts in his verdict, saying, it was a great deal of pity that so good a Beast should be disabled, and by degrees insinuates into the Gentlemans acquaintance, desiring him to send for a Farrier, who comes and searches his foot, but finds no cause of Lameness there, whereupon the Gentleman dispairing of his recovery is often pressed by the Jockey to sell him at half the worth, or swap him for some dull Jade that he or some of his Comrades have near at hand, who having got the Gentle-mans Horse, by uncramping or letting loose the vein render him as at first.

The Third Cheat they put upon Travellers is this, coming into a Country Inn, their first walk is into the Stable, where taking a view of the Horses, they single out the best for their purpose, demanding of the Hostler who that fine Horse belongs to, who ignorant of any design freely tells them, then they place their Horses next him, and seem only to feed, or rub them down, and order the Hostler to fetch a peck of Oats, the which whilst he is gone to do, they thrust a stone about the bigness of a Tennis-Ball into his Fundament, one of which they have always ready, it not having been in a quarter of an hour before the Horse begins to sweat mightily, and fall a trembling and staring as if his eyes were ready to start out of his head, so that a white foam soon after covers many places about him, which the Hostler observing, runs to the Gentleman that owns him, and tells him his Horse is a dying, at which starting up he runs to the Stable and finds him in a bad plight, not knowing what to think, or if he do, conjectures he is poisoned, and in a confused hurry enquires for a Farrier or Horse Doctor, when as Mr. Jockey steps in and asketh what is the matter, as if he poor lifeless fellow knew nothing of it, but quickly understanding the business, begins both to pity the Horse and Gentleman, the former for his miserable condition, and the latter for the danger he is in of losing his Horse, when thus he applys himself; Sir, I am sorry to see your Horse in so bad a plight, then puts in to buy him at a venture, live or die, the which if he cannot do handsomely, he undertakes to cure him, telling the Gentleman that though it is not his usual custom to meddle with, yet he will undertake for forty shillings to warrant his Life: The Gentleman consents rather than to lose a Horse worth twenty pounds; then for a shew he gives him a Drench, and then takes opportunity to withdraw the stone, and within half an hours space the Horse will be perfectly well, and so they fob the Ignorant.

Markham's Masterpiece, 1688

TO KNOW THE AGE OF A HORSE

William Cavendish, Duke of Newcastle, is the best known of the classic English writers on the art of horsemanship, and probably would still be even if the English did not so love a lord. Indeed, so great is his fame as the author of a treatise on the High School, the *New Method*, that it has cast into shadow his writing on horsemastership in general.

We give here a sample of the less-known aspect of Newcastle's work; from which it appears that for an author who has the reputation of writing for gentlemen only, he had a close acquaintance with some very ungentlemanly practices, including that form of bent dentistry nowadays known as 'bishoping'.

A Horse that is fit for Work should have forty Teeth; twenty four Grinders, which teach us nothing; and sixteen others, which all have their Names, and discover his Age.

As Mares have usually no Tusks, their Teeth are only thirty six. Those that have Tusks are esteemed barren; fit for Service, but not for the Stud: For, being warmer than others, they seldom have any Foals; except in a temperate Country, and some other Season than the Month of May; which however is the Time of getting them covered.

A Colt is foaled without Teeth. In a few Days he puts out four, which are called *Pincers*, or *Nippers*. Soon after appear the four *Separaters*, next to the *Pincers*. It is sometimes three of our Months before the next, called *Corner-Teeth*, push forth. These twelve *Colt's Teeth*, in the Front of the Mouth, continue without Alteration till the Colt is two Years, or two Years and a half old: Which makes it difficult, without great Care, to avoid being imposed on, during that Interval, if the Seller finds it for his Interest to make the Colt pass for either younger or older than he really is. The only Rule you have then to judge by, is his Coat, and the Hairs of his Mane and Tail. A Colt of one Year has a supple rough Coat, resembling that of a Water-Spaniel, and the Hair of his Mane and Tail feel like Flax, and hang like a Rope untwisted; whereas a Colt of two Years has a flat Coat, and strait Hairs, like a grown Horse.

At about two Years and a half old, sometimes sooner, sometimes later, according as he has been fed, a Horse begins to change his Teeth. Soft Nourishment, as Grass in particular, will forward, and a firm Diet in the Stable will retard his Change. The *Pincers*, which come the first, are also the first that fall; so that at three Years he has four Horse's, and eight Colt's Teeth, which are easily known apart, the former being larger, flatter, and

147. A set of studies by Baron Reis d'Eisenberg, now at Wilton House, of the Spanish court riding school in Vienna, the horses performing the conventional airs. Classical equitation was a sector of upper-class culture represented fairly evenly throughout western Europe of the seventeenth and eighteenth centuries. Now all the visible remains are contained in Vienna and in Saumur.

148. Typical quality half-bred hunters of the early nineteenth century, disfigured by the ugly habit of docking tails and cropping ears. (Detail from Stubbs' *John and Sophia Musters out riding at Colwick Hall*)

149. *Barnet Horse Fair*, by William Farley. At once more crowded and more restful than the same scene viewed by Yeats (Plate 144).

yellower than the other, and streaked from the End quite into the Gums. These four Horse *Pincers* have in the middle of their Extremities a black Hole, very deep; whereas those of the Colt are round and white. When the Horse is coming four Years old, he loses his four *Separaters*, or middle Teeth, and puts forth four others, which follow the same Rule as the *Pincers*. He has now eight Horse's Teeth, and Four Colt's. At Five

Years old he sheds the four *Corner*, which are his last *Colt's Teeth*, and is called a Horse. During this Year also his four *Tusks* (which are chiefly peculiar to Horses) come behind the others, the lower ones often four Months before the upper: But, whatever may be vulgarly thought, a Horse that has the two lower Tusks, if he has not the upper, may be judged to be under five Years old, unless the other Teeth shew the contrary:

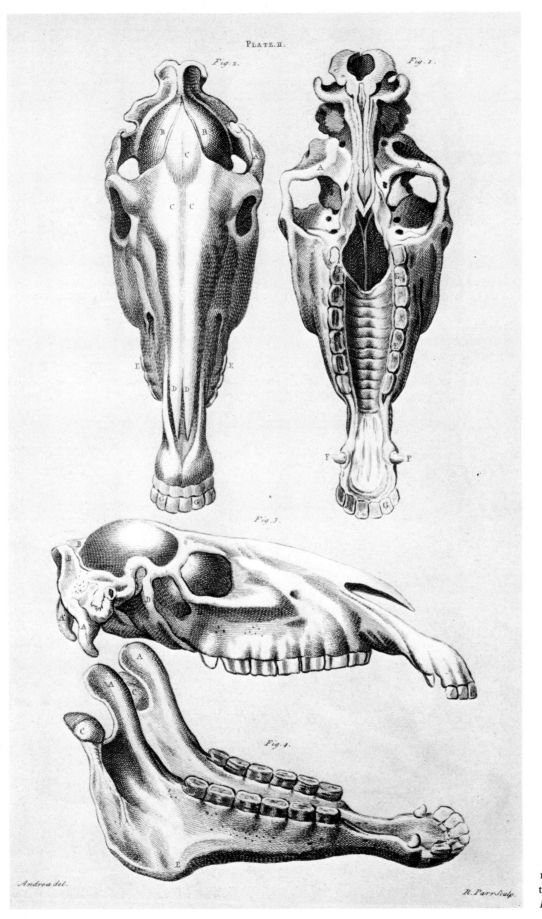

150. The skull and teeth of the horse. An illustration from the Duke of Newcastle's *The Perfect Knowledge of Horses*.

For some Horses, that live to be very old, never have any upper Tusks at all. The two lower Tusks are one of the most certain Rules that a Horse is coming five Years old, notwithstanding his Colt's Teeth may not be all gone.

It often happens that your Jockeys and Breeders, to make their Colts seem five Years old when they are but four, pull out their last Colt's Teeth: But if all the Colt's Teeth are gone, and no Tusks appear, you may be certain this Trick has been played. Another Artifice they use, is to beat the Bars every Day with a wooden Mallet, in the Place where the Tusks are to appear, in order to make them seem hard, as if the Tusks were just ready to cut.

When a Horse is coming six Years old, the two lower *Pincers* fill up, and, instead of the Holes above-mentioned, shew only a black Spot. Between six and seven, the two Middle Teeth fill up in the same Manner, and between seven and eight, the Corner Teeth do the like; after which it is said to be impossible to know certainly the Age of a Horse, he having no longer any Mark in his Mouth. You can indeed only have recourse to the Tusks, and the Situation of the Teeth, of which I shall now speak.

151. Veterinary chart from the Duke of Newcastle's *The Perfect Knowledge of Horses*.

152. Unexpected elevation, an illustration to an anecdote in Mark Twain.

For the Tusks, you must with your Finger feel the Inside of them, from the point quite to the Gum. If the Tusk be pointed, flat, and has two little Channels within-side, you may be certain the Horse is not old, and at the utmost only coming ten. Between eleven and twelve the two Channels are reduced to one, which after twelve is quite gone, and the Tusks are as round within, as they are without. You have no Guide then but the Situation of the Teeth. The longest Teeth are not always a Sign of the greatest Age, but their hanging over and pushing forwards; as their meeting perpendicularly is a certain Token of Youth. . . .

The artificial Manner is made use of by the Jews and Jockeys, who mark their Horses, after the Age of being known, to make them appear only six or seven years old. They do it in this manner: They throw down the Horse, to have him more at Command, and with a Steel-Graver, like what is used for Ivory, hollow the middle Teeth a little, and the corner ones somewhat more; then fill the Holes with a little Rosin, Pitch, Sulphur, or some Grains of Wheat, which they burn in with a Bit of hot Wire, made in proportion to the Hole. This Operation they repeat from time to time, till they give the Hole a lasting Black, in imitation of Nature. But, in spite of all they can do, the hot Iron makes a little yellowish Circle round these Holes, like what it would leave upon Ivory. They have another Trick therefore to prevent Detection; which is, to make the Horse foam from time to time, after having rubbed his Mouth, Lips, and Gums, with Salt, and the Crumb of Bread dried and powdered with Salt. This Foam hides the Circle made by the Iron.

Another thing they cannot do, is to counterfeit young Tusks, it being out of their power to make those two Crannies above-mentioned, which are given by Nature. With Files they may make them sharper or flatter, but then they take away the shining natural Enamel: So that one may always know, by these Tusks, Horses that are past seven, till they come to twelve or thirteen.

A General System of Horsemanship, 1657

9. Eastern and thoroughbred

The penetration of Europe by the oriental horse was a long process and a slow one, even if we interpret the word 'oriental' in the most liberal manner, to include, as is most commonly done, Barbs foaled in Morocco at a longitude of 8°W., which is a good deal more occidental than Penzance.

For practical purposes we cannot look further back than the Roman conquest of Gaul and Britain in the first century of our era, in terms of evidence verifiable by documentary sources. This expansion was a logical (from the Roman point of view) consequence of the conquest of Spain in the previous two centuries. Previous to that the 'imperialist' power in Spain had been Carthage, and the Carthaginian army owed its success to its cavalry arm, consisting of Numidian mercenaries mounted on North African ('Barb') horses. Thus at

153. Bahram Gur, the great hunter (reigned AD 420–438), transfixing a lion and a wild ass with a single arrow. A Persian miniature of *c.* 1490.

this early period Spanish horse stock was heavily tinged with North African blood. The Roman victory over the Carthaginians was in part due to their success in bribing the Numidian cavalry to change sides, and henceforward they, and the 'native' Iberian mounted auxiliaries, formed a considerable sector of Roman horsed units, including those in the garrisons of Britannia and Gaul. The prime source of military horses for all the western provinces was for a long time the state-owned studs in Spain, the most orientalized province (in terms of horses) in the whole Empire.

A less measurable, but probably more influential, element was introduced by the downfall of the Empire in the West, the result of a long process of attrition partly by Germans on foot but partly by Asiatic horse archers. Of this the Huns were the last of a long series of such peoples, whose lines of communication stretched far back into Central Asia, if not to Mongolia itself with its tough, serviceable but not aesthetically impressive horses, then at least as far as Turkestan, the breeding-ground of such races as the fabulous blood-sweating 'Heavenly Horses', to obtain a stock of which the Emperors of China had instructed their ambassadors to treat in terms of courtesy otherwise never extended to the rulers of the Outer Barbarians. No doubt the ordinary Hunnish troopers rode short-legged, big-headed, shaggy Type II ponies, strongly resembling the primeval Taki; but not such commanders as Attila and his captains.

I do not share the conviction of some writers that the Crusades 'must have' resulted in a large influx of Arab horses into 'Frankish' lands. There is but scanty written evidence for this; there is no proof, even, that the two 'most noble Arab horses' presented to Richard Coeur-de-Lion by Saladin ever reached the base on Cyprus, let alone England. Nor is it probable that many such imports took place. The fact that most of the time the Foul Paynim made rings round the Christian Dogs did not unduly influence Western military thinking. A fourteen-hand, seven-hundred-weight Saracen horse was not hefty enough to enable the owner to knock over another knight either in battle or in the 'friendly' tourney. Moreover, most Crusaders were flat broke at the end of their tour of duty, and transport of horses by sea is expensive. And few among them would want a souvenir—a reminder of the heat and the dust and the glare, the gritty stifling *khamseen*, the dysentery and the baksheesh, the intolerable thirst on duty and the almost complete absence, off duty, of drinkable wine.

Probably the Saracen offensive in Spain, which had reached far up into France in the years before Charlemagne's accession, had resulted in more oriental horses coming into Western hands than all the Crusades put together. So, too, had a less spectacular infiltration by way of Constantinople all the time it remained in Christian hands—well into the fifteenth century. In the markets by the Bosphorus Greek and Armenian middlemen bought selectively Saracen horses for wealthy 'Frankish' customers, for purposes that had

little to do with war. They made elegant, comfortable, tractable palfreys, pleasant to look on as to ride.

The most considerable channel through which oriental horses reached the West was, in the medieval period, Italy. Sicily was conquered by Muslim Emirs from North Africa in the eighth century. The struggle for power there and in southern Italy between the Saracens, the Byzantines, the Holy Roman Empire and the Papacy was finally resolved by the victory of Norman adventurers in the pay of the last-named. Norman Sicily was a unique and splendid blend of several different cultural traditions, but in matters of horsemanship, hunting, falconry, and above all in the type of horse ridden and bred, the Saracen element prevailed. The *cavallo gentile* of Renaissance Italy derived its quality from these oriental sources. It was known in

154. A prince with attendants, including on the right a European and a Mughal courtier. In front the horse would pass muster, in many respects, by the criteria of the Arab Horse Society. Behind, it is a classic demonstration, almost a caricature, of what are called 'sickle hocks'. A Persian miniature of *c.* 1680.

155. A game of polo, Persian miniature, *c.* 1600. 'My son, if your recreation is playing polo, do not be constantly indulging in it, for misfortune has overtaken many a man through so doing . . . Yet, if once or twice a year you find pleasure in polo, I regard it as permissible. But you should not indulge in a great deal of riding, because in that there is danger. The men riding should number not more than eight in all; you should be stationed at one end of the field and another man at the opposite end, with six men on the field actually playing the ball. When the ball comes in your direction, return it and bring your horse up; but take no part in the scrimmage, thereby avoiding collision. You can achieve your purpose merely by looking on.

That is how men of distinction play polo' (Kai-Kaus Ibn Iskander: *Qabus Nama—A Mirror for Princes*, 1082).

156. An Indian wall-hanging for comparison with the Bayeux Tapestry (Plate 13), but worked in the late eighteenth century. It shows the dead end of the Central Asian tradition of mounted warfare. Now most of the archers are dismounted. Signals are given by kettledrum (a Turkish invention) of a pattern still used by the Household Cavalry in England. The issue is not complicated, as most eighteenth-century battles between Indian rulers were, by the use of firearms or European mercenaries.

the rest of Europe as Apulian or Calabrian, but by the end of the fifteenth century it was as likely to have been bred in the Po valley as in the south. And it is here that the long and complicated story of the half-conscious English effort to 'create' the Thoroughbred really begins, with the acquisition by Henry VIII of stock from the Gonzaga rulers of Padua, from 1520 onwards, specifically as 'running horses'. By this time the royal stud at Tutbury was at least two centuries old. It was like that sort of pot-au-feu that bubbles away on the same hearth for generations—the elements of the original stock are untraceable, but its flavour is unmistakable. The Gonzaga additions are the earliest which can be identified and of which we have realistic pictures. There followed in the same century important contributions from Hungary, almost certainly of Turkish origin. But in 1580 a commercial treaty permitted for the first time for more than a century direct trading by ships of the English nation with Constantinople and certain other ports of the vast Turkish empire. Now that the Sultan had opened the door, if only by a crack, it was possible, at great expense, to acquire horses of the classic

157. Both the horses in this equine conversation-piece figured in several of James Ward's compositions; the little white Arab in *The Deerstealer* for instance. The model for the other is said to have been the race-horse Smolensko. (*L'Amour de Cheval* by Ward, 1827)

Arabian strains, besides Barbary horses and the 'Turk' horse proper, a tall, enduring and above all fast runner, originating in 'Great Tartary', i.e. Turkestan.

More such imports followed under James I, Charles I, the Commonwealth and Charles II, culminating, in the reign of Queen Anne, in the arrival of the identifiable Big Names to whom modern race-horses can trace their lineage. As explained in the Introduction, this was a side-effect of the Turkish withdrawal from the Danube valley. By the time the Turks had once more stabilized their position in Europe, England, at any rate, had acquired all the oriental horses it needed at home. Other nations thenceforward sent government missions to Turkish (including Arab) territory to buy foundation stock for the breeding of light cavalry horses. Britain sent none, except once, during the Crimean war, and this was to procure ready-made chargers for immediate service.

Quite apart from the highly specialized requirements of the race-course, there grew up in England a class of persons accustomed all their active lives to riding Arab horses. These were the servants, military and civil, of the East India Company. They found little to satisfy them in the horse stock of India itself, but were

mounted on Arab horses brought by sea from the Persian Gulf to Bombay, which they used for all purposes including sport and recreation. All these horses were entire stallions, hardly any of them of the quality or size seen in Stubbs's equestrian portrait of Warren Hastings. The tradition was inherited, unchanged, by officers of the post-Mutiny Indian Army and Civil Service; generations of Englishmen who had ridden Arab stallions every day for decades and never set eyes on an Arab mare. After the opening of the Suez Canal it became not uncommon for some retiring Anglo-Indian to bring home an Arab horse: but still never an Arab mare, and the stallions were not of known pedigree. Their history began on the dockside at Bombay, when they landed from the Gulf dhow.

Another 'special relationship' existed in France, dating from the Napoleonic adventure in Egypt. This expedition smashed the power of the ruling Mameluke military aristocracy in Egypt, who up to that time had owned more, and better, Arab horses than anyone else outside Arabia. All French soldiers from Napoleon downwards came to appreciate the virtues of the pure-bred Arabian horse as a charger, and French painters of the Romantic school adopted it, despite its relatively

small size, as the supreme model for the 'heroic' horse. So it came about that on the field of Waterloo both Napoleon and Wellington rode Arab horses, even if Wellington's was bred in Ireland.

❈ANCESTORS OF THE THOROUGHBRED

Nothing can exceed the attachment that exists between the poor Arab and his horse, often his whole stock of wealth. The mare and her foal inhabit the same tent with his family, and are caressed by all. The body of a mare is often the pillow of her master, and more frequently of his children, who roll about upon her and the foal, without the least risk.

The kindness thus engendered, is returned by the mare in many of those situations when the life of the child of the desert depends only on the sagacity and swiftness of his faithful courser.

When the Arab falls wounded from his mare, she will immediately stand still, and neigh until assistance arrives. Should fatigue compel him to lie down to sleep in the desert, she watches over him, and arouses him on the approach of man or beast. . . .

The poverty of the Arabs enables them to afford but scanty nourishment to their horses. Besides the dry aromatic herbage they may chance to pick up, the Arabian horse usually has but one or two meals in twenty-four hours. At night it receives a little water; and five or six pounds of barley or beans and a little straw . . . Very little water is given, as the Arabs conceive (and justly) that much liquid injures the horse's shape and affects his wind.

The colt is mounted after its second year, when the Arab on all other occasions so kind to his horse, puts it to a cruelly severe trial. The colt, or filly, is led out to be mounted for the first time; its master springs on its back, and rides at full speed for perhaps fifty miles, over sand and rock of the burning desert, without one moment's respite. He then plunges it into water enough to swim, and if immediately after this, it will eat as if nothing had happened, its purity of blood and staunchness are considered incontrovertible.

158. 'Autres pays, autres moeurs': in Morocco they put the saddle on before the bridle. (*Moroccan Saddling His Horse* by Eugène Delacroix, 1855)

Such is the account handed down to us by respectable authorities, who in their turn received it from the Arabs themselves; but some allowance should be made for the proneness to exaggerate for which all eastern nations are remarkable, more especially the Arabians; and glorying as they justly do in the prowess of their beautiful steeds, it is not to be wondered at, if they should sometimes enlarge upon it to foreigners.

The greatest care is exercised in breeding the kohlan, or kailhan, the noble race; much ceremony takes place as well at the union of these animals as at the birth of the foal; and a certificate is made out, and properly authenticated, within seven days after that event. It is generally believed that pedigrees of the noble race of horses exist of not less than five hundred years, with sire and dam distinctly traced. The following pedigree is mentioned by Weston, in his Fragments of Oriental Literature; it was found hanging round the neck of an Arabian horse purchased by Colonel Ainslie, during the last campaign in Egypt against the French.

'In the name of God, the merciful and compassionate, and of Seyd Mohammed, agent of the High God, and of the companions of Mohammed and of Jerusalem. Praised be the Lord, the omnipotent Creator. This is a high bred horse, and its colt's tooth is here in a bag about his neck, with his pedigree, and of undoubted authority, such as no infidel can refuse to believe. He is the son of Rabbaing, out of the dam Lahadah, and equal in power to his sire, of the tribe of Zazhalah. He is finely moulded, and made for running like an ostrich, and great in his stroke, covering much ground. In the honours of relationship he reckons Zaluah, sire of Mahat, sire of Kallack, and the unique Alket, sire of Manasseth, sire of Alshek, father of the race down to the famous horse the sire of Lakalala; and to him be ever abundance of green meat, and corn and water of life, as a reward from the tribe of Zazhalah, for the fire of his cover; and may a thousand branches shade his carcase from the hyena of the tomb, from the howling wolf of the desert; and let the tribe of Zazhalah present him with a festival within an enclosure of walls; and let thousands assemble at the rising of the sun, in troops, hastily, where the tribe holds up, under a canopy of celestial signs, within the walls, the saddle with the name and family of the possessor. Then let them strike the hands with a loud noise incessantly, and pray God for immunity for the tribe of Zoab, the inspired tribe.'

Next to the Arabian blood, we are indebted to the Barb for our present breed of thorough bred horses. . . .

Besides these two celebrated breeds, we have imported both Persian, Turkish and East Indian horses. . . .

The best breed of Turkish horses is descended from those of Arabia and Persia; but they greatly exceed the horses of both those countries in point of size. The body is even longer than the Arabians, and the crupper more elevated. They have contributed materially to the improvement of the English breed. . . .

The Turkish horses are . . . remarkable for their extreme docility, which is thus accounted for by Busbequius, who was ambassador at Constantinople in the seventeenth century; and it would be well, if both

159. *Racing in the Shadow of Windsor Castle* by Francis Barlow, 1687. Note the weighing-in arrangements in front of the royal box.

160. The steeplechase, nowadays represented by the point-to-point organized by hunts and by the professional steeplechase under National Hunt rules, which is run over a course differing from a flat racecourse only in as much as artificial obstacles have been built across it. Both originated in the steeplechase of the late eighteenth century, in which in counties like Leicestershire amateur riders competed across a line of typical hunting country on hunters that were all but thoroughbred. We show here Henry Alken's picture of the start of such an event in the first years of the nineteenth century.

masters and grooms would learn a lesson from the wisdom and humanity of this truly worthy and benevolent writer.

'Nothing,' writes Busbequius, 'can surpass the gentleness of the Turkish horses; and their obedience to their masters and grooms is very great. The reason is, they always treat them with great kindness. I myself saw, when I was in Pontus, passing through a part of Bithynia called Axillon, towards Cappadocia, how gentle the country people were to young colts, and how kindly they used them soon after they were foaled.

'They took them into their own habitations, cleansed, combed, and caressed them with as much affection as they would their own children. They hung something like a jewel about their necks, and a broad ribbon, which was full of amulets against poison, which they are most afraid of. They never strike them, the grooms that dress them being as gentle as their masters. In return for this treatment, these animals naturally acquire a great attachment to man, and are always most tractable and easily managed. The Turks take a pride in making them so tame that they will kneel to be mounted at the word of command, take up a stick or scimitar from the ground, and whenever the rider happens to fall off, immediately stand still. But alas! the horses of our christian grooms generally and with reason fear their keepers.'

James Christie Whyte,
History of the British Turf, 1840

For poets of the Romantic school the Arab horse was the horse worth writing about: think only of Byron.

Byron had a granddaughter called Anne Isabella King, a daughter of the Earl of Lovelace. She married Wilfrid Scawen Blunt, who is more remembered today for his poems than for his political views which brought him much notoriety in his lifetime. The first ten years of their married life were spent in almost ceaseless travel mostly on horseback, often in wild country, culminating in an expedition to Nejd in central Arabia, the classic breeding-ground of the pure Arabian horse. Blunt was convinced that a re-infusion of Arab blood would not only, after a few generations, add speed to the Thoroughbred, but would be the sole means of arresting a process of debilitation which must inevitably overtake it as a breed. He came, in time, to modify his views in both respects, but the initial impulse in the late 1870s led him to acquire a stock of Arab stallions and mares (hardly any of the latter had been seen before in England) that was unique and unrivalled. The Blunts had an establishment in Egypt and another in Sussex; at the latter the auctions of young stock bred from the desert horses brought back by them became famous throughout the Western world.

Wilfrid Blunt died a year or two before the date we have determined as the close of the Age of the Horse, and his wife a few years before that, but he lived long enough to be the first honorary president of the Arab Horse Society, founded to 'promote the breeding and importation of pure-bred Arabs, and to encourage the re-introduction of Arab blood into English light-horse breedings'. It was the first such society in the world, and has exercised a profound influence on that phase of equestrian history which the Blunts did not live to see —that age in which the horse ceased to count for anything in the productive economy of peace or the destructive effort of war, while at the same time playing an ever-increasing part in the leisure world of sport and recreation.

ARAB RECIPE FOR REARING A COLT

In *Bedouin Tribes of the Euphrates* and also in *A Pilgrimage to Nejd*, from which comes this extract, Lady Anne Blunt wrote an unrivalled and utterly unromantic account of her husband's and her romantic quest for the remnants of the authentic Arabian stock. The chapter on the rearing and breaking of colts seems much more credible than, and should be taken as a corrective to, the account given in Whyte.

'If,' said our informant, 'you would make a colt run faster than his fellows, remember the following rules:

' "During the first month of his life let him be content with his mother's milk, it will be sufficient for him. Then during five months add to this natural supply goat's milk, as much as he will drink. For six months more give him the milk of camels, and besides a measure of wheat steeped in water for a quarter of an hour, and served in a nosebag.

' "At a year old the colt will have done with milk; he must be fed on wheat and grass, the wheat dry from a nosebag, the grass green if there is any.

' "At two years old he must work, or he will be worthless. Feed him now, like a full-grown horse, on barley; but in summer let him also have gruel daily at midday. Make the gruel thus:—Take a double-handful of flour, and mix it in water well with your hands till the water seems like milk; then strain it, leaving the dregs of the flour, and give what is liquid to the colt to drink.

' "Be careful from the hour he is born to let him stand in the sun; shade hurts horses, but let him have water in plenty when the day is hot.

' "The colt must now be mounted, and taken by his owner everywhere with him, so that he shall see everything, and learn courage. He must be kept constantly in exercise, and never remain long at his manger. He should be taken on a journey, for work will fortify his limbs.

' "At three years old he should be trained to gallop. Then, if he be of true blood, he will not be left behind. Yalla!" '

GENERAL STUD BOOK

When J. Weatherby, Junior, published the first volume of *A General Stud Book* which has since become THE *General Stud Book* for all the world, it was already a hundred years after the end of the war in which Captain Byerly's Turk stallion served with such distinction, before serving all those mares with even greater distinction.

Some of the information which he had the foresight to include in his Introduction comprises all that we shall ever know about the founding fathers of the Thoroughbred race, for the sources from which he derived his notes have not all survived, and some of it was just oral family tradition. As he says in his preface, many horses constantly 'varied their titles with their owners' as they changed hands, and this gives some idea of the difficult problems of identity confronting the editor of this, the most comprehensive genealogical work the world has ever seen. This was sometimes

161. Detail of George Stubbs' *Race-horses belonging to the third Duke of Richmond at Exercise*, painted *c.* 1760–1.

complicated by political and social factors: for instance Curwen's Bay Barb was imported by a Cumbrian gentleman who was a Catholic, at a time when officially no Catholic might own a horse of more than five pounds value. Consequently he stood for a long time, mainly in Lincolnshire, as somebody else's Bay Barb.

These biographical notes also bring out very clearly the influence of the early imports outside the charmed circle of what was soon to become the fixed Thorough-bred breed: notably in the North Country, where Curwen's horse covered so many pony mares whose foals grew into 'very high-formed galloways'. Such matings are for the most part unrecorded but they must

have been far more numerous than those with the foundation mares of the Thoroughbred race, who were few in number; and they had an enormous influence on the development of British light horse stock in the mass as opposed to the élite of the race-course.

ARABIANS, BARBS AND TURKS

Place's White Turk, was the property of Mr. Place, Stud-master to Oliver Cromwell, when Protector, and was the sire of Wormwood, Commoner, and the great grand dams of Windham, Grey Ramsden, and Cartouch. *Royal Mares.* King Charles the Second sent abroad the master of the horses, to procure a number of foreign

162. *The Jockey*—
Toulouse-Lautrec's
impression of a race,
which clearly shows the
jockey's 'seat'—almost a
'stance'.

163. *The Three Younger
Sons of Shah Jehan out
Riding*, by Balchard.

165. *The Derby at Epsom* by Théodore Géricault. The 'flying gallop' is an artistic convention, not a real-life gait, but very useful nevertheless, having been exploited by the earliest oriental artists and by Bushmen in the last phase of South African rock painting.

164. In the age of Philip IV of Spain the boar hunt had become a ceremony more comparable with the Roman amphitheatre than the bull ring, largely an opportunity to display the dexterity of the lancer and the handiness of the Andalusian war-horses. Venery was nowhere; but this picture abounds in examples of the old-style Andalusian and of the mules which in Spain drew coaches and were bred out of Andalusian mares by Catalan jackasses. (Detail from *The Boar Hunt* by Velasquez)

horses and mares for breeding, and the mares brought over by him, (as also many of their produce) have since been called Royal Mares. . . .

Byerly Turk, was Captain Byerly's charger in Ireland, in King William's wars (1689, &c.) He did not cover many bred mares, but was the sire of the D. of Kingston's Sprite, who was thought nearly as good as Leedes; the D. of Rutland's Black-Hearty and Archer, the D. of Devonshire's Basto, Ld Bristol's Grasshopper, and Ld Godolphin's Byerly Gelding, all in good forms; Halloway's Jig, a middling horse; and Knightley's Mare, in a very good form. . . .

Curwen's Bay Barb, was a present to Lewis the Fourteenth from Muly Isamael, King of Morocco, and was brought into England by Mr. Curwen, who, being in France when Count Byram, and Count Thoulouse (two natural sons of Lewis the Fourteenth) were, the former, master of the horse, and the latter an admiral, he procured of them two Barb Horses, both of which proved most excellent stallions, and are well known by the names of the *Curwen Bay Barb*, and the *Thoulouse Barb*. Curwen's Bay Barb got Mixbury and Tantivy, both very high-formed galloways, the first of them was only thirteen hands two inches high, and yet there were not more than two horses of his time that could beat him, at light weights; Brocklesby, Little George, Yellow Jack, Bay Jack, Monkey, Dangerfield, Hip, Peacock, and Flatface, the first two in good forms, the rest middling; two Mixburys, full brothers to the first Mixbury, middling galloways; Long Meg, Brocklesby

166. Peytona and Fashion
in their Great Match for
$20,000 over the Union
Course, Long Island, 13
May 1845. Lithograph by
N. Currier. Artist,
C. Severin.

Betty, and Creeping Molly, extraordinary high-formed mares; Whiteneck, Mistake, Sparkler, and Lightfoot, very good mares; and several middling galloways, who ran for plates in the North. He got two full sisters to Mixbury, one of which bred Partner, Little Scar, Soreheels, and the dam of Crab; the other was the dam of Quiet, Silver Eye, and Hazard. He did not cover many mares except Mr. Curwen's and Mr. Pelham's. . . .

Darley's Arabian, was brought over by a brother of Mr. Darley, of Yorkshire, who being an agent in merchandise abroad, became member of an hunting club, by which means he acquired interest to procure this horse. He was sire of Childers, and also got Almanzor, a very good horse; a white legged horse of the D. of Somerset's, full brother to Almanzor, and thought to be as good, but meeting with an accident, he never ran in public; Cupid and Brisk, good horses; Daedalus, a very fleet horse; Dart, Skipjack, Manica, and Aleppo, good plate horses, though out of bad mares; Ld Lonsdale's mare, in a very good form; and Ld Tracy's mare, in a good one for plates. He covered very few mares except Mr. Darley's, who had very few well bred besides Almanzor's dam. . . .

Belgrade Turk, was taken at the siege of Belgrade, by General Merci, and sent by him to the Prince de Craon, from whom he was a present to the Prince of Loraine: he was afterwards purchased by Sir Marmaduke Wyvill, and died in his possession about 1740. . . .

Godolphin Arabian. Of this valuable stallion (strange as it will undoubtedly appear) scarce any records are extant; all that can be discovered, after strict enquiry, is, that he was a brown horse, about fifteen hands high, that he was first the property of Mr. Coke, and given by him to Mr. Roger Williams, keeper of the St. James's Coffee-House, by whom he was presented to Ld Godolphin, and that he continued in his Lordship's possession, as a private stallion, till his death. To those who are thoroughly conversant with the Turf, it would be superfluous to remark, that he undoubtedly contributed more to the improvement of the breed of horses in this country, than any stallion before or since his time: it would be equally unnecessary to enumerate his get: to those who are less acquainted with the annals of racing, the names of Cade, Regulus, Blank, Babraham, and Bajazet, may serve as a proof of the remark; and it may not be amiss to observe, that almost (if not entirely so) every *superior* horse of the present day, partakes of his valuable blood.—He died at Hogmagog, in 1753, in the 29th year of his age, and is buried in a covered passage, leading to the stable, with a flat stone over him, without any inscription.—In regard to his pedigree, from all that can be collected, none was brought over with him, as it was said, and generally believed he was stolen.—It may appear trifling to notice the extraordinary affection shewn by this horse to a cat, who lived in his stable, which was more particularly manifested by his extreme inquietude on the death of that animal. We mention this circumstance merely to account for the introduction of a cat in the portrait of the Godolphin Arabian, to which the reader is referred for an accurate representation of him.

167. *The Charge of the Scots Greys at Waterloo* by Lady Butler. This shows what Captain Bluntschli meant, in Shaw's *Arms and the Man*, by saying that the commonest wounds in cavalry charges were broken knees among troopers.

ARAB BLOOD IN AMERICA

The 1849 (Boston) edition of William Youatt's *The Horse* contained a great deal of matter specially added for the benefit of the American reader.

From this we reproduce one extract concerning what seems to be the first direct introduction of Arabian blood into American horse-breeding.

The second concerns that All-American speciality, the Standardbred racing trotter, whose public performances are, quantitatively, a more important spectator-sport than flat-racing or steeple-chasing in the United States, as also in some European countries and in New

Zealand, that most anglicized of all Commonwealth countries. The only foundation sire of Standardbreds was Messenger, son of the Thoroughbred Mambrino who traced back to the Darley Arabian and was one of the most Arabian-looking British race-horses of his day, if we are to take Stubbs's portrait of him seriously. Messenger also traced back to Marske and Eclipse, ultimately to the Darley Arabian.

The American editor of Youatt points out the peculiar social (and to some extent political) influences which favoured the trotter rather than the flat-racer in America from Revolutionary times onward. But also,

something must be ascribed to the regional traditions of the earlier English settlers. Of these, the majority came from the region between Suffolk and Lincolnshire, and it is precisely in this area around the Wash that the trotting horse was most successfully bred and held in the greatest esteem: indeed the Norfolk Trotter was at the height of its prestige in Messenger's lifetime. The majority of mares at the root of American Trotter pedigrees were called Canadian: they came from the Province of Quebec and were in fact of Norman origin, like the Quebec *habitants* themselves: and the Norman horse was famous for its trotting powers, as was the

168. The celebrated horse Lexington, showing, in the head, the largely Arabian ancestry of the American Standard-bred trotter. By Louis Maurer; lithograph by N. Currier, 1855.

169. The thoroughbred Mambrino was a descendant of the Flying Childers. His son Messenger was exported to the United States at about the time of Independence, and became the sire not only of celebrated American race-horses like Man o'War but also of an entire breed of trotting horses, the Standard-bred harness race-horses. (*Mambrino* by George Stubbs)

only other considerable element in the Quebec horse-stock—the *postier breton*, a hard-trotting roadster or cob type from Finisterre.

❀In *cavalry*, perhaps more than in any other weapon, our locality must always give us an advantage over any invading force. An enemy cannot bring cavalry with him. With something like a well arranged system in breeding our horses, this advantage may be turned to great account in time of war. With the forecast that distinguished his military administration, Napoleon had the sagacity to establish *Haras*, or studs, in the several departments of France, where thorough-bred stallions were placed at the service of the common farmer, on terms which barely paid the expense of their keep. But to come nearer home, while every one at all familiar with the incidents of our own Revolution, knows how much was effected in the South, by Lee's famous 'Legion'; few, comparatively, may be aware to what that celebrated corps chiefly owed its efficiency— and yet it is undeniable that in a great measure the *prevalence of blood in his horses* made it at once the scourge and the terror of the enemy. . . .

It was not, however, generally known, until the Repository offered by the 'TURF REGISTER' for the record of all extraordinary facts connected with these subjects, that to the remarkably accidental importation of the celebrated *Lindsey's Arabian* may

170. *The Celebrated American Trotting Horse Tom Thumb*, by E. J. Lambert, showing a racing sulky or 'machine'.

be traced some brilliant exploits of the battle-field, as well as of the turf in America. The curious history of that renowned Arabian is worthy of preservation here, as it was thus related to the editor, by a meritorious Maryland officer of the Revolution, the venerable General T. M. Forman, a yet living monument of the 'times that tried men's souls.' . . .

For some very important service, rendered by the Commander of a British frigate, to a son of the then Emperor of Morocco, the Emperor presented this horse (the most valuable of his stud) to the Captain, who shipped him on board the frigate, with the sanguine expectation of obtaining a great price for him, if

safely landed in England. Either in obedience to orders, or from some other cause, the frigate called at one of the English *West India* islands, where being obliged to remain some time, the Captain, in compassion to the horse, landed him for the purpose of exercise. No convenient securely inclosed place could be found but a large lumber-yard, into which the horse was turned loose; but delighted and playful as a kitten, his liberty soon proved nearly fatal to him. He ascended one of the piles, from which and with it he fell, and broke three of his legs. At this time in the same harbour, the English Captain met with an old acquaintance from one of our now Eastern states. To him he offered the horse, as an animal of inestimable value could he be cured. The Eastern Captain gladly accepted the horse, and knowing he must be detained a considerable time in the Island before he could dispose of his assorted cargo, got the horse on board his vessel, secured him in slings, and very carefully set and bound up his broken legs. It matters not how long he remained in the harbour, or if quite cured before he arrived on our shore; but he did arrive, and he must certainly have covered several seasons, before he was noticed as first mentioned. . . .

In Connecticut (I think) this horse was called Ranger; in Virginia (as it should be) he was called Lindsey's Arabian [after the captain who purchased him for the cavalry stud in about 1778]. He was the sire of Tulip and many good runners; to all his stock he gave great perfection of form; and his blood flows in the veins of some of the best horses of the present day.

EXTRAORDINARY TROTTING MATCH
A trotting match, for $1000 a-side, Three mile heats, under the saddle, came off on Saturday, Oct. 6, 1838, at 4 o'clock, over the Beacon Course, opposite this city. The annals of the turf furnish no parallel to it; every foot of the ground was severely contested, and the time made is by far the best on record.

Dutchman and Rattler were the contending horses; the first is a handsome bay gelding, of great size and substance, about 16 hands high; he is what is termed 'a meaty horse', and looks, when in fine condition, like an ordinary roadster in 'good order'. He was trained for the match and ridden by Hiram Woodruff. Rattler is a brown gelding, of about 15½ hands, and 'a rum 'un to look at'; he was drawn very fine, though one of those that seldom carry an ounce of superfluous flesh; we hear that his feed of late has seldom exceeded six quarts per day, while Dutchman's has been between twelve and sixteen. Rattler was trained and ridden by William Wheelan. His style of going is superior to Dutchman's; he spreads himself well, and strikes out clear and even. Dutchman does not appear to have perfect command of his hind legs; instead of throwing them forward, he raises them so high as to throw up his rump, and consequently falls short in his stride. The main dependence of his backers was based upon his

game; and a gentleman who 'put on the pot' to a heavy amount on Rattler, offered 2 to 1 on Dutchman before the start, provided the heats were broken.

The odds before the horses came upon the track were 5 to 4 on Dutchman; after the riders were up, 5 to 3 was current, and at length 2 to 1. As they were ridden up and down in front of the stand previous to starting, both appeared to be in superb condition, and to have their action perfectly. . . .

The Race. Rattler drew the track, but resigned it to Dutchman on the first quarter; he came in front on the backside, and at the half-mile post led by two lengths; he soon after broke up, when Dutchman headed him and led past the stand (2:42) round to the straight stretch on the backside, where the ground being descending, and more favourable to him, Rattler passed. Dutchman waited upon him, close up, to near the three-quarter mile post, where Rattler shook him off, and led past the stand (2:38) by four lengths; keeping up his rate, he led down the backside and round the turn to the straight stretch in front, where Hiram caught Dutchman by the head, and laid in the spurs up to the gaffs; the brush home was tremendous, but Rattler won by nearly a length, trotting the 3d mile in 2:34½, and the heat in 7:54½.

Second heat. Dutchman broke at starting, and 2 to 1 was offered against him. Down the backside the horses were lapped all the way; on the ascending ground, within about ten rods of the half-mile post, Dutchman gained a little, and came first to the stand (2:37). He drew out two lengths ahead round the 1st turn on the 2d mile, but Rattler gallantly challenged him down the backside and lapped him; at the half-mile post Dutchman was again clear, but by a desperate effort Rattler lapped him when they got into straight work in front, and thus they came to the stand (2:33). On the backside Rattler, as usual, drew out clear, but for an instant only; the spurs were well laid into D., and the struggle was desperate; Dutchman hung upon Rattler's quarter, and gradually gained to the half-mile post, when they were locked as perfectly as if in double harness. The contest was almost too much for Rattler, who skipped several times, and was only prevented from breaking by Bill's holding him up. They came up the quarter stretch at an immense pace, but opposite the four mile distance stand, Rattler unfortunately broke up, when nearly a length ahead, and Dutchman won the heat by six or eight lengths. When Rattler skipped, Wheelan should have taken him in hand, but he was so much ahead, and so near home, (within 180 yards,) that under the intense excitement of the moment, he neglected doing so; had he done so, however, at the rate Dutchman was going he would probably have won by a few feet, for Rattler could not have made up any lee-way, caused by pulling him up; nothing but his breaking lost him the heat. The instant Rattler broke, Hiram pulled up Dutchman, and he would have walked out had not the people in the stand called out to him to 'come on'. The last mile was performed in 2:40, and the heat in 7:50; had Dutchman kept up his stroke, the time of the heat would have been 7:48.

Third heat. Dutchman went off with a fine stride (2 to 1 offered on him) and led about half-way down the backside, when Rattler caught him; at the half mile post they were locked, and thus they came to the stand (in 2:42); they made the turn in the same position, and nothing but repeated injunctions from the Judges to keep silent, prevented cheers from the stands that would have made the welkin ring; it was a beautiful sight; both were going, D. under the spur, at a flight of speed, neck and neck; half-way down the backside, Rattler got almost clear, but Dutchman soon after lapped, and when they came to the stand (2:38½) was half a length ahead. When they got into straight work

on the backside, Rattler again collared him, and they went locked to near the half mile post, when Dutchman once more got in front, Wheelan having taken Rattler in hand for a brush up the straight side. This he made soon after; they were lapped as they swung round the turn, and the struggle that ensued revived recollections of *Bascombe* and *Post-Boy*. Profound silence was preserved on the stand, that neither horse might be excited or frightened into a break, and the interest of the scene was so great, that each of the spectators seemed to hold his breath as the horses neared the stand; it was a brush to the end, Dutchman coming out a throatlatch in front, caused by Hiram's giving up his pull, and giving him a push *à la Chifney*, which made him clearly the winner by a foot. The excited feelings of the crowd in the stand could no longer be repressed, but burst out in a tumultuous cheer that might have been heard three miles off. The last mile was done in 2:41½, and the heat in 8:02. The Judges, after some discussion, pronounced it a *dead heat*. . . .

Fourth heat. Dutchman led off from the score to half-way down the backside, by three lengths; Rattler, however, lapped him at the half mile post, but Dutchman soon after drew out in front again; Hiram kept him at his work from this point to the finish, and Rattler never got up to him afterwards, that we could *see*, for it was now so dark, neither horse nor rider could be distinguished; Rattler subsequently fell off in his stride, and was finally beaten handily by six lengths, after as game and honest a race as we ever saw, and by far the best, in point of time, on record.

THE ENGLISH MAIL-COACH

'The modern modes of travelling cannot compare with the old mail-coach system in grandeur and power', wrote De Quincey elsewhere in this essay of which we quote extracts. De Quincey's essay is already retrospective, and it so happens that the writing of grandeur and power on this subject was all done after the mail-coach had surrendered to its competitor the railway, or come to terms more humiliating than those on which the railway now co-exists with the airliner. But still the railway depended for its 'feeders' on horse-drawn vehicles, and this was fittingly symbolized at the re-opening, under private enterprise, of the Whitby–Pickering Railway at Easter 1973, when the royal party were taken to the station in a carriage behind a team of Cleveland Bays. This line, or rather the private sector between Grosmont and Goathland, now steam-operated, is a reminder that a compromise once existed. For the first decades of its existence its carriages ran on rails but were horse-drawn.

171. The coach in the Low Countries, bodywork predominantly of leather. (*Landscape With a Carriage* by S. Ruysdael, 1606–70)

172. *His Majesty King George IV travelling*, by James Pollard Junior, 1821. It was in the reign of this monarch that English coaching reached its apogee.

173. *The London and Dartford Stage*, an early nineteenth-century coaching print. Only macadamized roads made this light construction, and the use of blood-type horses, possible.

174. Pulling up to unskid. The driver in this coaching print is about to remove the skid, used for steep downhill gradients, from the rear wheel.

✻Some twenty or more years before I matriculated at Oxford, Mr. Palmer, at that time M.P. for Bath, had accomplished two things, very hard to do on our little planet, the Earth, however cheap they may be held by eccentric people in comets—he had invented mail-coaches, and he had married the daughter of a duke. . . .

These mail-coaches, as organized by Mr. Palmer, are entitled to a circumstantial notice from myself, having had so large a share in developing the anarchies of my subsequent dreams; an agency which they accomplished, first, through velocity, at that time unprecedented—for they first revealed the glory of motion; secondly, through grand effects for the eye between lamp-light and the darkness upon solitary roads; thirdly, through animal beauty and power so often displayed in the class of horses selected for this mail service; fourthly, through the conscious presence of a central intellect, that, in the midst of vast distances—of storms, of darkness, of danger—over-ruled all obstacles into one steady co-operation to a national result. For my own feeling, this post-office service spoke as by some mighty orchestra, where a thousand instruments, all disregarding each other, and so far in danger of discord, yet all obedient as slaves to the supreme *baton* of some great leader, terminate in a perfection of harmony like that of heart, brain, and lungs, in a healthy animal organization. But,

finally, that particular element in this whole combination which most impressed myself, and through which it is that to this hour Mr. Palmer's mail-coach system tyrannies over my dreams by terror and terrific beauty, lay in the awful *political* mission which at that time it fulfilled. The mail-coach it was that distributed over the face of the land, like the opening of apocalyptic vials, the heart-shaking news of Trafalgar, of Salamanca, of Vittoria, of Waterloo. . . .

The mail-coach, as the national organ for publishing these mighty events thus diffusively influential, became itself a spiritualized and glorified object to an impassioned heart; and naturally, in the Oxford of that day, *all* hearts were impassioned, as being all (or nearly all) in *early* manhood. In most universities there is one single college; in Oxford there were five-and-twenty, all of which were peopled by young men, the *élite* of their own generation; not boys, but men; none under eighteen. In some of these many colleges, the custom permitted the student to keep what are called 'short terms'; that is, the four terms of Michaelmas, Lent, Easter, and Act, were kept by a residence, in the aggregate, of ninety-one days, or thirteen weeks. Under this interrupted residence, it was possible that a student might have a reason for going down to his home four times in the year. This made eight journeys to and fro.

But, as these homes lay dispersed through all the shires of the island, and most of us disdained all coaches except his majesty's mail, no city out of London could pretend to so extensive a connection with Mr. Palmer's establishment as Oxford. Three mails, at the least, I remember as passing every day through Oxford, and benefiting by my personal patronage—viz., the Worcester, the Gloucester, and the Holyhead mail. Naturally, therefore, it became a point of some interest with us, whose journeys revolved every six weeks on an average, to look a little into the executive details of the system. With some of these Mr. Palmer had no concern; they rested upon bye-laws enacted by posting-houses for their own benefit, and upon other bye-laws, equally stern, enacted by the inside passengers for the illustration of their own haughty exclusiveness. These last were of a nature to rouse our scorn, from which the transition was not very long to systematic mutiny. Up to this time, say 1804, or 1805 (the year of Trafalgar), it had been the fixed assumption of the four inside people (as an old tradition of all public carriages derived from the reign of Charles II), that they, the illustrious quaternion, constituted a porcelain variety of the human race, whose dignity would have been compromised by exchanging one word of civility with the three miserable delfware outsides. Even to have kicked an outsider, might have been held to attaint the foot concerned in that operation; so that, perhaps, it would have required an act of Parliament to restore its purity of blood. What words, then, could express the horror, and the sense of treason, in that case, which *had* happened, where all three outsides (the trinity of Pariahs) made a vain attempt to sit down at the same breakfast-table or dinner-table with the consecrated four? I myself witnessed such an attempt; and on that occasion a benevolent old gentleman endeavoured to soothe his three holy associates, by suggesting that, if the outsides were indicted for this criminal attempt at the next assizes, the court would regard it as a case of lunacy, or *delirium tremens*, rather than of treason. . . .

No dignity is perfect which does not at some point ally itself with the mysterious. The connection of the mail with the state and the executive government—a connection obvious, but yet not strictly defined—gave to the whole mail establishment an official grandeur which did us service on the roads, and invested us with seasonable terrors. Not the less impressive were those terrors, because their legal limits were imperfectly ascertained. Look at those turnpike gates; with what deferential hurry, with what an obedient start, they fly open at our approach! Look at that long line of carts and carters ahead, audaciously usurping the very crest of the road. Ah! traitors, they do not hear us as yet; but, as soon as the dreadful blast of our horn reaches them with proclamation of our approach, see with what frenzy of trepidation they fly to their horses' heads, and deprecate our wrath by the precipitation of their crane-neck quarterings. . . .

Sometimes after breakfast his majesty's mail would become frisky; and in its difficult wheelings amongst

175. *The Louth mail stopt by the snow, assistance in prospect but not the time to hesitate, the letter bags sent forward with the guard in a post chaise and four.* By James Pollard Junior, 1836.

176. *James Selby's Brighton Coach*, 1888–9, by A. S. Bishop.

the intricacies of early markets, it would upset an apple-cart, a cart loaded with eggs, etc. Huge was the affliction and dismay, awful was the smash. I, as far as possible, endeavoured in such a case to represent the conscience and moral sensibilities of the mail; and, when wildernesses of eggs were lying poached under our horses' hoofs, then would I stretch forth my hands in sorrow, saying (in words too celebrated at that time, from the false echoes of Marengo), 'Ah! wherefore have we not time to weep over you?' which was evidently impossible, since, in fact, we had not time to laugh over them. Tied to post-office allowance, in some cases of fifty minutes for eleven miles, could the royal mail pretend to undertake the offices of sympathy and condolence? Could it be expected to provide tears for the accidents of the road? If even it seemed to trample on humanity, it did so, I felt, in discharge of its own more peremptory duties.

Upholding the morality of the mail, *a fortiori* I upheld its rights . . . Once I remember being on the box of the Holyhead mail, between Shrewsbury and Oswestry, when a tawdry thing from Birmingham, some 'Tallyho' or 'Highflyer', all flaunting with green and gold, came up alongside of us. What a contrast to our royal simplicity of form and colour in this plebeian wretch! The single ornament on our dark ground of chocolate colour was the mighty shield of the imperial arms, but emblazoned in proportions as modest as a signet-ring bears to a seal of office. Even this was displayed only on a single pannel, whispering, rather than proclaiming, our relations to the mighty state; whilst the beast from Birmingham, our green-and-gold friend from false, fleeting, perjured Brummagem, had as much writing and painting on its sprawling flanks as would have puzzled a decipherer from the tombs of Luxor. For some time this Birmingham machine ran along by our side—a piece of familiarity that already of itself seemed to me sufficiently jacobinical. But all at once a movement of the horses announced a desperate intention of leaving us behind. 'Do you see *that?*' I said to the coachman.—'I see,' was his short answer. He was wide awake, yet he waited longer than seemed prudent; for the horses of our audacious opponent had a disagreeable air of freshness and power. But his motive was loyal; his wish was, that the Birmingham conceit should be full-blown before he froze it. When *that* seemed right, he unloosed, or, to speak by a stronger word, he *sprang*, his known resources: he slipped our royal horses like cheetahs, or hunting-leopards, after the affrighted game. How they could retain such a reserve of fiery power after the work they had accomplished, seemed hard to explain. But on our side, besides the physical superiority, was a tower of moral strength, namely, the king's name, 'which they upon the adverse faction wanted'. Passing them without an effort, as it seemed, we threw them into the rear with so lengthening an interval between us, as proved in itself the bitterest mockery of their presumption; whilst our guard blew back a shattering blast of triumph, that was really too painfully full of derision.

177. The North Yorkshire waggon—a load of paving-stones drawn by four horses in tandem. The path on which the waggoner is standing is the old packhorse 'trod', predating the road. Nineteenth-century photograph by Frank Meadow Sutcliffe.

178. While the road in Europe and America saw the development of wheeled transport in the eighteenth and nineteenth centuries, in Japan it was the domain of the pack-horse. This print by Keisi Yeisen (1792–1848) shows packhorses and porters travelling past Mount Fuji.

THE OVERLAND CONDUCTOR

What the Americans called a stage-coach was in fact the English mail-coach all over again, its life prolonged in the New World past the middle of the nineteenth century, whereas in Britain its doom was sealed from the moment that mails were first loaded on to a railway train. Only it took longer to build railways from the Atlantic to the Pacific than from London to Thurso or Falmouth. And there were no hostile redskins beyond the Tyne or the Tamar.

The excellence of the American service was of the same order as the British. It was not so much the high quality of the material, or of the personnel, as the meticulous organization of routes and relays and the reliable quartermastership in general: and all achieved by capitalistic enterprise with not an atom of governmental assistance in either case.

Our new conductor (just shipped) had been without sleep for twenty hours. Such a thing was very frequent. From St. Joseph, Missouri, to Sacramento, California, by stage-coach, was nearly nineteen hundred miles, and the trip was often made in fifteen days (the cars do it in four and a half, now), but the time specified in the mail contracts, and required by the schedule, was eighteen or nineteen days, if I remember rightly. This was to make fair allowance for winter storms and snows, and other unavoidable causes of detention. The stage company had everything under strict discipline and good system. Over each two hundred and fifty miles of road they placed an agent or superintendent, and invested him with great authority. His beat or jurisdiction of two hundred and fifty miles was called a 'division'. He purchased horses, mules harness, and food for men and beasts, and distributed these things among his stage stations, from time to time, according to his judgment of what each station needed. He erected station buildings and dug wells. He attended to the paying of the station-keepers, hostlers, drivers and blacksmiths, and discharged them whenever he chose. He was a very, very great man in his 'division'—a kind of Grand Mogul, a Sultan of the Indies, in whose presence common men were modest of speech and manner, and

in the glare of whose greatness even the dazzling stage-driver dwindled to a penny dip. There were about eight of these kings, all told, on the overland route.

Next in rank and importance to the division-agent came the 'conductor'. His beat was the same length as the agent's—two hundred and fifty miles. He sat with the driver, and (when necessary) rode that fearful distance, night and day, without other rest or sleep than what he could get perched thus on top of the flying vehicle. Think of it! He had absolute charge of the mails, express matter, passengers and stage-coach, until he delivered them to the next conductor, and got his receipt for them.

Consequently he had to be a man of intelligence, decision and considerable executive ability. He was usually a quiet, pleasant man, who attended closely to his duties, and was a good deal of a gentleman. It was not absolutely necessary that the division-agent should be a gentleman, and occasionally he wasn't. But he was always a general in administrative ability, and a bull-dog in courage and determination—otherwise the chieftainship over the lawless underlings of the overland service would never in any instance have been to him anything but an equivalent for a month of insolence and distress and a bullet and a coffin at the end of it. There were about sixteen or eighteen conductors on the overland, for there was a daily stage each way, and a conductor on every stage.

Next in *real* and official rank and importance, *after* the conductor, came my delight, the driver—next in real but not in *apparent* importance—for we have seen that in the eyes of the common herd the driver was to the conductor as an admiral is to the captain of the flag-ship. The driver's beat was pretty long, and his sleeping-time at the stations pretty short, sometimes; and so, but for the grandeur of his position his would have been a sorry life, as well as a hard and a wearing one. We took a new driver every day or every night (for they drove backward and forward over the same piece of road all the time), and therefore we never got as well acquainted with them as we did with the conductors; and besides, they would have been above being familiar with such rubbish as passengers, anyhow, as a general thing. Still, we were always eager to get a sight of each and every new driver as soon as the watch changed, for each and every day we were either anxious to get rid of an unpleasant one, or loath to part with a driver we had learned to like and had come to be sociable and friendly with. And so the first question we asked the conductor whenever we got to where we were to exchange drivers, was always, 'Which is him?' The grammar was faulty, maybe, but we could not know, then, that it would go into a book some day. As long as everything went smoothly, the overland driver was well enough situated, but if a fellow driver got sick suddenly it made trouble, for the coach *must* go on, and so the potentate who was about to climb down and take a luxurious rest after his long night's siege in the midst of wind and rain and darkness, had to stay where he was and do the sick man's work. Once, in the Rocky Mountains, when I found a driver sound asleep on the box, and the mules going at the usual break-neck pace, the conductor said never mind him, there was no danger, and he was doing double-duty—had driven seventy-five miles on one coach, and was now going back over it on this without rest or sleep. A hundred and fifty miles of holding back of six vindictive mules and keeping them from climbing the trees! It sounds incredible, but I remember the statement well enough.

The station-keepers, hostlers, etc., were low, rough characters, as already described; and from western Nebraska to Nevada a considerable sprinkling of them might be fairly set down as outlaws—fugitives from justice, criminals whose best security was a section of country which was without law and without even the pretence of it. When the 'division-agent' issued an order to one of these parties he did it with the full understanding that he might have to enforce it with a navy six-shooter, and so he always went 'fixed' to make things go along smoothly. Now and then a division-agent was really obliged to shoot a hostler through the head to teach him some simple matter that he could have taught him with a club if his circumstances and surroundings had been different. But they were snappy, able men, those division-agents, and when they tried to teach a subordinate anything, that subordinate generally 'got it through his head'.

Mark Twain, *Roughing It*, 1872

PONY EXPRESS

The story of the mail is a long one. All postal services began as royal messenger organizations, and from early times the monarch might show favour to a subject by allowing him or his messages to travel by the royal post. The last relic of this, the privilege of 'franking' letters, survived in England as a form of patronage until the early nineteenth century. At what period it first occurred to a government to defray the expense of its private information service by conveying mail for a fee is not known, but certainly the Roman *cursus publicus* in the West, which was primarily for official use, did convey paying passengers and private missives. Procopius, writing of the *cursus publicus* in the Eastern Empire under Justinian, regards it primarily as a means of conveying official messages and places it in the same category as the military intelligence system.

The mail system of the Empire from the time of Augustus onwards was predominantly a vehicular one. Over most of the stages it was carried in a two-horse vehicle not unlike the 'post chaise' of much more recent times. In some provinces, however, the nature of the roads was such that the Imperial messengers had to ride post. Both the original Persian messengers and those of Alexander's successors who took over from them were riding posts according to Herodotus; so also were the Mongol couriers described by Marco Polo. The Royal Mail in England was carried on horseback until 1784.

The service described by Mark Twain (again in *Roughing It*) in fact ran only for two years—in 1860 and 1861—and closed down as a financial failure, despite the high fees charged, when a combination of rail and telegraph was about to make it redundant. The Overland Route, from St Joseph to Sacramento, was, by British standards, on a vast scale—almost exactly ten times the distance from London to York, for which the record coach time was 22 hours.

Twain was wrong about weapons. Most pony-riders *were* armed with a carbine and two revolvers. Otherwise they would have been dead men, in Indian country. These weapons and the ammunition weighed far more than all the rest of their equipment.

179. *Whistlejacket*, the race-horse, probably the most beautiful animal ever painted by Stubbs in all the glory of his full mane and tail, his mood expressed by the cocked position of the ears, unmutilated.

180. One of Thomas Rowlandson's hunting scenes (*The Kill*, 1787).

181. *Stage coach in flight* by Frederic Remington.

182. Heavy horses at heavy labour—
an etching by L. D. Luard.

In a little while all interest was taken up in stretching our necks and watching for the 'pony-rider'—the fleet messenger who sped across the continent from St. Joe to Sacramento, carrying letters nineteen hundred miles in eight days! Think of that for perishable horse and human flesh and blood to do! The pony-rider was usually a little bit of a man, brimful of spirit and endurance. No matter what time of the day or night his watch came on, and no matter whether it was winter or summer, raining, snowing, hailing, or sleeting, or whether his 'beat' was a level straight road or a crazy trail over mountain crags and precipices, or whether it led through peaceful regions or regions that swarmed with hostile Indians, he must be always ready to leap into the saddle and be off like the wind! There was no idling-time for a pony-rider on duty. He rode fifty miles

183. 'Here he comes'.

without stopping, by daylight, moonlight, starlight, or through the blackness of darkness—just as it happened. He rode a splendid horse that was born for a racer and fed and lodged like a gentleman; kept him at his utmost speed for ten miles, and then, as he came crashing up to the station where stood two men holding fast a fresh, impatient steed, the transfer of rider and mail-bag was made in the twinkling of an eye, and away flew the eager pair and were out of sight before the spectator could

hardly get the ghost of a look. Both rider and horse went 'flying light'. The rider's dress was thin, and fitted close; he wore a 'round-about', and a skull-cap, and tucked his pantaloons into his boot-tops like a race-rider. He carried no arms—he carried nothing that was not absolutely necessary, for even the postage on his literary freight was worth *five dollars a letter*. He got but little frivolous correspondence to carry—his bag had business letters in it, mostly. His horse was stripped of all unnecessary weight, too. He wore a little wafer of a racing-saddle, and no visible blanket. He wore light shoes, or none at all. The little flat mail-pockets strapped under the rider's thighs would each hold about the bulk of a child's primer. They held many and many an important business chapter and newspaper letter, but these were written on paper as airy and thin as gold-leaf, nearly, and thus bulk and weight were economized. The stage-coach travelled about a hundred to a hundred and twenty-five miles a day (twenty-four hours), the pony-rider about two hundred and fifty. There were about eighty pony-riders in the saddle all the time, night and day, stretching in a long, scattering procession from Missouri to California, forty flying eastward, and forty toward the west, and among them making four hundred gallant horses earn a stirring livelihood and see a deal of scenery every single day in the year.

We had had a consuming desire, from the beginning, to see a pony-rider, but somehow or other all that passed us and all that met us managed to streak by in the night, and so we heard only a whiz and a hail, and the swift phantom of the desert was gone before we could get our heads out of the windows. But now we were expecting one along every moment, and would see him in broad daylight. Presently the driver exclaims: *'HERE HE COMES!'*

Every neck is stretched further, and every eye strained wider. Away across the endless dead level of the prairie a black speck appears against the sky, and it is plain that it moves. Well, I should think so! In a second or two it becomes a horse and rider, rising and falling, rising and falling, sweeping toward us nearer and nearer—growing more and more distinct, more and more sharply defined—nearer and still nearer, and the flutter of the hoofs comes faintly to the ear—another instant a whoop and a hurrah from our upper deck, a wave of the rider's hand, but no reply, and man and horse burst past our excited faces, and go winging away like a belated fragment of a storm!

So sudden is it all, and so like a flash of unreal fancy, that but for the flake of white foam left quivering and perishing on a mail-sack after the vision had flashed by and disappeared, we might have doubted whether we had seen any actual horse and man at all, maybe. . . .

We passed Fort Laramie in the night, and on the seventh morning out we found ourselves in the Black Hills, with Laramie Peak at our elbow (apparently) looming vast and solitary—a deep, dark, rich indigo blue in hue, so portentously did the old colossus frown under his beetling brows of storm-cloud. He was thirty or forty miles away, in reality, but he only seemed removed a little beyond the low ridge at our right. We breakfasted at Horse-Shoe Station, six hundred and seventy-six miles out from St. Joseph. We had now reached a hostile Indian country, and during the afternoon we passed Laparelle Station, and enjoyed great discomfort all the time we were in the neighbourhood, being aware that many of the trees we dashed by at arm's length concealed a lurking Indian or two. During the preceding night an ambushed savage had sent a bullet through the pony-rider's jacket, but he had ridden on, just the same, because pony-riders were not allowed to stop and inquire into such things except when killed. As long as they had life enough left in them they had to stick to the horse and ride, even if the Indians had been waiting for them a week, and were entirely out of patience. About two hours and a half before we arrived at Laparelle Station, the keeper in charge of it had fired four times at an Indian, but he said with an injured air that the Indian had 'skipped around so's to spile everything—and ammunition's blamed skurse, too.' The most natural inference conveyed by his manner of speaking was, that in 'skipping around', the Indian had taken an unfair advantage. The coach we were in had a neat hole through its front—a reminiscence of its last trip through this region. The bullet that made it wounded the driver slightly, but he did not mind it much. He said the place to keep a man 'huffy' was down on the Southern Overland, among the Apaches, before the company moved the stage-line up on the northern route. He said the Apaches used to annoy him all the time down there, and that he came as near as anything to starving to death in the midst of abundance, because they kept him so leaky with bullet holes that he 'couldn't hold his vittles'. This person's statements were not generally believed.

184. Changing horses.

MEDICINE DOG

Part of the value of eye-witness accounts such as Catlin's of the last days of independent life among the Plains Indians is that the same sort of episodes are being re-enacted, thousands of years later, as must have taken place in the Old World at the time of the migrations of the horseborne nomads and their clashes with the military forces of the sedentary agricultural and urban empires of antiquity. Only now it was the 'settled' white agriculturalists that were on the move, exerting intolerable pressure on the frontiers of the Red Man's hunting ground. The resemblance between the fully developed horse culture of the Amerindians and that of the nomads between Manchuria and Turkestan is the more remarkable since the horse had only played a part in Indian life for less than two centuries before Catlin's day, and in the case of some tribes for a much shorter period than that. Yet these Comanches thought and behaved as if they had many centuries or millennia of equestrian tradition behind them. One may compare the cavortings of their herald between the armies with the display put on by the Gothic King Totila (Chapter 3), and what Catlin called the 'most picturesque' mixture of dress and equipment in the column of US Cavalry troopers in sober blue uniform interspersed with motley-clad bands of Cherokee and Comanche allies and tributaries is reminiscent of a Roman *agmen* like Arrian's command in which the utilitarian dress of the regular Roman cohorts alternated with the barbaric costume of the Celtic or Numidian or Iberian auxiliaries and the no less barbaric trappings of their horses.

But more than that; it is clear enough from what Catlin says about the stampede from the horse-lines by night that this was one of the principal ways, if not *the* way, in which the mustang population of the Great Plains originated, and this too has its parallel in the Old World. There are areas outside the latitudes bounding the original habitat of the Wild Horse, notably the Arabian Peninsula, where archaeology can show no trace of an indigenous wild horse previous to the era of domestication. And yet there exists a strong local tradition of wild horses of the mountain or the desert, from among which some legendary culture-hero first tamed the horse in that region. The horses in question must have been feral horses, the equivalent of the American mustang or the Australian brumby, descendants of those stampeded from the picket lines of the Assyrian, Babylonian, Hittite or Egyptian invading columns in just this way, and brought back into human service by the Bedouin, perhaps after many generations. In just the same way the Plains Indians acquired horses less by actual capture from the palefaces than by picking up the wild progeny of horses which had strayed from settlements, mostly at a time when these were being raided by the Indians.

Noticeable throughout all accounts of the American West is the part played by the mule, not least in the traces of the stage-coach, and it is a pity that Catlin did not see fit to state whether the mules seen grazing among the Comanche stock had been stolen, traded for, or bred by the Comanche themselves.

The great difference between the equestrian Indian and the wandering horseborne Asiatic tribesman is of course that in the former case the horse is not an integral part of a stock-breeding economy. It remained, until the free Indian way of life died with Sitting Bull, the sole domestic animal apart from the dog. And like the dog it served purely as an aid to hunting, and by extension to warfare.

Our course was about due West, on the divide between the Washita and Red Rivers, with our faces looking towards the Rocky Mountains. The country over which we passed from day to day, was inimitably beautiful; being the whole way one continuous prairie of green fields, with occasional clusters of timber and shrubbery, just enough for the uses of cultivating-man, and for the pleasure of his eyes to dwell upon. The regiment was rather more than half on the move, consisting of 250 men, instead of 200 as I predicted in my Letter from that place . . . We advanced on happily, and met with no trouble until the second night of our encampment, in the midst of which we were thrown into 'pie' (as printers would say), in an instant of the most appalling alarm and confusion. We were encamped on a beautiful prairie, where we were every hour

185. The artistic convention of the 'flying gallop' showing all four legs extended, which is anatomically impossible, is common in early European art and lasted until the nineteenth century. The same convention was independently adopted by the Bushmen artists of South Africa and, as here, by the Plains Indians. (Painted buffalo robe: Cheyenne, Wyoming, 1850–75)

apprehensive of the lurking enemy. And in the dead of night, when all seemed to be sound asleep and quiet, the instant sound and flash of a gun within a few paces of us! and then the most horrid and frightful groans that instantly followed it, brought us all upon our hands and knees in an instant, and our affrighted horses (which were breaking their lasos), in full speed and fury over our heads, with a frightful and mingled din of snorting, and cries of 'Indians! Indians! Pawnees!' &c., which rang from every part of our little encampment! In a few moments the excitement was chiefly over, and silence restored; when we could hear the trampling hoofs of the horses, which were making off in all directions (not unlike a drove of swine that once ran into the sea, when they were possessed of devils); and leaving but now and then an individual quadruped hanging at its stake within our little camp. . . .

After an instant preparation for battle, and a little recovery from the fright, which was soon effected by waiting a few moments in vain, for the enemy to come on;—a general explanation took place, which brought all to our legs again, and convinced us that there was no decided obstacle, as yet, to our reaching the Camanchee towns; and after that, 'sweet home', and the arms of our wives and dear little children, provided we could ever overtake and recover our horses, which had swept off in fifty directions, and with impetus enough to ensure us employment for a day or two to come.

At the proper moment for it to be made, there was a general enquiry for the cause of this *real misfortune*, when it was ascertained to have originated in the following manner. A 'raw recruit', who was standing as one

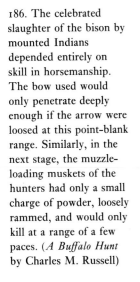

186. The celebrated slaughter of the bison by mounted Indians depended entirely on skill in horsemanship. The bow used would only penetrate deeply enough if the arrow were loosed at this point-blank range. Similarly, in the next stage, the muzzle-loading muskets of the hunters had only a small charge of powder, loosely rammed, and would only kill at a range of a few paces. (*A Buffalo Hunt* by Charles M. Russell)

of the sentinels on that night, saw, as he says 'he supposed', an Indian creeping out of a bunch of bushes a few paces in front of him, upon whom he levelled his rifle; and as the poor creature did not '*advance* and *give the countersign*' at his call, nor any answer at all, he 'let off!' and popped a bullet through the heart of a poor dragoon horse, which had strayed away on the night before, and had faithfully followed our trail all the day, and was now, with a beastly misgiving, coming up, and slowly poking through a little thicket of bushes into camp, to join its comrades, in servitude again!

The sudden shock of a gun, and the most appalling groans of this poor dying animal, in the dead of night, and so close upon the heels of sweet sleep, created a long vibration of nerves, and a day of great perplexity and toil which followed, as we had to retrace our steps twenty miles or more, in pursuit of affrighted horses; of which some fifteen or twenty took up wild and free life upon the prairies, to which they were abandoned, as they could not be found. After a detention of two days in consequence of this disaster, we took up the line of march again, and pursued our course with

187. Burning grass is a primitive but effective technique, at the right season, for improving grazing. Here it is being used either to drive game or as a stratagem of war. (*Indians Firing the Prairie* by Frederic Remington)

188. *Captain Stewart Leading his Party* by Alfred Jacob Miller. A reminder, not often seen in 'heroic' paintings of the American expansion over the great plains, that the ass and the mule (right foreground) played almost as great a part in the conquest as the horse.

189, 190. George Catlin's
pictures of Indians
chasing and roping the
wild mustang.

vigour and success, over a continuation of green fields, enamelled with wild flowers, and pleasingly relieved with patches and groves of timber.

On the fourth day of our march, we discovered many fresh signs of buffaloes; and at last, immense herds of them grazing on the distant hills. Indian trails were daily growing fresh, and their smokes were seen in various directions ahead of us. And on the same day at noon, we discovered a large party at several miles distance, sitting on their horses and looking at us. From the glistening of the blades of their lances, which were blazing as they turned them in the sun, it was at first thought that they were Mexican cavalry, who might have been apprized of our approach into their country, and had advanced to contest this point with us. On drawing a little nearer, however, and scanning them closer with our spy-glasses, they were soon ascertained to be a war-party of Camanchees, on the look out for their enemies.

The regiment was called to a halt, and the requisite preparations made and orders issued, we advanced in a direct line towards them until we had approached to within two or three miles of them, when they suddenly disappeared over the hill, and soon after shewed themselves on another mound farther off and in a different direction. The course of the regiment was then changed, and another advance towards them was commenced, and as before, they disappeared and shewed themselves in another direction. After several such efforts which proved ineffectual, Col. Dodge ordered the command to halt, while he rode forward with a few of his staff, and an ensign carrying a white flag. I joined this advance, and the Indians stood their ground until we had come within half a mile of them, and could distinctly observe all their numbers and movements. We then came to a halt, and the white flag was sent a little in advance, and waved as a signal for them to approach; at which one of their party galloped out in advance of the war-party, on a milk white horse, carrying a piece of white buffalo skin on the point of his long lance in reply to our flag.

This moment was the commencement of one of the most thrilling and beautiful scenes I ever witnessed. All eyes, both from his own party and ours, were fixed upon the manoeuvres of this gallant little fellow, and he well knew it.

191. The herd of
mustangs, showing the
variety of colours
observed by Catlin.

192. A 'gallant little fellow'.

The distance between the two parties was perhaps half a mile, and that a beautiful and gently sloping prairie; over which he was for the space of a quarter of an hour, reining and spurring his maddened horse, and gradually approaching us by tacking to the right and the left, like a vessel beating against the wind. He at length came prancing and leaping along till he met the flag of the regiment, when he leaned his spear for a moment against it, looking the bearer full in the face, when he wheeled his horse, and dashed up to Col. Dodge, with his extended hand, which was instantly grasped and shaken. We all had him by the hand in a moment, and the rest of the party seeing him received in this friendly manner, instead of being sacrificed, as they undoubtedly expected, started under 'full whip' in a direct line towards us, and in a moment gathered, like a black cloud, around us! The regiment then moved up in regular order, and a general shake of the hand ensued, which was accomplished by each warrior riding along the ranks, and shaking the hand of every one as he passed. This necessary form took up considerable time, and during the whole operation, my eyes were fixed upon the gallant and wonderful appearance of the little fellow who bore us the white flag on the point of his lance. He rode a fine and spirited wild horse, which was as white as the drifted snow, with an exuberant mane, and its long and bushy tail sweeping the ground. In his hand he tightly drew the reins upon a heavy Spanish bit, and at every jump, plunged into the animal's sides, till they were in a gore of blood, a

193. The hunting of the buffalo—another Catlin illustration showing exactly how the Indians went about catching their staple food.

huge pair of spurs, plundered, no doubt, from the Spaniards in their border wars, which are continually waged on the Mexican frontiers. The eyes of this noble little steed seemed to be squeezed out of its head; and its fright, and its agitation had brought out upon its skin a perspiration that was fretted into a white foam and lather. The warrior's quiver was slung on the warrior's back, and his bow grasped in his left hand, ready for instant use, if called for. His shield was on his arm, and across his thigh, in a beautiful cover of buckskin, his gun was slung—and in his right hand his lance of fourteen feet in length.

Thus armed and equipped was this dashing cavalier; and nearly in the same manner, all the rest of the party; and very many of them leading an extra horse, which we soon learned was the favourite war-horse; and from which circumstances altogether, we soon understood that they were a war-party in search of their enemy.

After a shake of the hand, we dismounted, and the pipe was lit, and passed around. And then a 'talk' was held, in which we were aided by a Spaniard we luckily had with us, who could converse with one of the Camanchees, who spoke some Spanish.

Colonel Dodge explained to them the friendly motives with which we were penetrating their country —that we were sent by the President to reach their villages—to see the chiefs of the Camanchees and Pawnee Picts—to shake hands with them, and to smoke the pipe of peace, and to establish an acquaintance, and consequently a system of trade that would be beneficial to both.

They listened attentively, and perfectly appreciated; and taking Colonel Dodge at his word, relying with confidence in what he told them; they informed us that their great town was within a few days' march, and pointing in the direction—offered to abandon their war-excursion, and turn out and escort us to it, which they did in perfect good faith. We were on the march in the afternoon of that day, and from day to day they busily led us on, over hill and dale, encamping by the side of us at night, and resuming the march in the morning.

During this march, over one of the most lovely and picturesque countries in the world, we had enough continually to amuse and excite us. The whole country seemed at times to be alive with buffaloes, and bands of wild horses.

We had with us about thirty Osage and Cherokee, Seneca and Delaware Indians, employed as guides and hunters for the regiment; and with the war-party of ninety or a hundred Camanchees, we formed a most picturesque appearance while passing over the green fields; and consequently, sad havoc amongst the herds of buffaloes, which we were almost hourly passing. We were now out of the influence and reach of bread stuffs, and subsisted ourselves on buffaloes' meat altogether; and the Indians of the different tribes, emulous to shew their skill in the chase, and prove the mettle of their horses, took infinite pleasure in dashing into every herd that we approached; by which means, the regiment was abundantly supplied from day to day with fresh meat. . . .

The tract of country over which we passed, between the False Washita and this place, is stocked, not only with buffaloes, but with numerous bands of wild horses, many of which we saw every day. There is no other animal on the prairies so wild and so sagacious as the horse; and none other so difficult to come up with. So remarkably keen is their eye, that they will generally run 'at the sight', when they are a mile distant; being, no doubt, able to distinguish the character of the enemy that is approaching when at that distance; and when in motion, will seldom stop short of three or four miles. I made many attempts to approach them by stealth, when they were grazing, and playing their gambols, without ever having been more than once able to succeed. In this instance, I left my horse, and with my friend Chadwick, skulked through a ravine for a couple of miles; until we were at length brought within gunshot of a fine herd of them, when I used my pencil for some time, while we were under cover of a little hedge of bushes which effectually screened us from their view. In this herd we saw all the colours, nearly, that can be seen in a kennel of English hounds. Some were milk white, some jet black—others were sorrel, and bay, and cream colour—many were of an iron grey; and others were pied, containing a variety of colours on the same animal. Their manes were very profuse, and hanging in the wildest confusion over their necks and faces— and their long tails swept the ground. . . .

The Indian, when he starts for a wild horse, mounts one of the fleetest he can get, and coiling his laso on his arm, starts off under the 'full whip', till he can enter the band, when he soon gets it over the neck of one of the number; when he instantly dismounts, leaving his own horse, and runs as fast as he can, letting the laso pass out gradually and carefully through his hands, until the horse falls for want of breath, and lies helpless on the ground; at which time the Indian advances slowly towards the horse's head keeping his laso tight upon its neck, until he fastens a pair of hobbles on the animal's two forefeet, and also loosens the laso (giving the horse chance to breathe), and gives it a noose around the under jaw, by which he gets greater power over the affrighted animal, which is rearing and plunging when it gets breath; and by which, as he advances, hand over hand, towards the horse's nose, he is able to hold it down and prevent it from throwing itself over on its back, at the hazard of its limbs. By this means he gradually advances, until he is able to place his hand on the animal's nose, and over its eyes; and at length to breathe in its nostrils, when it soon becomes docile and conquered; so that he has little else to do than to remove the hobbles from its feet, and lead or ride it into camp.

This 'breaking down' or taming, however, is not without the most desperate trial on the part of the horse, which rears and plunges in every possible way to effect its escape, until its power is exhausted, and it becomes covered with foam; and at last yields to the power of man, and becomes his willing slave for the rest of its life. By this very rigid treatment, the poor animal seems to be so completely conquered, that it makes no further struggle for its freedom; but submits quietly ever after, and is led or rode away with very little difficulty. Great care is taken, however, in this and in subsequent treatment, not to subdue the spirit of the animal, which is carefully preserved and kept up, although they use them with great severity; being, generally speaking, cruel masters.

The wild horse of these regions is a small, but very powerful animal; with an exceedingly prominent eye, sharp nose, high nostril, small feet and delicate leg; and undoubtedly, have sprung from a stock introduced by the Spaniards, at the time of the invasion of Mexico;

which having strayed off upon the prairies, have run wild, and stocked the plains from this to Lake Winnepeg, two or three thousand miles to the North.[1] . . .

The Camanchee horses are generally small, all of them being of the wild breed, and a very tough and serviceable animal; and from what I can learn here of the chiefs, there are yet, farther South, and nearer the Mexican borders, some of the noblest animals in use of the chiefs, yet I do not know that we have any more reason to rely upon this information, than that which had made our horse-jockeys that we have with us, to run almost crazy for the possession of those we were to find at this place. Amongst the immense herds we found grazing here, one third perhaps are mules, which are much more valuable than the horses.

George Catlin, *Letters and Notes of the Manners, Customs and Condition of the North American Indians*, 1841

[1] There are many very curious traditions about the first appearance of horses amongst the different tribes, and many of which bear striking proof of the above fact. Most of the tribes have some story about the first appearance of horses; and amongst the Sioux, they have beautifully recorded the fact, by giving it the name of Shonk a-wakon (the medicine dog).

194. The Red Indian chief on his horse, about 1910: note the saddle and stirrups.

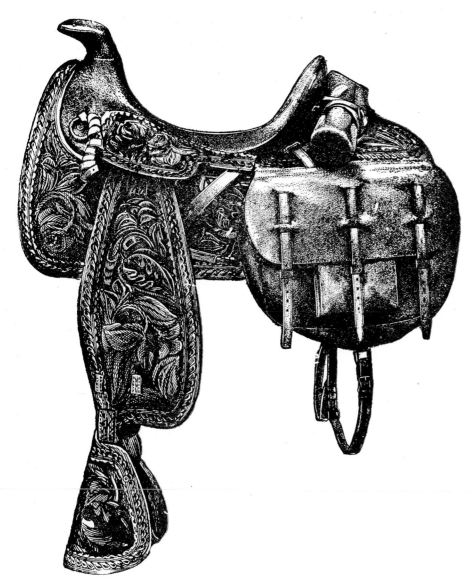

195. The 'Whitman modified Mexican', an example from the catalogue of the Mehlbach Saddle Company, New York, 1907. A 'super quality, hand-embossed, best selected oak stock, solid nickel trimmings, super furniture, without bags and poncho holder' sold for $65.

WESTERN EQUIPMENT

The historical antecedents of the Western saddle, stretching back through Mexico to Andalusian and ultimately to Moroccan prototypes, are correctly described by Rollins; but why did the Mexicans call it *basto*, which means pack-saddle, not riding-saddle? (Cf. French bât = pack-saddle.)

The plate, which really has no equivalent in English saddle construction, is the foundation of certain saddles recently in use in the Western Mediterranean, notably in Provence, where the half-barrel-like structure was even more pronounced. But this type of saddle is intended primarily not for horsemen but for muleteers.

One wonders which particular ethnic section of Texans used the anglicism 'girth' for 'cinch'.

The *tapadero* type of stirrup was in common use in many European countries, including England, in the fifteenth and sixteenth centuries.

The thongs dependent from the saddle are of even more respectable antiquity. On the oldest known saddle, recovered deep-frozen from the tombs of Pazyrik in the Altai mountains of Western Siberia, where it had been buried about 430 BC, there are four pairs of thongs placed exactly as in the Mexican *basto*.

What no Western film ever seems to show adequately is the appalling discomfort of the cowboy's life, including frequently lack of sleep, bed or no bed. On the movies, it always seems to be summer. Who ever filmed the goodies chasing the baddies in a blizzard? And what Western film ever gave us the faintest taste of the monotonously indigestible and hellishly unpalatable fare described in this extract? How many cowboys died of scurvy?

❋The riding saddle of the cowboy merits description, not only because it was the cowboy's work-bench or his throne, according as one cares to picture it, but also because one cannot understand the puncher's ability to ride the bronco except one understands the saddle. . . .

The riding saddle universally used upon the Range was of the type which, throughout the West, was known as 'cow saddle', 'Range saddle', or, more commonly, as 'stock-saddle', and in the East was called 'Mexican saddle', 'Western saddle', or 'cowboy saddle'. It perhaps should have been termed Moorish rather than Mexican, for, in almost its present basic form, the Moors carried it from Africa to Spain over a thousand years ago. . . .

All stock-saddles were alike in fundamentals, though they varied in incidental details.

The height and angles of the horn and cantle, and whether the seat were short or long, wide or narrow, whether it were of approximately uniform width or more or less triangular, whether it were level or sloped upward toward either the horn or the cantle or toward both, whether the horn were vertical or inclined forward, and whether its top were horizontal or were higher at its front edge than at its rear were all matters purely of the rider's choice; save that the cantle had to be high enough to prevent the lariat-thrower from slipping backward when his cow-horse after the throw squatted on its haunches and braced itself. Also followers of the Texan custom of fastening the lariat's home end to the horn before the lariat was thrown required at least a fairly high horn. Such men had to have not only the space thus occupied but also additional room for 'snubbing', because, the instant the lariat caught its prey, the lariat had to be wound for a few turns around the horn; *i.e.* to be snubbed. . . .

Extremely stout construction was required to withstand successfully the terrific strains from roping.

Upon the front end of a strongly built hardwood 'tree', comprised of longitudinal 'fork' and transverse 'cantle', was bolted a metal horn; and the whole, covered with rawhide, was fastened down onto a broad, curved, leathern plate which rested on the horse's back. This plate in its entirety was called the 'skirt', unless one preferred to differentiate and to refer to the half of the plate on the horse's left side as one skirt, the 'near' or 'left' skirt, and to the half on the horse's right side as another skirt, the 'off' or 'right' skirt, and thus, when mentioning the two halves collectively, to term them as 'skirts' instead of as a skirt.

Synonyms for skirt and skirts were respectively 'basto' and 'bastos' (from Spanish 'basto', a pad or a pack-saddle), though some men restricted these latter terms to the leathern lining of the skirt, a lining known as the 'sudadero' [sweat-catcher].

On each side of the horse there lay on top of the skirt a leathern piece which was shorter and narrower than the skirt, fitted closely around the base of the horn and cantle, and had its outer edges parallel with, but well inside of, the borders of the bottom and rear edges of the skirt. This leathern piece was the so-called 'jockey'. It usually was in two sections, its portion forward of the stirrup-leather being termed the 'front jockey', while so much as was aft of the stirrup-leather was styled the 'rear jockey'.

The composite structure fitted onto the horse's back in the same way as would have done a headless barrel if halved lengthwise, and to the entire barrel-like portion of the saddle was colloquially applied the term bastos, although that term had technically the more restricted meaning stated above.

In infrequent instances the skirt and the rear jockey extended backward no farther than to the cantle, and then there was sewn to the latter's base an 'anquera', a broad plate of leather which covered the otherwise exposed portion of the horse's hips, and protected the clothing of the rider from his animal's sweat.

The skirt of usual size stretched from the horse's withers to his rump, and well-nigh half-way down both his flanks. It had so much bearing surface that the saddle tended to remain in position even without the aid of a 'cinch'. A large skirt was necessary when riding buckers or when roping; but for ordinary pottering about a few ranch owners used a saddle the skirt of which was much curtailed.

Whether the saddle should contain a 'roll' was a matter of the rider's individual choice. Some men used the attachment, others did not. A roll was a long welt which stuck out for a third of an inch or more from the front face of the cantle just under its top rim. This cornice-like addition tended to keep the rider from sliding backward out of the saddle during roping and from moving skyward when his pony was bucking.

The saddle was attached to the horse either by one 'cinch' passing under the animal at a point approximately even with the stirrups, or by two 'cinches', respectively designated as the 'front' and the 'hind' or

196. Red Indian horsemanship included only exercises that were of direct utility in hunting or in battle. Some of them bear a close resemblance to those practised by European plainsmen such as the Cossacks. A painting by George Catlin.

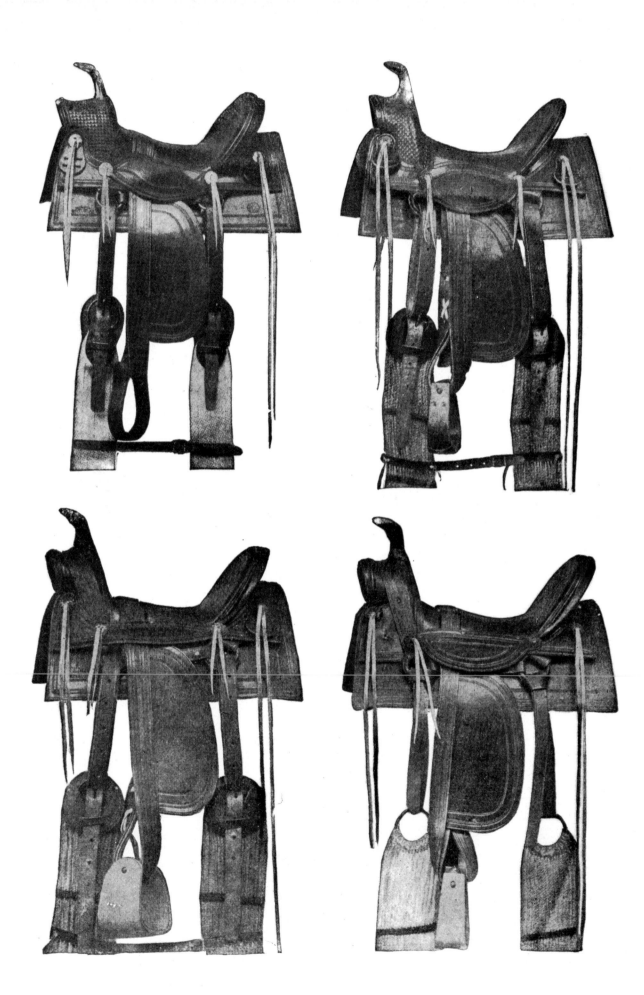

198. Whitman stock or ranch saddles from the Mehlbach Company. 'All trees in these saddles are steel fork, hide covered, skirts wool lined and the seats of solid leather, with steel strainer and beaded roll cantle. Stirrup leathers in Styles 1 and 2 are $2\frac{1}{2}$ inches, in Style 3, $2\frac{1}{4}$ inches and in Style 4, $1\frac{3}{4}$ inches wide.'

197. The ancestors of the Red Indians migrated from eastern Asia over the top of the world to Alaska and pushed on through the American continents before the horse had been domesticated but not before the invention of the travois drawn by the only domesticated animal, the dog. In about 4000 BC Asiatic nomads began to use a larger-sized travois behind the newly domesticated horse, but no pictorial record of this exists. The plains Indians in general had no horses before 1700, but they immediately took the step that had been taken in Asia six thousand years earlier. This picture by George Catlin shows a scene in nineteenth-century America that might belong to Neolithic Mongolia. This is the father of all horse-drawn vehicles, eastern or western.

199. *The Cowboy* by Frederic Remington.

THE FRONTIER | 237

'rear cinch', and passing one just behind the animal's front legs and one some twelve inches further to the rear. The saddle of two cinches was designated technically as 'double-rigged' or 'double rig'. . . .

Some Texans called the cinches 'girths', and the rearward of them the 'flank girth'.

Whether a saddle should be single or double rigged was a matter of its owner's preference. The single as compared with the double was more easily put on and taken off, was a bit more flexible in riding motion, but it was more apt to shift position during roping and bucking and upon steep trails. . . .

The 'cincha' or, as usually termed, the cinch was a broad, short band made of coarsely woven horsehair or sometimes of canvas or cordage, and terminating at either end in a metal ring. On each side of the saddle-tree was attached, for each cinch, a second metal ring called the 'rigging ring', 'tree ring', or 'saddle-ring', and from which hung a long leathern strap called a 'latigo'. This strap, after being passed successively and usually twice through both the cinch ring and the corresponding tree-ring, was fastened below the latter by much the same method as that in which the present-day masculine 'four-in-hand' necktie is knotted. The latigo on the saddle's off side was permanently left thus fastened, and, in saddling and unsaddling, operations were restricted to the strap upon the near side. . . .

While camped within a forest, punchers had carefully to guard their latigos, because, for some inscrutable reason, the latter bore to porcupines the same relation that candy does to children. It was no uncommon thing to see a dismounted puncher, when not using his saddle as a pillow, hang it from a limb or place it on a pole fastened horizontally and high above the ground.

Each stirrup-leather hung . . . from the saddle's tree. These two leathers at their starting-point almost met behind the horn, and, severally leaving, one to the saddle's right, the other to the saddle's left, rested in shallow grooves cut in the wood of the tree. In some saddles, the seat's leathern covering, starting forward from the cantle, went only to this groove's rear edge. In other saddles, this covering extended over the entire seat and completely hid the upper portion of the stirrup-leathers. Technical names were given to these two forms of seat covering. They were respectively 'three-quarter seat' and 'full seat'.

Where each stirrup-leather emitted from the saddle's side, was overlaid a flat leathern plate. This plate, known indiscriminately as the 'seat jockey' or 'leg jockey', shielded the rider's leg from chafing.

Sewn to the back of each stirrup-leather was a vertical, wide leathern shield, the 'rosadero' [dew-catcher]; sometimes, though incorrectly, called the 'sudadero'. It protected from the horse's sweat and offered stout defence to the rider's leg.

At the bottom of each stirrup-leather, was a stirrup made of a wide piece of tough wood bent into shape, bolted together at the top, and so sturdy as to defy crushing by a falling horse. Into the stirrup went the rider's foot clear to the latter's heel, his toe pointing inward and either horizontally or downward. The sides and front of the stirrup were ordinarily enclosed by a wedge-shaped, leathern cover open toward the rear. The technical name of this cover was 'tapadero', though colloquially this almost always was shortened into 'tap'.

Commonly each side of each of the 'taps' was in the form of a triangle with apex pointing downward, and was so long that this apex barely escaped the ground; but some men used 'taps' which following the historic Spanish model, were shaped somewhat like horizontally laid coal-scuttles. The 'taps' prevented the rider's feet from passing completely through the stirrups, being snagged by brush, or being bitten by a savage horse. When long and flapped under a ridden steed, they were of no small use as a whip.

'Open' stirrups, i.e., 'tapless' ones, were rarely seen upon the Range.

From each side of every saddle hung four sets of thongs, two thongs in each set. One of these sets was at the saddle's front, one near its rear, while the other two were spaced so that the rider's leg just passed between them. The two sets of rear thongs embraced whatever might be laid across the saddle behind the cantle, almost invariably the 'slicker', which was a long rain-coat of yellow oilskin such as coastal fishermen wear; though in the Southwest the thongs instead of this sometimes confined a Mexican 'serape'. The front and side thongs held any package of the moment.

If a cowboy were starting on a trip which, while forcing him to camp overnight, did not call for many supplies and a consequent pack-horse, he would, nevertheless, not limit himself to the traditional Hudson Bay Company's ration of a rabbit track and a cartridge, but would insert within the folds of the 'slicker' tied at his saddle's rear the journey's necessaries. These were a frying-pan, some flour, bacon, coffee, salt, and, as a substitute for yeast, either a bottle of sour dough or a can of baking-powder.

When halting time arrived, the camp was pitched wherever both forage for the horse and drinkable water met. The water, though drinkable, was not always pleasing . . . Occasionally, in the desert, [it] was either non-existent or else so alkalinely saturated as hopelessly to 'rust the boilers' of whoever drank it. In the latter case, although the horses were left grimacingly to gulp the biting fluid and run the risk of being 'alkalied', the men might have recourse to canned tomatoes. The liquid portion of the can's contents assuaged thirst and counteracted the effect of the already swallowed alkali dust, while the solid vegetable

200. The Foremost Cow Punchers at the American Legion Rodeo. Western horsemen (and one horsewoman) of the Henry Ford era.

201. *Two cowboys chasing and preparing to lassoo a steer*, by Charles M. Russell. The longhorn breed of cattle of Spanish origin, now vanished from the Western states, was the immediate beneficiary of the exterminated 'buffalo'.

wiped across one's face would heal the bleeding cuts which that cannibalistic dust had made. A tomato might occasionally be pressed against a pony's lips for their comforting.

The can-opener was irresistible, since it was a pistol fired horizontally at the can's top edge.

The pitching of camp was a simple process. It consisted of stripping the saddle and bridle from the horse, of turning the latter loose to graze either at the end of a picket rope or within the grip of hobbles, and finally of building a fire. Lighting the fire was not always an easy matter, for matches might be wet or lost. Then it would call for powder from a dissected cartridge, and the igniting of it by a pistol-shot. Careless aiming might 'hang the kindlings on the scenery'.

If, as was usually the case, the camp's coffee were unground, its beans were mashed on a rock with the butt of a pistol. The resultant mixture of vegetable and mineral substances was set aside until the frying-pan should have cooked, first, bread and, next, bacon.

The bread was quite eatable. With a thick batter spread thinly over the bottom of the pan, the latter was

laid upon hot coals for a moment and until a lower crust had commenced to form. Then, tipped on edge, it was held far enough from the fire for a little heat to reach it and to raise the loaf. This achieved, the pan, still on edge, was pushed to within baking distance of the coals, and was left there until the pan's contents were done.

The thus baked bread, the historic 'frying-pan bread' of the West, vacated the pan, and into the latter went strips of bacon. When these had been fried, the pan was rapped against a rock or tree, to expel such of the grease as readily would leave, and then received a charge of water and the coffee-gravel mixture. When the boiling fluid was fairly well covered with fat melted from the utensil's sides, the dose-like beverage was ready for consumption. . . .

In cold weather the puncher . . . customarily took to bed with him his horse's bridle, that the bit might be kept warm and the horse be spared the pain which mouthing frigid metal would have caused.

Camping in the colder climates was often a trying process marked by nocturnal contests between soporific desire and rheumatic pains, a contest which vacillated according as a sleepy hand dropped fuel upon the fire or the embers chilled.

However, the topic under consideration is the cowboy's saddle and not his troubles.

There might be at the base of the saddle's horn a 'buck strap', which was a loop that offered a convenient handhold during pitching. Its owner never bragged about its presence. Top riders scorned it, and excluded it from their saddles.

Not infrequently a pair of leathern pockets bestrode the saddle, sometimes behind the cantle, more rarely at the horn. These receptacles were called either 'cantineses' or saddle pockets. . . .

The leather of the entire saddle, inclusive of taps and stirrup-leathers, usually was covered with handsomely impressed designs of leaves and flowers. A saddle, if so decorated, would cost, in the decades of the seventies and eighties, some fifty dollars. In the Southwest, occasionally not only was silver laid into the groundwork of the impressed designs, but both the horn and cantle were subject to be ornamented with precious metal. Then the cost assuredly mounted. Ten months' wages often went into decoration. At least one ranch owner had a horn and cantle each of solid gold.

Often on the cowboy's saddles there was applied a homemade ornamentation consisting of brass nails or, again, of rattlesnake skins plastered flat and permanently stuck fast by their own glue.

The saddle's colouring was usually light brown; but sometimes, and especially in the less expensive saddles, it was cherry-red.

Each saddle best fitted its special owner, for it gradually acquired tiny humps and hollows that registered with his anatomy, and induced both comfort and security of seat. These little mouldings, which suited well the owner, would often fight the contour of a stranger's legs. Wherefore each man swore by his own saddle and at all others. . . .

Moreover, it was a bit disgraceful to sell one's saddle. It was akin to disposing of the ancestral plate and family jewels. The phrase 'He's sold his saddle', became of general usage, and was employed in a figurative way to denote that anybody in any calling had become financially or morally insolvent. . . .

Because the saddle from its shape and large bearing surface had so good a hold on the horse's back, riders usually, except when on fractious animals or in a mountainous country, let the cinches sag loosely. This gave comfort to the lungs within the confining straps. The horses aided in procuring this sag, for Western steeds, when being saddled, puffed themselves like adders at the first pull on the latigo. They might be momentarily thrown off their guard by a kick behind the ribs, but the beasts reconcentrated their attention upon inhaling before the strap could be pulled again.

To 'cinch up' any bronco (he was 'cinched up', not merely 'cinched'), one had to place one's foot against the brute's ribs and, in the case of the front cinch, to pull with almost all one's strength upon the latigo, meanwhile standing ready to dodge precipitate bites from the indignant head-tossing bronco. Pulling upon the rear cinch exacted much less muscular effort, but much greater circumspection; for bites were apt to be more frequent, and good measure might throw in a kick or two.

202. *Hunting Rheas in South America* by George Catlin. On the South American pampas large grazing mammals used to be much rarer than on the North American prairie. To some extent large flightless birds were a substitute for them as game. They were eliminated to make room for cattle and horses.

The cowboy's saddle was not suitable for racing. It was too heavy, thirty pounds at the very least and usually forty pounds or over. But the usual and useful gaits of the Range were not of racing speed. They were the running walk, the jiggling trot, the lope, with now and then a short dash after errant live stock.

The cowboy's saddle well-nigh inhibited jumping of hurdles. Its occupant, the instant he assumed the posture necessary to encourage his horse to 'take off', lost his balanced seat, and was, from the saddle's shape, unable to cling, as on the English tree, by constrictive force. But there were few hurdles upon the Range.

Nor could a rider, when in this saddle, rise to the trot. But the cowboy did not wish to rise. In his own language, he 'postage-stamped' the horse.

Nevertheless the saddle was ideal for the service in which it was used.

P. A. Rollins, *The Cowboy* (1922)

There were the White Anglo-Saxon Protestant cowboys (of whom a surprisingly large number were Negroes, though they too appear seldom in the Western celluloid epic). Known to the other Americans as *los Norte-americanos*, they ranged over about a quarter of the cattle-country in the Americas. South of the Rio Grande, and intermittently all the way to Cape Horn, Iberian-mestizo Catholic cowboys known by such names as vaqueros, gauchos, etc., lived much the same sort of life, their culture derived from that of the mounted herdsmen of Spain and Portugal. We refer the reader to the works of W. H. Hudson (*Far Away and Long Ago*,

A Little Boy Lost, and *El Ombu*) for the life of the gauchos on the pampas, and of the vast herds of horses on which they depended for living, in all its extravagance. For it was incredibly wasteful of livestock. A gaucho would kill a steer just for one meal, or would kill a colt just to make a pair of boots from the skin of its forelegs. This manner of life has now passed away as utterly as that of the old-style Texas cattleman, with the introduction of barbed-wire paddocks, 'tame' breeds of cattle like the Hereford in place of the all-but-feral Spanish Longhorn, artesian wells and the internal combustion engine.

203. *The Battle of Bull Run, Va., 21 July 1861*—the gallant charge of the Zouaves and defeat of the rebel Black Horse Cavalry. A Currier and Ives lithograph. 'Rebel' equals confederate. 'Zouaves' do not imply French intervention in the Civil War. They were simply an American imitation of an admired corps of infantry which was itself an imitation of North African, Turkish-style troops. Compare the international cavalry fashion for hussars at the same period.

12. The horse in the railway age

BUSMAN'S HOLIDAY

Less written-up, because less spectacular, than the mail-coach, is the passenger and goods traffic drawn by horses and supplementing the railway; its urban and suburban volume was enormous. In London it was documented by two social observers of great talent, Mayhew in 1851 and Gordon in 1893. Both examined in great detail the conditions of labour, both human and equine, and the economic background of the traffic to and from the station in the late Victorian period. Gordon in particular quotes not only the price of forage and fodder, rents of stables, the economics of manure disposal, but also the going prices for draught and harness horses of all grades, and what they fetched at the knacker's in a worn-out state. His last chapter is an analysis of the cat's meat and bone-meal trade of London.

At the end of Queen Victoria's reign there were about four million horses in Great Britain, three hundred thousand of them in London, the vast majority of both figures working in harness. One London knacker alone (Harrison Barber) killed 26,000 annually, at an average age of eleven years. This figure was not far below the peak of the British horse population, on the eve of the Kaiser's War. In the United States this

204. *Omnibus passing the Three Compasses Inn, Clapton, 1850,* by Pollard. Land transport in England was inseparably connected with public houses.

peak was reached in 1915, with 21,431,000 head. But the American mule population went on growing until 1925, when there were 5,918,000 mules in the United States.

The total number of omnibuses traversing the streets of London is about 3,000. . . . The number of conductors and drivers is about 7,000. . . . The receipts of each vehicle vary from 2*l.* to 4*l.* per day. Estimating the whole 3,000 at 3*l.*, it follows that the entire sum expended annually in omnibus hire by the people of London amounts to no less than 3,285,000*l.*, which is more than 30*s.* a-head for every man, woman, and child, in the metropolis. The average journey as regards length of each omnibus is six miles, and that distance is in some cases travelled twelve times a-day by each omnibus, or, as it is called, 'six there and six back'. . . .

The extent of individual travel performed by some of the omnibus drivers is enormous. One man told me that he had driven his 'bus' seventy-two miles (twelve stages of six miles) every day for six years, with the exception of twelve miles less every second Sunday, so that this man had driven in six years 179,568 miles.

ORIGIN OF OMNIBUSES

This vast extent of omnibus transit has been the growth of twenty years, as it was not until the 4th July, 1829, that Mr. Shillibeer, now the proprietor of the patent mourning coaches, started the first omnibus . . . Mr. Shillibeer was a naval officer, and in his youth stepped

205. A metropolitan horse-drawn tram photographed in Dalston, London, 1895.

206. Paris in the 1890s,
with omnibuses. An
original photograph.

from a midshipman's duties into the business of a
coach-builder, he learning that business from the late
Mr. Hatchett, of Long Acre. Mr. Shillibeer then
established himself in Paris as a builder of English
carriages, a demand for which had sprung up after the
peace, when the current of English travel was directed
strongly to France. In this speculation Mr. Shillibeer
was eminently successful. He built carriages for
Prince Polignac, and others of the most influential men
under the dynasty of the elder branch of the Bourbons,
and had a bazaar for the sale of his vehicles. He was
thus occupied in Paris in 1819, when M. Lafitte first
started the omnibuses which are now so common and
so well managed in the French capital. Lafitte was the
banker (afterwards the minister) of Louis Philippe, and
the most active man in establishing the Messageries
Royales. Five or six years after the omnibuses had been
successfully introduced into Paris, Mr. Shillibeer was
employed by M. Lafitte to build two in a superior style.
In executing this order, Mr. Shillibeer thought that so
comfortable and economical a mode of conveyance
might be advantageously introduced in London. He
accordingly disposed of his Parisian establishment, and
came to London, and started his omnibus as I have

narrated. . . . His speculation was particularly and at
once successful. His two vehicles carried each twenty-
two, and were filled every journey. The form was that
of the present omnibus, but larger and roomier, as the
twenty-two were all accommodated inside, nobody
being outside but the driver. Three horses yoked
abreast were used to draw these carriages. . . .

Mr. Shillibeer's success continued, for he insured
punctuality and civility; and the cheapness, cleanliness,
and smartness of his omnibuses, were in most advantageous contrast with the high charges, dirt, dinginess,
and rudeness of the drivers of many of the 'short
stages'. The short-stage proprietors were loud in their
railings against what they were pleased to describe as a
French innovation. In the course of from six to nine
months Mr. Shillibeer had twelve omnibuses at work.
The new omnibuses ran from the Bank to Paddington,
both by the route of Holborn and Oxford-street, as well
as by Finsbury and the New-road. Mr. Shillibeer feels
convinced, that had he started fifty omnibuses instead
of two in the first instance, a fortune might have been
realized. In 1831–2, his omnibuses became general in
the great street thoroughfares; and as the short stages
were run off the road, the proprietors started omnibuses

in opposition to Mr. Shillibeer. The first omnibuses, however, started after Mr. Shillibeer's were not in opposition. They were the Caledonians, and were the property of Mr. Shillibeer's brother-in-law. The third started, which were two-horse vehicles, were foolishly enough called 'Les Dames Blanches'; but as the name gave rise to much low wit in *équivoques* it was abandoned. The original omnibuses were called 'Shillibeers' on the panels, from the name of their originator; and the name is still prevalent on those conveyances in New York, which affords us another proof that not in his own country is a benefactor honoured, until perhaps his death makes honour as little worth as an epitaph.

The opposition omnibuses, however, continued to increase as more and more short stages were abandoned; and one oppositionist called his omnibuses 'Shillibeers', so that the real and the sham Shillibeers were known in the streets. The opposition became fiercer. The 'busses', as they came to be called in a year or two, crossed each other and raced or drove their poles recklessly into the back of one another; and accidents and squabbles and loitering grew so frequent, and the time of the police magistrates was so much occupied with 'omnibus business', that in 1832 the matter was mentioned in Parliament as a nuisance requiring a remedy, and in 1833 a Bill was brought in by the Government and passed for the 'Regulation of Omnibuses (as well as other conveyances) in and near the metropolis'. . . . As the beginning of 1834, Mr. Shillibeer abandoned his metropolitan trade, and began running omnibuses from London to Greenwich and Woolwich, employing 20 carriages and 120 horses; but the increase of steamers and the opening of the Greenwich Railway in 1835 affected his trade so materially, that Mr. Shillibeer fell into arrear with his payments to the Stamp Office, and seizures of his property and re-seizures after money was paid, entailed such heavy expenses, and such a hindrance to Mr. Shillibeer's business, that his failure ensued. . . .

OMNIBUS DRIVERS

The driver is paid by the week. His remuneration is 34s. a-week on most of the lines. On others he receives 21s. and his box—that is, the allowance of a fare each journey for a seat outside, if a seat be so occupied. In fine weather this box plan is more remunerative to the driver than the fixed payment of 34s.; but in wet weather he may receive nothing from the box. The average then the year through is only 34s. a-week; or, perhaps, rather more, as on some days in sultry weather the driver may make 6s., 'if the 'bus do twelve journeys', from his box. . . .

From a driver I had the following statement:

'I have been a driver fourteen years. I was brought up as a builder, but had friends that was using horses, and I sometimes assisted them in driving and grooming when I was out of work. I got to like that sort of work, and thought it would be better than my own business if I could get to be connected with a 'bus; and I had friends, and first got employed as a time-keeper; but I've been a driver for fourteen years. I'm now paid by the week, and not by the box. It's fair payment, but we must live well. It's hard work is mine; for I never have any rest but a few minutes, except every other Sunday, and then only two hours; that's the time of a journey there and back. If I was to ask leave to go to church, and then go to work again, I know what the answer there would be—"You can go to church as often as you like, and we can get a man who doesn't want to go there." The cattle I drive are equal to gentlemen's carriage-horses. One I've driven five years, and I believe she was worked five years before I drove her. It's very hard work for the horses, but I don't know that they are over-worked in 'busses. The starting after stopping is the hardest work for them; it's such a terrible strain. I've felt for the poor things on a wet night, with a 'bus full of big people. I think that it's a pity that anybody uses a bearing rein. There's not many uses it now. It bears up a horse's head, and he can only go on pulling, pulling up a hill, one way. Take off his bearing rein, and he'll relieve the strain on him by bearing down his head, and flinging his weight on the collar to help him pull. If a man had to carry a weight up a hill on his back, how would he like to have his head tied back? Perhaps you may have noticed Mr. ——'s horses pull the 'bus up Holborn Hill. They're tightly borne up; but then they are very fine animals, fat and fine: there's no such cattle, perhaps, in a London 'bus—

207. *The Milk Man*, from a series of watercolours of New York tradesmen by Nicolino Calyo, about 1840.

leastways there's none better—and they're borne up for show. Now, a jib-horse won't go in a bearing rein, and will without it. I've seen that myself; so what can be the use of it? It's just teasing the poor things for a sort of fashion. I must keep exact time at every place where a time-keeper's stationed. Not a minute's excused—there's a fine for the least delay. I can't say that it's often levied; but still we are liable to it. If I've been blocked, I must make up for the block by galloping; and if I'm seen to gallop, and anybody tells our people, I'm called over the coals. I must drive as quick with a thunder-rain pelting in my face, and the roads in a muddle, and the horses starting—I can't call it shying, I have 'em too well in hand—at every flash, just as quick as if it was a fine hard road, and fine weather. It's not easy to drive a 'bus; but I can drive, and must drive, to an inch: yes, sir, to half an inch. I know if I can get my horses' heads through a space, I can get my splinter-bar through. I drive by my pole, making it my centre. If I keep it fair in the centre, a carriage must follow, unless it's slippery weather, and then there's no calculating. I saw the first 'bus start in 1829. I heard the first 'bus called a Punch-and-Judy carriage, 'cause you could see the people inside without a frame. The shape was about the same as it is now, but bigger and heavier. A 'bus changes horses four or five times a-day, according to the distance. There's no cruelty to the horses, not a bit, it wouldn't be allowed. I fancy that

'busses now pay the proprietors well. The duty was $2\frac{1}{2}d.$ a-mile, and now it's $1\frac{1}{2}d.$ Some companies save twelve guineas a week by the doing away of toll-gates. The 'stablishing the threepennies—the short uns—has put money in their pockets. I'm an unmarried man. A 'bus driver never has time to look out for a wife. Every horse in our stables has one day's rest in every four; but it's no rest for the driver.'

Henry Mayhew, *London Labour and the London Poor*, 1851

THE CARRIER'S HORSE

Gordon's book was published by—of all people—the Religious Tract Society, in 1893. His world is substantially the world of *Black Beauty*, but, as he says, the treatment afforded the London working horse was, by then, considerably better than that common in Anna Sewell's lifetime, owing almost entirely to the humanitarian movement triggered off by that all-time best-seller. No one knows the total number of copies printed, since very many impressions were pirated in the United States where British copyright was not respected: it sold as well after its period of copyright had expired as before, and probably its total circulation has about equalled that of *Robinson Crusoe* and *Pilgrim's Progress*.

The carrying trade of these days is in the hands of the railway companies, and the carrier's horse is for all practical purposes the railway horse. Of the 84,000,000 tons of general merchandise hauled along the railroads of this island in 1890, the bulk was collected and distributed in railway vans.

A railway company is obliged to keep several varieties of horse in its stables. It must have horses that walk for the heavy traffic, and horses that trot for the light; or to put it differently, waggon horses, goods horses, parcels horses, horses for shunting, and horses for omnibuses in the cases in which its omnibuses are not horsed by contract. And, taking all these varieties together, we find that the companies collecting and delivering goods in the metropolis have amongst them a stud of 6,000. These we shall not be over-valuing at 60l. apiece all round, which means that railway shareholders have some 360,000l. invested in horseflesh in London alone, to say nothing of the vans and drays, which would be worth quite as much.

The typical railway horse is the van horse, of which ten-thirteenths of the stud consist. He is not specially bred for his calling; he is but a dray horse whom the association of certain merits has peculiarly fitted for railway work. There is no mistaking this horse; he is a Britisher to the backbone, but he is not so easy to get as he used to be, owing to the foreigners collecting so many specimens of him. He is as good a horse as we

208. *London Cab Stand*, 1888, by R. Dollman. On the right are hansoms, on the left four-wheeled 'growlers'.

209. London Bridge at
noonday, 1872: a horse-
borne traffic jam.

have, being power personified, with nothing about him in wasteful excess. Well-moulded in every muscle, standing not an inch too high on his well-shaped legs—'give me legs and feet', said the Midland superintendent to us, 'and I will look after the rest'—broad and strong, with nothing of tubbiness in the barrel or scragginess about the neck and head, he is admirably adapted for the work for which he is chosen; and that work he does well. . . .

The Great Western prides itself on having as good a stud as any company in London, and the stables in which it is housed are admittedly excellent. In the new block in South Wharf Road there are four floors of horses one over the other, the top floor being almost as high as the hotel, with a look-out down on to the station roof. Sunday is the railway horse's day of rest, a day which all of them know, though they may not call it by that name, and for seeing the horse at home, quiet and contented, under exceptionally favourable circumstances, there is no place better than Paddington. In the new stables there are about 500 horses; close by,

nearer the goods station, there is another lot of 140, comfortably installed under lofty arches, which are sensibly ventilated and lighted electrically; and further on there is the infirmary, with three dozen stables for invalids. Altogether, the Great Western has about 1,100 horses working in London. . . .

The Great Western horses are under the superintendence of Captain Milne, and there is a certain army precision and smartness about the management which is not apparent in all railway stables. As much as possible the colours are kept separate, one stable being of greys, another of chestnuts, another of bays, and so on; and right well do the carefully groomed animals look, standing in their neat straw litter, with a glint of sunlight on them, clean as a picture against the white background leading up to the varnished pine roof overhead, while most of the smooth arched blue brick gangways are as clean as a man-o'-war deck, the only thing on them being the two fodder sacks, like a huge ottoman, at the far end. . . .

Over each horse's head is his number, answering to

210. *The Smith Brothers Brewery*, *c.* 1861, on Eighteenth Street between Seventh and Eighth Avenues, New York. From a lithograph by 'L. M.' (possibly Louis Maurer). This detail shows horse-drawn beer waggons, called 'drays' in England.

the number branded on his hoof, and behind him is his harness, all in due order as if it were a trooper's; but there is not a collar to be seen. When the Great Western horse comes home at night his collar goes not to the stable but to the drying-room, whence it comes in the morning ready for wear, warm and comfortable as a clean pair of socks.

At two o'clock on Monday morning the week's work begins. The Covent Garden vans then go out. At eight o'clock the stables are in full bustle, and the runs that slope from floor to floor are alive with the descending crowd, as, to the jingle of the harness, they come cautiously down. Some of them, before the day is out, will have been as far as Woolwich Dockyard and back; some of them will be out for eighteen hours, to rest on the morrow, some of them for six, to take a longer turn next day. So many vans have to be horsed, and so much work has to be done, and somehow it has to be got through, or there would be an accumulation which it would be difficult to deal with. Early on the Monday

morning the silent goods-yard surlily wakes to life, and it knows no rest till Saturday night. What the trains bring the vans must take, what the vans bring the trains must take, be it much or little. Of course there is an average; and provision is made for the tide which begins to rise at Michaelmas and breaks its last big wave at Easter.

The heaviest railway van weighs two tons, and will carry seven or more. Such a van, with its load drawn by its four-horse team, will be a moving mass of thirteen tons, one of the heaviest things going through the streets of London, as the railway parcels cart is one of the fastest. The team walks; the single horse trots, and is not supposed to go more than eight miles an hour, but he does, although it is not every one who would give him credit for the rate at which he slips along. There is no vehicle in the Great Western service worked with that most extravagant arrangement, a tandem team, but some of the heavy drays have three horses abreast, an economical device, giving almost the

211. *The Buffalo Hunt.* George Catlin explains why these seemingly incredible feats were possible. In a sense the buffalo was blind and only its stupidity and false sense of security induced by thousands of years during which its chief enemy had operated on foot and without fire-arms enabled the hunters, red and white alike, to do their vast execution.

212. *The Grand Drive, Central Park.* A Currier and Ives lithograph of New York in the summer of 1869.

213. *The Life of a Fireman: The Metropolitan System.* A Currier and Ives lithograph, New York 1866. There were special designs of horse-drawn vehicle for all fire-fighting purposes.

power of four horses in two-and-two, and having only the disadvantage of heating the middle horse rather more than the outsiders. Like the fours, and threes, and unicorns, the pairs are supposed to walk, and it is these vans which do most of the work. Their average tare is a ton. Like a train, they are fitted with a powerful brake, which eases the strain of the stoppages, but the starting pull is at times tremendous, particularly with thoughtless drivers, and it is this effort, as much as the constant jarring of the feet, which makes a horse's London life so short. . . .

Weather will age a horse more than it will a man, owing to its affecting the work so much; and it will be

quite as prejudicial to its health. In dry weather almost as many horses slip down as in the rain, and quite as many are run into; but the dry weather has nothing to answer for in the chafings by the wet harness, and the colds and sore throats which lead on to other troubles that make short work of the London horse of all sorts and conditions. . . .

Pickfords [the North Western agents] do an enormous business, and have a stud of some 4,000 horses, of which about two out of ten pass through their stables in a year. The firm has a long pedigree, and dates back to the days of their old team waggons, the driver of which did not ride on the vehicle, but on a handy cob,

from whose back he worked the string of horses by means of a long whip. One of the first of these drivers was the founder of the oldest firm of shipping carriers in London, John Smither & Co.; and this reminds us that just as the goods-yards have their feeders and distributors, so have the wharves and docks. Some of these shipping horses are as good as those in the railway service, but as a rule they are of poorer quality. Some are doing their twenty-five miles a day, and in one stud there is a horse that is twenty-five years old, but their average London life is six years; and they are bought at six, when they can be got at a profitable price. . . .

The largest of [the firms of carriers] is Carter Paterson's, who have a stud of 2,000 stabled at their twenty London depots, the headquarters being in the Goswell Road. The system on which these carrying companies work is practically that of the railways. The parcels are collected from the senders on information received at the numerous order stations, which the public know by the show-boards. From the houses and shops of the consignors the parcels are taken as a rule by one-horse vans to the nearest depot, where they are transhipped into vans drawn by pairs or teams, and find their way across London to the depot nearest the address of the consignee, from which depot they are sent out to their destination in the local single-horse vans. . . .

The horses are generally of a lighter type than the railway horse, as befits the lighter trade, and they are worked on a different system. Sunday is the rest day, and the horse does nine trips a week; one day he has two trips, the next day he has one, the next he has two, the next one, and so on—three trips every two days. The length of the trip depends very much on the season, and during the fever heat of Christmas time the carrier's horse has quite as much work to do as he can manage. . . .

Pickfords, who do heavier work in connection with the North Western, and the other firms who have a good deal of railway agency, have heavier horses to suit the trade. One of the noticeable things on Thanksgiving Day in 1872 was the ease with which the Speaker's coach, usually drawn by six horses, was hauled along by a pair of Pickford's Clydesdales, engaged for that occasion only, behind whom it seemed to be as light as an empty dray. The Parcels Delivery Company are at the other end of the scale, and average a much lighter build of animal; in fact, the carrier's horse is of all varieties. . . .

Some of them are evidently of an advanced age, but then it is not every carrier's horse that has made its first appearance in London in that character. The more hours they rest the longer they last, and the more they fetch when 'cast'; but in a good many instances the casting is the final one to that dark bourne whence no horse returns except as 'meat'. These, however, are the great minority; the majority having yet another, and perhaps another, experience before they face the slaughterman. Some last a few months; of others there are very extraordinary stories, but we refrain; and even including the patriarchs, we should not have an average of much more than five years of London hard labour.

W. J. Gordon, *The Horse-World of London*, 1893

JADING AND DRAWING A HORSE

George Ewart Evans in his works on East Anglian folklore and folk life has preserved for us much of the tradition and described in detail the hereditary skills of the last generations of horsemen who worked with the great horses on the land and on the roads in the Eastern Counties, especially in Suffolk and Cambridgeshire. The youngest of these 'owd bors' is now something like seventy-five, and the pride of their youth was overcast by the years of the First World War. But their world, of which the great red Suffolk Horse was the undoubted king, did not finally pass away until just after the Second World War. When the last of them is gone, our last link with the squires and pages and 'stede-men' who lived in the service of the Great Horse of chivalry, and whose skills were transmitted to a certain generation of ploughmen and waggoners at that point when the Great Horse renounced the battlefield for the cornfield, will be snapped for ever.

One of the most interesting and spectacular devices of the old farm horsemen was the stopping of a horse

214. *Newgate Prison from St Sepulchre's Church*, 1901. A painting of horse-drawn London by M. Durham.

dramatically so that it would not move. This was called in East Anglia *jading* a horse; and it was from this practice more than any other that the horsemen sometimes earned the name of *horse-witches* because they were able to make the horse stand as though it were paralysed or bewitched. A note in Gibbon shows how ancient this practice was. It concerns the sixth-century Frankish king, Clovis:

'After the Gothic victory, Clovis made rich offerings to St Martin of Tours. He wished to redeem his warhorse by the gift of one hundred pieces of gold, but the enchanted steed could not move from the stable till the price of his redemption had been doubled. This *miracle* provoked the king to exclaim: '*Vere, B. Martinus est bonus in auxilio, sed carus in negotio.*' (Indeed, St Martin may be a good friend when you're in trouble, but he's an expensive one to do business with.) It is evident that the priests who served St Martin knew how to jade a horse and to attribute its state to the Saint's intervention; and if Gibbon had had the slightest suspicion of how the *miracle* had been performed he would have used a much stronger form of irony than a mere italicizing of the word itself. For the priests, in fact, were doing exactly the same trick, and probably by exactly the same means, as the old East Anglian and Scottish horsemen who made out and actually believed that the horse's immobility was the result of some secret and magical device they had resorted to. This incident concerning the Saint is also an example of early Christianity's adaptation of the old pagan beliefs, with politic foresight, for its own purpose; and, as already shown, traces of the sacred horse-cult remained in Christian ceremony for centuries after this event recorded by Gibbon. . . .

The following example of horse jading happened in Suffolk just after the First World War. It is typical of how an older horseman who had in his possession most of the ancient secrets, was able to deal with a situation that had baffled a younger man. The older horseman tells the story: 'I was coming home with three lovely black horses which we always used on the road; and I used to glory in trimming them up, because they wore the worsted—red, white and blue—and they used to look lovely. I found I'd come to the Wetherden *May-pole*, and there was a chap there with his horses. He said to me:

' "Hullo, Charlie. You're just the chap I want to see."

'I said: "What's the matter now, mate?"

' "Somebody's been *a-doing the saddle up* on my horses and I cannot get these horses away. The trace-horse is backing and the *fill'us* [shaft-horse] is going another way!"

' "Wait here a minute, bo'," I said; "I'll tell you what: you've been a-braggin' again, haven't you?"

' "No" ' he say, "I haven't said a lot."

' "I told you," I said, "you must not brag what you can do, because there's allus somebody as good a man as yourself. Here now," I said, "wait a minute. . . . "

' "What about your horses?" he said.

' "I ain't frightened my horses will run away: it's yours I'll have to look after."

'So I just went a-front there with my milk and vinegar; rubbed it in my palm and fingers; and then I rubbed it inside the horses' nose and then round their nostrils. I then said to this young horseman: "Now hop on your waggon and be off!" and he done so.'

As can be inferred from the above account there is no magical practice involved. Someone had played a trick on the young horseman and had put down a substance that was so obnoxious to the horses' delicate sense of smell that they would not move. The older and more knowledgeable horseman knew exactly what had happened and took immediate steps to neutralize this smell. The substance or substances were placed down either on an object in front of the horse or somewhere on the front of the horse himself. Until the smell of the substance is neutralized the horse will not move forward an inch, resisting all kinds of persuasion and even force. One horseman revealed that he could jade a horse standing, say, on the sandy apron outside an inn simply by walking round him and unobtrusively dropping one of the obnoxious powders in the sand, especially in front of him: 'You didn't have to touch the horse, but that would stop him.' The same horseman also revealed that if this particular device had been used there was no need to use a neutralizing substance. A well-informed horseman simply had to grasp the horse's head firmly and give it a sharp turn and *back*

215. The last pit ponies at Easington Colliery, Co. Durham, coming up for the last time.

him out of the area that had been contaminated by the jading substance. . . .

Many of these secret jading substances are organic; and their number is added to by, for instance, an observant horseman adapting something for his own use. While out ploughing a horseman had noticed a stoat some distance away stalking a rabbit. The stoat was gradually moving round unobserved by the rabbit. But as soon as the stoat got into the wind and the rabbit scented it, the rabbit set up a shriek and remained as though paralysed. It was easy then, as the horseman saw, for the stoat to make its kill. The incident remained in his mind and was reinforced by another experience he had shortly afterwards. He was ploughing a *stetch* not far from the headlands when his two horses suddenly stopped dead. He was too wise and experienced a horseman to attempt to force them to go forward: instead he turned them short and proceeded to plough another *stetch*. A little while later he gave his horses a rest, and returned to the spot they had refused to pass. He found a dead stoat lying near the hedge. Reasoning from this he made himself a jading substance compounded of stoat's liver and rabbit's liver, dried and

powdered up and added to *dragon's blood*[1] which was a code name among the old horsemen for one of their more powerful jading substances. The same horseman, a stallion-leader, gave another instance of how he made use of the horse's hyper-sensitive power of smell. When his horse staled he kept some of the urine. He corked it down in a bottle until the smell was particularly aggressive. If he wanted to keep his horse away from a certain mare he had only to rub some of the liquid on the stallion's bridle or on the mare to ensure that the horse would not go near her.

In addition to the repellent or jading substances there are the *drawing* or *calling oils*. They have the opposite effect: they *draw* or *call* a horse towards the horseman; but they, too, depend for their effect on the horse's keen sense of smell. The drawing oils are nearly all aromatic oils to which the horse is attracted. The following will show how the name *drawing* arose: To catch a frisky horse or a young colt in a field the horseman placed a little of the mixture of oil of origanum, oil of rosemary, oil of cinnamon, and oil of fennel about his person.

[1] The actual substance is red-gum resin which exudes from a kind of palm-fruit.

216. *Cart and Horses* by John Constable. The thill-and-trace tandem team, with harness essentially the same as that seen in English illuminated manuscripts of the fourteenth century.

The instructions with this recipe which came from an old horseman's notebook were: *Set this mixture by the wind;* that is, the horseman was advised to stand in the wind so that as soon as the colt or horse scented him he would advance towards him. On a warm day, the instructions said, it would be sufficient for the horseman to place a few drops on his perspiring forehead to *call* his horses from a fair distance without saying a word, or making any sound. Another device was to bake sweet-scented cakes to give to the horse as tit-bits. . . .

The castor or wart that grows on the inside of the horse's foreleg was also used as the basis for a drawing powder: 'Dry it in your pocket; great [*sic*] it into powder with a bright file or rasp. And it will be a pure white powder. Put it in a verey Close Box for the purpose. This powder has a great attraction for all animals, and the horse itself. The oil of rhodium possesses peculiar properties: all animals cherish a fondness for it and it exercises a subduing influence over them. Oil of Cumin: the horse has an instinctive passion for this. Both are natives of Arabia. With this knowledge horse taming becomes easy, and when the horse scents the odour he is drawn toward it.'

Drawing oils and jading substances were sometimes used with spectacular effect. A Norfolk man answered an advertisement for a horse-leader in Essex. He went down to the farm and applied for the job. They told him that the horse's previous leader—an old man—had died suddenly. He asked to see the horse and they took him to the stable. When he got to the horse's stall he found it was locked. Then the farmer admitted that there had been many applicants for the job already, but each had been driven out of the stall by the horse.

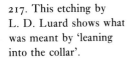

217. This etching by L. D. Luard shows what was meant by 'leaning into the collar'.

219. The hussar tradition naturalized in Western Europe—the officer's horse, a detail from Géricault's *Officier de Chasseurs.*

Latterly they had been feeding him by dropping his fodder from a loft above the stall, and lowering down pails of water on a string. The farmer warned him of the danger of entering the stall. But the Norfolk man said: 'Never mind. Give me the keys.' He opened the door, took off his cap and threw it into the stall: 'If that's welcome,' he said, 'so am I.' In a short time the horse came to the door: they put the bridle on him and shortly afterwards the Norfolk man was taking the horse to the smithy to be shod. . . .

Drawing oils were also used in a more quiet way. A stallion leader had a walking stick which he invariably carried with him when he travelled a horse. The stick had a special feature about it; the horseman had split it at the end, just above the ferrule, and he had inserted

a piece of cotton wool which he impregnated with a drawing oil mixture . . . A similar appreciation of the horse's acute sense of smell induced an old blacksmith to keep a bunch of violets in the forge whenever the season permitted. He believed that the smell of the flowers had a soothing effect on the horses brought to him to be shod. In this connection it is worth adding that it was once considered the fashion to wear a little bunch of violets in the coat when riding to hounds.

Many of the drawing oils were allied to the conditioning powders which were sold in great quantities up to recent times. These powders helped to keep the horse in good condition; and their essence or oil was often the kind of tit-bit that made an effective drawing substance as well. An advertisement in an eighteenth-

220. (*Overleaf*) France was the first and is still the most important country to have been conquered by the English style of racing and its ancillary, thoroughbred breeding. (*Racecourse* by Edgar Degas)

218. A waggon and team of horses by Rosa Bonheur. Six Percherons like this could pull a waggon steadily at a fast trot.

century newspaper shows that in East Anglia they have varied hardly at all over a period of two hundred years:

ADVERTISEMENT

Having fix'd up two large Mills which I work with Horses, for grinding the following Powders with which I'll supply Country Shopkeepers, upon Cheaper Terms than any Man in London; I sell for Ready Money, and no less Quantities than 14 lb of a Sort; and to any Person that takes 56 lb of an Sort at a Time, I'll allow 2s for every 56 lb on Account of Carriage, or 4s for 112 lb.

Fine Powder Liquorice at 6d per Pound	Powder Gentian at 7d
	Powder Bay-berries at 6d
Ditto second sort at 3d	Root of Liquorice at 5d
Powder Elecampane at 4d	Powder of White Helle-
Powder Turmerick at 6d	bore Root at 16d
Powder Fenugreek at 4d	Fine Powder of Ginger at
Powder Horse Spice at 4d	34s per cwt.
Powder Aniseeds at 6d	Ditto second sort at 18s
Powder Cummin seeds at 6d	per cwt.
	Pepper Dust at 30s per
Powder Diapente at 6d	cwt.

N.B.: Please to direct for JOHN ROWLEY, Druggist at the Red Cross in the Poultry, London; where may be had all Sorts of Drugs, Chymicals and Galenicals upon Reasonable Terms.

The Pattern under the Plough, 1966

This catalogue has many items in common with those recommended by a Kentish horseman nearly two centuries earlier:

'These things are most excellent to put in horses provender to preserve them from . . . all diseases.
The Powder of a Wolfes Liver
The Powder of Ennula Compana ('ellicampane')
The Powder of Pollipodium of the Oake
The fine cut peeces of ruebarbe
The Powder of Brimstone made very fine
The Powder of licorish, Anniseedes, Fenegreke, Turmericke, Bay-berries,
Long-pepper, Agrimony, Camamile, Wormewood, Sauen, Linseed, Smalage,
Persely, Rue, Isop, Coltesfoote, Horehownd, and such like.'

The same author has left us the following gruesome diagnosis and prognosis:

'*The Mourning of the Chine: The Signes to Know the Disease.*
First, the continuall distilling reume in the head
Secondly, the continueing knobs between the Iawes
Thirdly, the keeping of his hair without casting
Fourthly, the continuall running of thicke stinking matter at the nose
Fifthly the fastning or growing of a knob as big as a walnut, to the inside of one of the Iawes, and then commit his carcasse to the croes, for then he is past helpe.'

(From Nicholas Morgan, *Perfection of Horsemanship*, 1609.)

The Mourning of the Chine is nowadays known as strangles. It is the equine equivalent of mumps, and about as infectious, though no more dangerous.

THE HORSEMAN'S WORD

At some time between the middle of the seventeenth century, when the Great Horse in Britain passed out of military service to employment in coach, waggon and plough teams, and the second half of the eighteenth century when the Agricultural Improvers converted all but a fringe of British farmers from ox husbandry to horse husbandry, there grew up a unique institution known as the Society of Horsemen. Its existence seems to have been confined to the eastern side of Britain, but it extended from Kent to Aberdeenshire and beyond. The early stages of its history are entirely undocumented, but must have been fascinating, because initially its membership will have consisted half of ploughmen and waggoners brought up in the ox-drawn tradition, and half of grooms and drivers from the households of the gentry who had followed the Great Horse into its new field of activity. These diverse elements combined to form what was neither a friendly society, nor a clandestine trade union, nor a working-men's club, nor a craft guild: yet the Society partook, one way or another, of the nature of all these bodies,

221. (*Previous page*) One of the advantages of the canal system which spread its net over England in the half-century preceding the railway era was the great scope it gave to draught horses, a single one of which could pull a barge weighing many times as much as the waggon drawn by a team of six horses. When the Ouse navigation was opened at Boroughbridge in mid-Yorkshire one barge was said to have the capacity of six hundred packhorse loads. (Detail from *Flatford Mill* by John Constable)

222. *Broadway in the Snow, near Spring Street*, a lithograph of 1857 by H. Sebron.

and there was added to its ritual a strong element reminiscent of witchcraft as revealed by the 'confessions' of convicted witches about the ceremonies of the cult practised in Cromwellian times. The initiation ceremonies had much in common with those of the witch-coven, and the most important of the craft secrets, such as the power to 'bind and loose' horses so that they would either refuse to move from or refuse to stop in a certain place were in effect 'white' witchcraft.

The last members of this Society are still alive in Britain, all of them upwards of seventy, but probably there are no more practising branches. In effect, most shoeing-smiths were honorary members. The following is the form of oath taken by initiates in the East Anglian region, but it is not likely that this varied much from district to district.

※I of my own free will and accord do hereby most solomly vow and swear before God and all these witnesses that I will always heal conceal and never reveal any art or part of this secret of horsemanry which is to be revealed to me at this time or any other time hereafter except to a true and faithful brother after finding him to be so after the trial and strict examination. Further more I vow and swear that I will not give it or see it given to a fool nor to a madman nor to a drunkard nor to any one in drink nor to any one who would abuse or bad use (?) his own or his master's horses. Further more I vow and swear that I will not give it nor see it given to a tradesman except to a blacksmith or a farier or to a worker of horses. Further more I vow and swear that I will not give it nor see it given to any one under 18 or above 45 years of age nor without the sum of £1

223. A barge horse in about 1905. Compare the photograph with the horse painted by Constable in Plate 221.

224. Indian Army Cavalry in 1911: the reception of King George V at the Durbar, Delhi.

sterling or anything of the same value being placed on the table as I do at this time before three lawful sworn brethren after trial and examination finding them to be so. Further more I vow and swear that I will not give it nor see it given to any one after the sun sets on Saturday night nor before he rises on Monday morning nor in a public house. Further more I vow and swear that I will always be at a brother's call within the bounds of three miles except I can give a lawful excuse such as my wife in childbed or my mares in foaling or myself in bad health or in my master's employment. Further more I vow and swear that I will not give nor see it given to my Father nor Mother Sister nor Brother nor to a woman at all. Further more I vow and swear that I will not write it nor endite it paint nor print it carve nor engrave it in the valleys nor on the hillside on rock nor gravel sand nor snow silver nor gold brass nor copper iron nor steel woolen nor silk, or anything moveable or unmoveable under the great canopy of heaven or so much as wave a signal (?) of it in the air whereby the secrets of horsemanry might be revealed.

And if I fail in any of these obligations that I go under at this time or any other time hereafter, I to my heart wish and desire that my throat may be cut from ear to ear with a horseman's knife and my body torn to pieces between wild horses and blown by the four winds of heaven to the utmost parts of the earth, my heart torn from my left breast and its blood wrung out and buried in the sands of the sea shore where the sea ebbs and flows thrice every 24 hours that my rememberance may be no more heard among true and faithful brethren. So help me God to keep this solom obligation.

The Society cannot be simply classified as a workers' syndicate 'against' the employer. It is true that it formed an influential pressure group since it controlled the source of power in the pre-machine age; in some areas where neither wind nor water mills were used, even grist was ground in horse-operated mills. It could make life hell for a farmer who wished a member to do something contrary to the traditions of his craft. But outside those districts, such as parts of Northum-

225. (*Left*) Horses entraining for veterinary hospitals in France during the First World War. On the Eastern Front between 1914 and 1918 vast numbers of cavalry were deployed, and decisive actions fought, between the mounted arms of the Russian, German and Austrian forces. In 1939 the Polish army took the field with division after division of cavalry supported by horse artillery which found itself helpless in the face of aircraft and armour.

On the Western Front almost equally large cavalry forces spent their time behind the front, waiting for the tactical situation which would justify their employment and which never came. More horses died from shellfire in the picket lines where they stood tethered inactively, or died of exposure to the elements there, than were killed in any sort of action. It is true, of course, that by far the greater part of the artillery on the Western Front was horse-drawn, though not Horse Artillery in the technical sense which implies such mobility as will enable the batteries to move at the pace of the squadrons which they support; and artillery remount depots swallowed horses of all kinds, from vanners to heavy draught, by the thousand over those years. This and the next three paintings are by Edwin Noble.

226. (*Left*) Evacuated from the front line, horses and mules on the way back to casualty clearing stations in France.

227. (*Top right*) Birth of the motor horse-box, first used as an ambulance on the Western Front.

228. (*Right*) Horses draw horses out of Flanders mud. The equine counterpart of the stretcher-bearer on the Western Front.

berland, where very large farms were the rule, many of the younger men who worked with the Suffolk Punch, the Shire, the Old Lincolnshire Black Horse, the Cleveland Bay and the Clydesdale, were themselves the sons of farmers, and had reasonable expectations of succeeding to the lease- or freehold of the family farm or else of setting up for themselves elsewhere in early middle age. Such men would not regard themselves as part of a rural proletariat, nor for that matter would 'horsemen'—that is, ploughmen and waggoners—in general, for they were the agrarian aristocracy of labour.

THE HORSE IN THE TWENTIETH CENTURY

The introduction of horses, or of any large animals, on to the stage, is always attended nowadays with a slight air of the ridiculous. *Hassan* with real camels is scarcely an improvement on *Hassan* without camels. There have been periods in the history of the theatre when such entries would have been perfectly feasible: you could for instance have brought several horses on to the stage of the Roman Theatre at Orange, but no one ever did. The design of London theatres in the great age of English drama, for a few decades either side of 1600, was such that only people were able to get on to the stage, access to which was by ladders and narrow pass-

ages. But the type of heroic historical spectacle which drew the biggest audience tended to present characters who always moved on horseback, and actions which in real life would be performed by mounted persons. For this reason Elizabethan stage dialogue comprises some of the most impressive verbal painting of the horse in action that has ever been written. And it was better that way.

However, for a brief period in the nineteenth century there was a class of London theatrical performance known as hippodrama which had its counterparts in Paris and New York. Astley's Amphitheatre specialized in it, but examples of the genre were also put on at regular theatres such as the Royal, Drury Lane, and the Covent Garden Opera House. Some of these flesh-and-blood horse operas were specially written, but others were adaptations of such Shakespearian plays as *Richard II*, cut so as to point up the equestrian scenes and bring White Surrey further down-stage; or else they were spectacular dramatizations of Sir Walter Scott's novels. Obviously *Ivanhoe* with its tournament offered much scope.

In that quarter of the twentieth century in which the triumph of the motor-car over the horse became first inevitable and then complete, a similar triumph of the cinema over the live theatre was accomplished. The theatre was forced back almost exclusively into capital cities; but the cinema which had supplanted it was a

229. *Colt Hunting in the New Forest* by Lucy Kemp Welch. This is the annual 'Drift of the Forest' which was incumbent on tenants of many manors as part of services due to their feudal lord. 'Colt' in the New Forest, and on Exmoor, means foal of either sex: the distinction is between 'mare-colts' and 'horse-colts'.

silent one, as well as a black-and-white one, and word-painting was something outside the horizon of those who directed it. Violent action in the open air was its forte, whether in the presentation of the cowboys-v.-Indians formula or of historical drama set in any period in any country. Steadily, as the horse lost employment in the armies and the transport undertakings of the Western world, more opportunities were opened for it on the silent, monochrome screen. It was essential that the audience should be able to tell one horse from another, since it became increasingly difficult to distinguish one actor, once mounted and placed at a certain range from the camera, from another except by their clothes; the more so in the frequent instances where the actors could not really ride, and if the action called for paces faster than a walk had to be replaced by extras who could. Monochrome film does not distinguish readily between bay, brown and chestnut horses. A very bright, classically-coloured palomino is recognizable by its silver mane, but the only safe way is to mount the hero on a white (or grey will do) and the villain on a black. Thus photogenic horses of these hues

230. Ploughing, rolling and broadcasting seed by hand, though at this time it was common to sow seed from a horse-drawn drill. (*Seed-Time*, 1854–6, by J. F. Herring)

were at one time at a premium in California. This situation also created a steady demand for extras who could sit on a horse and look as if they belonged there, or could drive a buggy or a stage-coach, not to mention stuntmen (and stuntwomen) capable of more advanced feats.

Russian cinema, with its historical spectaculars, has always relied heavily on equestrian effects. What would *Battleship Potemkin* be without the shots of the Cossacks roughing up the populace in the Odessa Steps sequence? Or Eisenstein's *Dmitri Donskoi* without the massed squadrons of the Teutonic Knights advancing so relentlessly at the first battle of Tannenberg? Often such episodes taxed the directors' historical advisers beyond their powers. It was said of Eisenstein that he knew everything, that he was such a polymath he needed no specialist advisers. If that is so, then the Tannenberg sequence was his Waterloo, since it shows a crashing anachronism. Part of the effect is gained by the rhythmic rise and fall of the armoured colossi in their stirrups as they trot towards the waiting Russians. But in fact the medieval knight did not rise from the saddle at the trot, he did not go tittup-tittup-tittup but joggle-joggle-joggle, he just 'sat it out'. The nearest modern equivalent to the way the knights rode is to be seen, nowadays, in the Household Cavalry when they are escorting the royal coach on ceremonial occasions. The contrast is more marked because the postillions on the coach team are actually rising to the trot. That is why it is called 'posting'. This is the kind of thing both cinema and television tend to get wrong nine times out of ten.

231. *Timber-Hauling* by Lucy Kemp Welch.

During the last quarter-century the most interesting, the least expected, and the most hopeful new departure in horsemanship, riding as therapy, has come into being. Following on the widespread poliomyelitis epidemic of 1947, hospitals in England and Norway had the idea of letting child patients who were convalescent but still severely disabled perform their remedial exercise on horseback. The results were so good that the method was applied to other patients: to limbless children, for example, and to spastics of all ages, and finally to sufferers from mental as well as physical disabilities. Even that most daunting psychological disability, autism, has been helped by riding therapy. Great care is needed in the selection of suitable horses, that quality known as 'confidential' being required to the utmost degree. It is significant that the majority of animals employed in this new role consists of ponies. This is not solely due to the fact that most disabled riders are children; whatever their age mounting and dismounting are the most difficult parts of the exercise, and not the part from which most benefit is derived. We are in fact back with the palfrey of Queen Anne's time and earlier, which was never very tall, partly because it was used in activities that entailed frequent mounting and dismounting, and partly because it was overwhelmingly of what we now call pony blood, and those breeds such as the Connemara which formerly ambled and paced now provide, with their 'easy' gait, the ideal therapeutic vehicle. It is notable that American physiotherapists use for this purpose the *paso fino* which is the Latin-American descendant of the original Spanish ambler. In the field of dressage it is possible for severely disabled persons to compete at international level, as the record of Lis Hartel shows. In Britain the Riding for the Disabled Association which has 150 local groups not only benefits patients but also the members of the group who volunteer to help. It takes, in the initial stages, three attendants to start a disabled rider on his way to recovery; and members of such teams may well feel gratified that by skills gained in the exercise of their own chosen sport they are able to contribute to the relief of human suffering.

Among other ailments which the horse can contribute to curing is the gastric ulcer, of the type induced by the urban rat-race. It is noticeable that the horse revival began in the European country which first achieved total mechanization—Great Britain. To a certain extent present-day interest in horses and the sports which depend on them is a revulsion from the car-centred civilization, from the Brave New World whose chronology, according to Aldous Huxley's prophecy, would be counted in Years of Our Ford. It is significant that a new monthly magazine, *Riding*, its title later expanded to *Riding and Driving*, appeared in London as early as 1936. Today it is one of five such monthlies published in the United Kingdom, besides the weekly *Horse & Hound* which is a uniquely British institution. Having survived all the expansions and contractions of the British horse world since 1884, the number of its classified advertisements of horses for sale and wanted at any given time (taking the season of the year into account) is a fair index of the extent of private horse ownership in the country. One has only to try and buy or sell a horse anywhere else in Europe to realize that there is no continental equivalent, not even in Germany which is probably the West European country with the greatest recent expansion in horsemanship for pleasure, though the special circumstances of territorial dismemberment, the ruin of the rural gentry, and the discrediting of the military caste have combined to create a different equestrian image from that of, say, present-day France. Consider only that East Prussia, home not only of the Junker but of the most famous German breed and the most famous stud complex (Trakehnen), no longer belongs to either of the German Republics; and that of all Western armies, the Bundeswehr offers the least encouragement to riding as a sport for officers or other ranks. An essentially bourgeois country like Holland, where the part played by the horse in agriculture is today minimal, yet has a surprisingly large number of horses per head of human population, though the equine population is largely transient. Holland is a kind of entrepôt, and the Dutch international horse-dealer is to be found operating in France and in Italy. Dutch dealers advertise Welsh ponies 'direkt aus England' (*sic*) in German periodicals.

The new horse-culture of European leisure is based,

like an earlier one, on British example. (Unlike the earlier one it is shared by the Japanese, who are currently the biggest buyers of hunter-type horses from New Zealand.) That vocabulary which was once a symbol of continental anglomania has been greatly expanded. To take only its baneful influence on the French language: there was an existing substratum of borrowings, mainly of Regency period, consisting partly of words denoting things for which there was no French term: thus *le* (loose-)*box* and *le dog-cart* make sense in their way. But this stratum also contains elements of illogical *franglais* like *le groom*, *le foal* and *le yearling*: of course there were (and still are) perfectly good real French equivalents. Such words are always mispronounced and wherever possible mis-spelt. But in our day, there has been added a new range of coinings, not totally accurate counterfeits, and monstrous derivations like *ponette* (pony-mare), *double-poney* (cob, more or less), *le cross* (cross-country phase of three-day event) and *le steeple* (Phase B of the same). This is only the Gallic revenge for the Anglophone massacre of French terms in the arts of ballet and dressage. Similar gems now decorate the vocabulary of other languages: even if the German for Phase B is *Rennbahngallop*, the

232. Three original glass-plate photographs by Frank Meadow Sutcliffe of nineteenth-century rural scenes, the first showing horses ploughing. The horses are Cleveland Bays, a popular breed in the United States today, where there are Cleveland Bay societies whose members breed and show them, though they do not plough with them.

233. Horses and a cart. The difference between a cart and a waggon is the number of wheels. Carts (two wheels) were generally used in more hilly districts, and waggons (four wheels) in flatter areas, though there were exceptions to this rule.

234. Horses used for dragging fishing boats ashore on a shallow beach, on the Yorkshire coast.

German horse still gets *ein Mash* after his exertions and at regular intervals during *das Training* (pronounced *Trynink*).

As European middle-class life achieves an increasingly dead level of uniformity, as the differences between Mediterranean culture and that north of the Alps steadily decrease, as even the quality of life in Western capitalist Europe ceases more and more to differ from that in Marxist Europe beyond the Elbe, a more or less standard dose of equestrianism will probably be injected into the life-style, at any rate of the professional classes, everywhere from Spain to Scandinavia, from Connemara to Cracow. Maybe no country will ever achieve that density of pony-club population (80,000) found in the country of origin; or the number of adults (a million) who ride for pleasure at least once a week in Britain. Probably in none is there such pressure by female children on parents to let them ride, at the same time so little matched by similar blackmail on the part of boys. The Mediterranean standard horse-situation is the señorita on her balcony admiring the caballero's display of *gineta*, the same in the twentieth century as in the age of the Cid. Uniquely in Britain can one see some such phenomenon as an incredibly handsome young man following the foxhounds on a bicycle, just to keep in sight his beloved who dismounted looks rather undistinguished but appears to great advantage on a well-turned-out hunter.

The increasing publicity value of equestrian sports at international level has had some curious side-effects. Prestige demands that nationals of one state shall shine as brilliantly as those of another in the stadia of Aachen and Rome and Wembley and Tokyo, on the same terms and under the same rules: among other things at dressage riding, which is essentially a legacy of the aristocratic West European court-culture of the seventeenth and eighteenth centuries. With what twinges of conscience, then, must the Soviet Master of Sport put on the obligatory costume of the manège, comprising as it does items drawn from the wardrobe of the effete Regency aristocracy, even a cut-down version of that unmistakable symbol of the monopoly-capitalist, the cylindrical silk hat?

Riding for women and girls does not seem to have much encouragement east of the Oder-Neisse line and its southward prolongation, as is shown by the all-male composition of the Russian, Polish and Bulgarian teams in the 1973 European Championship Junior *Concours Complet d'Equitation* held at Pompadour. A visit to a Hungarian collective farm in August 1972 provided another illustration of this: it culminated in a display, for the benefit of foreign sightseers, of horsemanship by the children of the collective farm-workers. Whereas the majority of English pony-club members likely to be seen in such an event would be girls, all these Hungarian riders were boys. This is the more puzzling as professional sexual equality, in theory and in practice, in the Marxist half of Europe is absolute. The cause must therefore be psychological, but its exact nature eludes this writer.

An essential basis for a widespread 'popular equitation' movement does still exist in East and East Central Europe, namely the presence of considerable stocks of light horses even in the 1970s. This is due to the traditional nature of the rural economy before mechanization. The fact that the heavy clay soils so typical of the British Isles and many parts of Western Europe are largely absent east of a certain line meant that heavy horses of the stamp of the Boulonnais or the Shire or the Jutland were not needed for arable farming, and even today one may see horses of pronounced 'oriental' type ploughing in Poland and Rumania. Owing to a different policy concerning collectivization and mechanization the same considerations do not apply with the same force in Hungary or the eastern, less industrialized parts of Czechoslovakia, but these countries too share a formative period of history when the political scene for centuries was dominated by Turkish pressure against the frontiers, and often by actual Turkish rule. This meant that the native horse-stock was saturated with oriental blood, Turkish or Turcoman or Arab, so that the common horse of the countryside was of 'warm-blooded' riding type: otherwise it was a pony of the stamp of the Polish *konik*, the Hungarian *goral* or the Rumanian *hucul*.

There is thus a tradition of peasant ownership, of peasant breeding, and of peasant riding, largely in the course of daily work as a herdsman, of horses of a kind

235. Cleaning the plough body, Berkshire.

which in other parts of Europe were inseparably connected in popular tradition with the aristocracy and their henchmen. If no ideological taboo operates, and if material prosperity advances at the speed which has recently been manifested, for example, in East Germany and Rumania, it is very possible that the leisure horse will become as much an everyday feature of East European life in the 1980s as of, say, Holland in the 1970s. Let no one be deceived into thinking that this common bond of interest will constitute a unifying influence that will make for wider understanding, world peace, the relief of tension and similar stock phrases. Recollect that it is less than a hundred years since all classes in all countries in Europe had a great deal more to do with horses than they do now; which contributed not at all to mutual understanding. As to international sport, it has patently contributed more to international ill-will in the last few Olympiads than the first organizers of the 1912 meeting ever dreamed of.

And so we come to the last bottle in our rack. It holds such wine as needs no bush, but yet I must read the label to you. Edwin Muir (1887–1959) may or may not have been a member of the Society of Horsemen, but he had all the qualifications. His working life began following the plough on the Isle of Wyre in Orkney, where his father farmed at the ancient Norse holding of Bu, mentioned in the Sagas. Orkney is at the far end of the Lands of the Great Horse: beyond that lie only Shetland, Faeroe, Iceland, where only ponies live and work. Muir as a verbal painter of the insular scene of his youth is worthy of respect, but he is not a mere 'regional' poet, and most of his work is contained in wider horizons. He was born well within the Age of the Horse, but outlived it, and what many regard as the last and the best of his major poems must have been inspired by the memory of those days of youth in Bu of Wyre. It may be that the man-made cataclysm of his prophetic but not hopeless nightmare will never come; or again, it may come in such a way that there will be no horses left to pull us out of the scrap-Neolithic sub-culture in which the survivors of nuclear ruin will exist. Yet this rescue is imaginable. We may come to it, not in the end, but in a new beginning.

236. Draught horses, an etching by Anton Lock.

✵ THE HORSES

Barely a twelvemonth after
The seven days war that put the world to sleep,
Late in the evening the strange horses came.
By then we had made our covenant with silence,
But in the first few days it was so still
We listened to our breathing and were afraid.
On the second day
The radios failed; we turned the knobs; no answer.
On the third day a warship passed us, heading north,
Dead bodies piled on the deck. On the sixth day
A plane plunged over us into the sea. Thereafter
Nothing. The radios dumb;
And still they stand in corners of our kitchens,
And stand, perhaps, turned on, in a million rooms
All over the world. But now if they should speak,
If on a sudden they should speak again,
If on the stroke of noon a voice should speak,
We would not listen, we would not let it bring
That old bad world that swallowed its children quick
At one great gulp. We would not have it again.
Sometimes we think of the nations lying asleep,
Curled blindly in impenetrable sorrow,
And then the thought confounds us with its strangeness.
The tractors lie about our fields; at evening
They look like dank sea-monsters couched and waiting.

We leave them where they are and let them rust:
'They'll moulder away and be like other loam'.
We make our oxen drag our rusty ploughs,
Long laid aside. We have gone back
Far past our fathers' land.
                                    And then, that evening
Late in the summer the strange horses came.
We heard a distant tapping on the road,
A deepening drumming; it stopped, went on again
And at the corner changed to hollow thunder.
We saw the heads
Like a wild wave charging and were afraid.
We had sold our horses in our fathers' time
To buy new tractors. Now they were strange to us
As fabulous steeds set on an ancient shield
Or illustrations in a book of knights.
We did not dare go near them. Yet they waited,
Stubborn and shy, as if they had been sent
By an old command to find our whereabouts
And that long-lost archaic companionship.
In the first moment we had never a thought
That they were creatures to be owned and used.
Among them were some half-a-dozen colts
Dropped in some wilderness of the broken world,
Yet new as if they had come from their own Eden.
Since then they have pulled our ploughs and borne
                                    our loads,
But that free servitude still can pierce our hearts.
Our life is changed; their coming our beginning.

List of illustrations

Acknowledgements

THE PUBLISHERS would like to thank the following for permission to reproduce excerpts from works copyrighted by them:

Sheed & Ward, London & New York, for *The Mongol Mission* edited by C. H. Dawson; Faber & Faber Ltd., London, for *The Pattern under the Plough* by George Ewart Evans; J. M. Dent & Sons Ltd., London, for *The Poem of the Cid* translated by M. S. Merwin; Hutchinson Ltd., London, for *Breaking and Riding* by James Fillis, translated by M. H. Hayes and published by Hurst & Blackett Ltd.; Barrie & Jenkins Ltd., London, for *A Mirror for Princes* by Kai-Kaus Ibn Iskander, published by The Cresset Press; Faber & Faber Ltd., London, and Oxford University Press Inc., New York, for 'The Horses' from *Collected Poems 1921–1958* by Edwin Muir, © 1960 by Willa Muir; Charles Scribner's Sons, New York, for *The Cowboy* by P. A. Rollins, © 1922 by Charles Scribner's Sons; J. A. Allen & Co. Ltd., London, for *The Caprilli Papers* edited by P. Santini, © the Santini Estate; Columbia University Press, New York, for *An Arab-Syrian Gentleman and Warrior in the Time of the Crusades*, translated by P. K. Hitti.

The publishers also wish to acknowledge the kindness of the museums and institutions etc. who own or have the copyright of the paintings, drawings or photographs reproduced in this book. Their names are given in the list of illustrations.

Bibliography

The works quoted in this book are listed below:

ALFRED THE GREAT: *Whole Works*, Oxford & Cambridge 1852–3.

BLUNT, LADY ANNE: *Bedouin Tribes of the Euphrates*, London 1879.

BUTLER, JOHN: *The Horse and How to Ride Him*, London 1861.

CAPRILLI, FEDERICO: *The Caprilli Papers*, ed. P. Santini, J. A. Allen & Co. Ltd., London 1967.

CASSIODORUS, FLAVIUS MAGNUS AURELIUS: *The Letters of Cassiodorus*, trans. Thomas Hodgkin, London 1886.

CATLIN, GEORGE: *Letters and Notes of the Manners, Customs and Condition of the North American Indians*, 1841.

The *Chronicle of Ely* (twelfth century).

CLEMENS, SAMUEL L. (MARK TWAIN): *Roughing It*, Hartford (Conn.) 1873.

DAWSON, C. H.: *The Mongol Mission*, Sheed & Ward, London & New York 1955.

DE QUINCEY, THOMAS: *The English Mail Coach*, London 1854.

EVANS, GEORGE EWART: *The Pattern Under the Plough*, Faber & Faber Ltd., London 1966.

FILLIS, JAMES: *Breaking and Riding*, trans. M. H. Hayes, London 1902.

GIRALDUS CAMBRENSIS: *Historical Works*, Bohn Edition 1847.

GORDON, W. J.: *The Horse World of London*, 1893.

GREENE, ROBERT: *A Notable Discovery of Coosnage* (1591), Bodley Head, London 1923.

GUERINIÈRE, FRANÇOIS ROBICHON DE LA: *Ecole de Cavallerie*, Paris 1733.

GUISCHARDT, C. T.: *Mémoires Militaires sur les Grecs et les Romains . . . et de La Tactique d'Arrien*, The Hague 1758.

HAYES, ALICE: *The Horsewoman*, London 1893.

Herodotus, Bohn Edition, London 1849.

HITTI, P. K.: *An Arab-Syrian Gentleman and Warrior in the time of the Crusades* (Usamah ibn Munquidh), Cambridge 1924.

HOMER: *The Iliad*, trans. E. V. Rieu, Penguin, London 1950.

HROZNY, BEDRICH: *Archiv Orientální*, Journal of the Czechoslovak Oriental Institute, Prague & Paris 1929–31.

HULL, ELEANOR: *The Cuchullin Saga in Irish Literature*, London 1898.

JUSTINUS: *History of the World*, Bohn Edition, London 1853.

KAI-KAUS IBN ISKANDER: *Qabus Nama, A Mirror for Princes*, The Cresset Press, London 1951.

LIVY: *History of Rome*, Bohn Edition, London 1848.

MARKHAM, GERVASE: *Markham's Masterpiece*, London 1688.

MAYHEW, HENRY: *London Labour and the London Poor*, 1851.

MORGAN, NICHOLAS: *The Perfection of Horsemanship*, London 1609.

MUIR, EDWIN: *Collected Poems 1921–1958*, Faber & Faber, London & Oxford University Press Inc., New York 1960.

NEWCASTLE, WILLIAM CAVENDISH, DUKE OF: *A General System of Horsemanship in All its Branches*, London 1743.

PAUSANIAS: *Description of Greece*, Bohn Edition, London 1886.

PLINY: *Natural History*, Bohn Edition, London 1848.

PLUTARCH: *The Lives of the Noble Grecians and Romanes . . . translated . . . into Englishe by T. North*, London 1579.

Poem of the Cid, A Verse Translation by M. S. Merwin, J. M. Dent & Sons, London 1959.

POLO, MARCO: *The Most Famous and Noble Travels of Marco Polo . . . The Translation of Marsden revised by T. Wright*, London 1904.

PROCOPIUS: *History of the Wars*, trans. H. B. Dewing, Loeb Edition, London 1914.

ROLLINS, P. A.: *The Cowboy*, Charles Scribner's Sons, New York 1922.

THOMPSON, CHARLES: *Rules for Bad Horsemen*, London 1762.

WEATHERBY, J.: *Introduction to a General Stud Book*, London 1791.

WHYTE, J. C.: *History of the British Turf*, London 1840.

XENOPHON: *The Art of Horsemanship*, trans. M. H. Morgan, Boston 1893.

YOUATT, WILLIAM: *The Horse*, Philadelphia 1845.

Index